T0324660

A.U.A. Language Center
Thai Course

Book 3

Prepared by

J. Marvin Brown

Published by
Cornell University Southeast Asia Program
Ithaca, N.Y.
1992

Originally published by the American University Alumni Association Language Center, Bangkok, Thailand. Reprinted with permission.

ISBN 0-87727-508-4

Cover by Amporn Kompipote. Illustrations by Thanit Docragglang.

The A.U.A. Thai Course

Thai Book 1
Thai Book 2
Thai Book 3
Thai Book A (Small Talk)
Thai Book B (Getting Help)
Thai Book R (Reading)
Thai Book W (Writing)

A.U.A. Thai Course Books can be ordered from:

> SEAP Publications
> Cornell University
> East Hill Plaza
> Ithaca, NY 14850
>
> (607) 255-8038

Tapes are available for Books 1, 2, 3, A, and B. Order from:

> Tape Sales
> G11 Noyes Lodge
> Cornell University
> Ithaca, NY 14853
>
> (607) 255-7394

For a master set of A.U.A. tapes, institutions should order directly from A.U.A. Language Center, 179 Rajadamri Road, Bangkok 10330, Thailand.

PREFACE

This edition of Book 3 of the AUA Language Center Thai Course is a direct continuation of Book 1 (1967) and Book 2 (1968) and should be used only by students who have studied from those books; for without this background, the sections on tone manipulation and tone distinctions might prove too difficult even for students who are in other respects far beyond the level of this book. In any case a student using Book 3 should have copies of Books 1 and 2 since they are frequently referred to (especially in the glossary). And the general information about the course as a whole appears only in the introduction to Book 1.

The main change from Books 1 and 2 in lesson content is the use of narratives instead of dialogs and questions on the narratives instead of grammar drills in every other lesson; the subject of each narrative is the dialog of the preceding lesson. The sections on vowels and consonants, tone production, and numbers-time-days-months have been dropped, and sections on tone distinctions and particles have been added. The ten sections of each lesson are shown below.

1. Vocabulary and expansions.
2. Tone manipulation.
3. Patterns / Sentence structure.
4. Tone identification.
5. Dialog / Narrative.
6. Tone distinctions.
7. Grammar drills / Questions on the narrative.
8. Conversation.
9. Particles.
10. Writing.

The reading selections included in review lessons and the writing section of each lesson are completely separate from the programming of the rest of the book and can be skipped completely if desired.

The present edition is a major revision of the earlier course and has benefited greatly from suggestions made by the following teachers who taught that course: Matana Chutrakul, Niphapharn Chutrakul, Nitaya Amaraket, Saengthong Beokhaimook, Srim Nolrajsuwaj, and Preecha Ratanodom. These same teachers (excepting Khun Niphapharn) read the revision and made corrections. As in the preceding books, most of the dialogs (the first five of the eight in this book) are revisions of earlier dialogs written by Churee Indaniyom. The last three dialogs, the narratives, and the reading selections were written by or with the help of Preecha and Wipha Ratanodom. My own contributions have been made with the constant assistance of Khun Preecha and Khun Wipha.

J. M. B.

Bangkok, Thailand
April 1969

CONTENTS

v

ix

The regular text appears on the right-hand pages only. On the pages facing from the left, all Thai words and sentences are printed in normal Thai writing.

บทที่ ๔๑

๔๑.๑ คำศัพท์

หรอก	ตก
	สีตก
เซนต์	สีไม่ตก
ฟุต	หด
อาจ	ควร
หน้า	เช้ต
	หรือ เสื้อเช้ต
กว้าง	คง
นิ้ว	ม้า
หลา	ที่
ลด	กระดาน
	กระดานดำ
ไหม	
ผ้าไหม	จุด
ผ้าไหมไทย	จุดบุหรี่
ซัก	ยก
ซักน้ำ	
ซักแห้ง	สอน

LESSON 41

41.1 Vocabulary and expansions.

lɔk	A particle which gives the feeling 'contrary to what you seem to think'.
sen	Centimeter.
fút	A foot in length.
ʔàat	May, might, maybe.
nâa	Face, surface, page.
kwâaŋ	To be wide, broad.
níw	Fingers, toes, inches.
lǎa	A yard in length.
lót	To reduce in price or weight.
mǎy	Silk.
phâa mǎy	Silk cloth.
phâa mǎy thay	Thai silk.
sák	To wash clothing, to launder.
sák náam	To wash in water. To rinse.
sák hɛ̂ɛŋ	To dry-clean.
tòk	To fall.
sǐi tòk	The color runs or fades.
sǐi mây tòk	The color is fast (it won't run or fade.)
hòt	To shrink.
khuan	Should, ought to.
chə́ət	(From the English 'shirt'.)
sûa chə́ət	A dress shirt.
khoŋ	Most likely, sure to, bound to.
máa	Horse.
thii	A particle used in requests: 'Do it just this once.'
kradaan	A board, a plank.
kradaan dam	A blackboard.
cùt	To light a fire.
cùt burìi	To light a cigarette.
yók	To lift, to raise.
sɔ̌ɔn	To teach.

๔๑.๒ แบบฝึกหัดการสลับเสียงสูงต่ำ

ช่วยลุงหน่อยนะตุ่ม
    ตุ่มช่วยไม่ได้หรอกลุง

ช่วยปู่หน่อยนะต้อย
    ต้อยช่วยไม่ได้หรอกปู่

ช่วยแม่หน่อยนะแอ๊ด
    แอ๊ดช่วยไม่ได้หรอกแม่

ช่วยน้าหน่อยนะศรี
    ศรีช่วยไม่ได้หรอกน้า

ช่วยป๋าหน่อยนะแดง
    แดงช่วยไม่ได้หรอกป๋า

ช่วยลุงหน่อยนะต้อย
    ต้อยช่วยไม่ได้หรอกลุง

ช่วยปู่หน่อยนะแอ๊ด
    แอ๊ดช่วยไม่ได้หรอกปู่

ช่วยพ่อหน่อยนะศรี
    ศรีช่วยไม่ได้หรอกพ่อ

ช่วยน้าหน่อยนะแดง
    แดงช่วยไม่ได้หรอกน้า

ช่วยป๋าหน่อยนะตุ่ม
    ตุ่มช่วยไม่ได้หรอกป๋า

๔๑.๓ โครงสร้างของประโยค

กว้างกี่นิ้ว
สูงกี่เซนต์
ยาวกี่ฟุต

หลาละ ๓๕ บาท
เมตรละ ๕๐ บาท
กิโลละ ๓๐ บาท

ลดบ้างได้ไหม
กินบ้างได้ไหม
ช่วยบ้างได้ไหม

ถ้าจะให้ดี
ถ้าจะให้สวย
ถ้าจะให้ไป

ควรซักก่อนตัด
ควรแก้ก่อนใช้
ควรจอดก่อนลง

ควร (จะ) พอ
คง (จะ) พอ
อาจจะพอ

Response drill. (The meaning of lɔk in the following sentences is shown in English by an emphatic stress on the word **can't**.)

chûay luŋ nɔ̀y ná, tùm.
   tùm chûay mây dây lɔk, luŋ.

chûay pùu nɔ̀y ná, tôy.
   tôy chûay mây dây lɔk, pùu.

chûay mɛ̂ɛ nɔ̀y ná, ʔɛ́ɛt.
   ʔɛ́ɛt chûay mây dây lɔk, mɛ̂ɛ.

chûay náa nɔ̀y ná, sǐi.
   sǐi chûay mây dây lɔk, náa.

chûay pǎa nɔ̀y ná, dɛɛŋ.
   dɛɛŋ chûay mây dây lɔk, pǎa.

chûay luŋ nɔ̀y ná, tôy.
   tôy chûay mây dây lɔk, luŋ

chûay pùu nɔ̀y ná, ʔɛ́ɛt.
   ʔɛ́ɛt chûay mây dây lɔk, pùu.

chûay phɔ̂ɔ nɔ̀y ná, sǐi.
   sǐi chûay mây dây lɔk, phɔ̂ɔ.

chûay náa nɔ̀y ná, dɛɛŋ.
   dɛɛŋ chûay mây dây lɔk, náa.

chûay pǎa nɔ̀y ná, tùm.
   tùm chûay mây dây lɔk, pǎa.

Please help me, Toom
   I *can't* help you, Uncle.

Please help me, Toy.
   I *can't* help you, Grandpa.

Please help me, At.
   I *can't* help you, Mother.

Please help me, Sri.
   I *can't* help you, Nah.

Please help me, Daeng.
   I *can't* help you, Papá.

Please help me, Toy.
   I *can't* help you, Uncle.

Please help me, At.
   I *can't* help you, Grandpa.

Please help me, Sri.
   I *can't* help you, Father.

Please help me, Daeng.
   I *can't* help you, Nah.

Please help me, Toom.
   I *can't* help you, Papá.

41.3   Patterns.   **41.3**

kwâaŋ kìi níw.
sǔuŋ kìi sen.
yaaw kìi fút.

How many inches wide?
How many centimeters tall?
How many feet long?

lǎa la cèt sìp hâa bàat.
méet la hâa sìp bàat.
kiloo la sǎam sìp bàat.

75 baht a yard.
50 baht a meter.
30 baht a kilogram.

lót bâaŋ dây máy.
kin bâaŋ dây máy.
chûay bâaŋ dây máy.

Can you reduce the price a bit?
Can I eat some?
Can you help me a little?

thâa ca hây dii,
thâa ca hây sǔay,
thâa ca hây pay,

If you want to have it good,
If you want to make it pretty,
If you want me to go,

khuan sák kɔ̀ɔn tàt.
khuan kɛ̂ɛ kɔ̀ɔn cháy.
khuan cɔ̀ɔt kɔ̀ɔn loŋ.

You should wash it before cutting.
You should fix it before you use it.
You should stop before you get out.

khuan (ca) phɔɔ.
khoŋ (ca) phɔɔ.
ʔàat ca phɔɔ.

It should be enough.
It is most likely enough.
It is probably enough.

๔๑.๔ แบบฝึกหัดการฟังเสียงสูงต่ำ

เพชรบุรี	สนามหลวง
พญาไท	เจริญกรุง
ราชเทวี	ราชดำเนิน
หัวลำโพง	ประตูน้ำ

๔๑.๕ บทสนทนา

ก. ผ้านี่หน้ากว้างกี่นิ้ว
    ข. ๓๖ นิ้วครับ

ก. ขายยังไง
    ข. หลาละ ๓๕ บาทครับ

ก. ลดบ้างได้ไหม
    ข. ไม่ได้ครับ นี่เป็นไหมไทยอย่างดีที่สุด
    ซักน้ำได้ ไม่ต้องซักแห้ง
    สีไม่ตกเลย

ก. หดมากไหม
    ข. หดนิดหน่อยเท่านั้น
    ถ้าจะให้ดีควรซักก่อนตัด

ก. เสื้อเชิ้ตแขนสั้นตัวหนึ่ง ใช้ผ้าสอง
หลาคงพอนะ
    ข. พอครับ

The tone identification sections of Book 3 contain words chosen for their usefulness, not for their tones as in Book 2. After the student has identified the tones and written them in, he should make an effort to remember the words. This section provides additional vocabulary as well as practice in tone identification.

Streets and places in Bangkok.

phetburii	One of Bangkok's major streets.
phayathay	One of Bangkok's major streets.
raat (cha) theewii	The intersection of Phetburi and Phayathai streets.
hualamphooŋ	The name of the central railway station and surrounding district.
sanaamluaŋ	'The Royal Arena'. A large oval field near the Grand Palace originally designed for royal cremations. It is used now mainly for week-end markets.
caraankruŋ	'New Road'. Bangkok's oldest street.
raat (cha) damnəən	Bangkok's widest street.
pratuunaam	The intersection of Phetburi and Rajdamri streets.

41.5 Dialog.

A. phâa níi nâa kwâaŋ kìi níw.   How many inches wide is this cloth?

  B. săam sìp hòk níw khráp.   36 inches.

A. khăay yaŋŋay.   How do you sell it?

  B. lăa la cèt sìp hâa bàat khráp.   75 baht a yard.

A. lót bâaŋ dây máy.   Can you come down a little?

  B. mây dây khráp.   No, sir.
  nîi pen măy thay yàaŋ dii thîisùt.   This is the best kind of Thai silk.
  sák náam dây.   It can be washed in water.
  mây tôŋ sák hɛ̂ɛŋ.   It doesn't have to be dry-cleaned.
  sĭi mây tòk ləəy.   And the color won't run at all.

A. hòt mâak máy.   Does it shrink much?

  B. hòt nítnɔ̀y thâwnán.   Just a little.
  thâa ca hây dii,   To play it safe (if you want it good),
  khuan sák kɔ̀ɔn tàt.   you should wash it before having it cut.

A. sûa chɔ́ɔt khɛ̂ɛn sân tua nuŋ   For a short-sleeved shirt,
  cháy phâa sɔ̌ɔŋ lăa khoŋ phɔɔ ná.   using 2 yards of cloth will probably be enough, don't you think?

  B. phɔɔ khráp.   Yes, sir.

7

๔๑.๖ ความแตกต่างระหว่างเสียงสูงต่ำ

หมาอยู่ในบ้าน   ม้าอยู่ข้างนอก

หมาอยู่ที่ไหน
    ในบ้าน หมาอยู่ในบ้าน

หมาอยู่ในบ้านใช่ไหม
    ใช่ หมาอยู่ในบ้าน

ม้าอยู่ที่ไหน
    ข้างนอก ม้าอยู่ข้างนอก

ม้าอยู่ข้างนอกใช่ไหม
    ใช่ ม้าอยู่ข้างนอก

อะไรอยู่ในบ้าน
    หมา หมาอยู่ในบ้าน

หมาอยู่ข้างนอกใช่ไหม
    ไม่ใช่ หมาอยู่ในบ้าน

อะไรอยู่ข้างนอก
    ม้า ม้าอยู่ข้างนอก

ม้าอยู่ในบ้านใช่ไหม
    ไม่ใช่ ม้าอยู่ข้างนอก

๔๑.๗ แบบฝึกหัดไวยากรณ์
ก.

อยากได้กางเกงขายาวสักตัวหนึ่ง
(สั้น)

อยากได้เสื้อแขนสั้นสักตัวหนึ่ง
(ยาว)

อยากได้กางเกงขาสั้นสักตัวหนึ่ง
(เสื้อ)

อยากได้เสื้อแขนยาวสักตัวหนึ่ง
(กางเกง)

ข.

คุณควรจะไปหาหมอ   (ใช้มีด)
คุณควรจะใช้มีด   (คอยอีกหน่อย)
คุณควรจะคอยอีกหน่อย (ทำเสร็จแล้ว)
คุณควรจะทำเสร็จแล้ว (บอกเขา)
คุณควรจะบอกเขา   (ไม่)

คุณไม่ควรจะบอกเขา   (กินมากอย่างนี้)
คุณไม่ควรจะกินมากอย่างนี้(ใส่พริกไทย)
คุณไม่ควรจะใส่พริกไทย (สูบบุหรี่)
คุณไม่ควรจะสูบบุหรี่

41.6 Tone distinctions.

In this section of each lesson, most of the time should be spent drilling without books. After the students have repeated and answered with books to work up fluency, the teacher should put the information on the board (either in writing or by pictures) and ask the questions in random order.

mǎa yùu nay bâan. máa yùu khâŋ nɔɔk.   The dog is in the house. The horse is outside.

mǎa yùu thîi nǎy.

   nay bâan. mǎa yùu nay bâan.   mǎa yùu nay bâan, chây máy.

máa yùu thîi nǎy.   chây. mǎa yùu nay bâan.

   khâŋ nɔɔk. máa yùu khâŋ nɔɔk.   máa yùu khâŋ nɔɔk, chây máy.

ʔaray yùu nay bâan.   chây. máa yùu khâŋ nɔɔk.

   mǎa. mǎa yùu nay bâan.   mǎa yùu khâŋ nɔɔk, chây máy.

ʔaray yùu khâŋ nɔɔk.   mây chây. mǎa yùu nay bâan.

   máa. máa yùu khâŋ nɔɔk.   máa yùu nay bâan, chây máy.

      mây chây. máa yùu khâŋ nɔɔk.

41.7 Grammar drills.

a. Substitution drill.

yàak dây kaŋkeeŋ khǎa yaaw sák tua nɯŋ.   I want to get a pair of long pants.
(sân)   (short)

yàak dây kaŋkeeŋ khǎa sân sák tua nɯŋ.   I want to gat a pair of short pants.
(sɯ̂a)   (shirt)

yàak dây sɯ̂a khɛ̌ɛn sân sák tua nɯŋ.   I want to get a short-sleeved shirt.
(yaaw)   (long)

yàak dây sɯ̂a khɛ̌ɛn yaaw sák tua nɯŋ.   I want to get a long-sleeved shirt.
(kaŋkeeŋ)   (pants)

b. Substitution drill.

khun khuan ca pay hǎa mɔ̌ɔ. (cháy mîit)   You should go see a doctor. (use a knife)

khun khuan ca cháy mîit.   You should use a knife.
(khɔɔy ʔiik nɔ̀y)   (wait a little longer)

khun khuan ca khɔɔy ʔiik nɔ̀y.   You should wait a little longer.
(tham sèt lɛ́ɛw)   (have finished by now)

khun khuan ca tham sèt lɛ́ɛw.   You should have finished by now.
(bɔ̀ɔk kháw)   (have told him)

khun khuan ca bɔ̀ɔk kháw. (mây)   You should have told him. (not)

khun mây khuan ca bɔ̀ɔk kháw.   You shouldn't have told him.
(kin mâak yaŋŋíi)   (eat so much)

khun mây khuan ca kin mâak yaŋŋíi.   You shouldn't eat so much.
(sày phrík thay)   (put pepper on it)

khun mây khuan ca sày phrík thay.   You shouldn't have put pepper on it.
(sùup burìi)   (smoke)

khun mây khuan ca sùup burìi.   You shouldn't smoke.

ค.

เขาคงจะอยู่บ้าน	(ไปแล้ว)
เขาคงจะไปแล้ว	(ลืมบอก)
เขาคงจะลืมบอก	(ชอบอาหารไทย)
เขาคงจะชอบอาหารไทย	(ไม่)
เขาคงจะไม่ชอบอาหารไทย	(สบาย)
เขาคงจะไม่สบาย	(มีเงินพอ)
เขาคงจะไม่มีเงินพอ	

๔๑.๘ การสนทนาโต้ตอบ

๔๑.๕ วลีท้ายประโยค

ที่ หน่อย

ขอพูดที	ช่วยจุดบุหรี่ที
ขอนั่งที	ช่วยบอกเขาที
ขอยืนที	ช่วยทิ้งบุหรี่ที
ขอทิ้งบุหรี่ที	ช่วยยกเก้าอี้ให้ที
ขอไปห้องน้ำที	ช่วยเขียนคำว่า "ทราบ" ให้ที

ขอพูดกับเขาหน่อย	ช่วยบอกเขาหน่อย
ขอถามอะไรหน่อย	ช่วยสอนภาษาไทยหน่อย
ขอสูบบุหรี่หน่อย	ช่วยส่งหนังสือให้หน่อย
ขอยืมหนังสือหน่อย	ช่วยยกโต๊ะให้หน่อย
ขอเขียนที่กระดานดำหน่อย	ช่วยฉายไฟให้หน่อย

c. Substitution drill.

kháw khoŋ ca yùu bâan. (pay lέεw)	He's most likely at home. (gone already)
kháw khoŋ ca pay lέεw. (lʉʉm bɔɔk)	He must have gone already. (forget to tell me)
kháw khoŋ ca lʉʉm bɔɔk.	He must have forgotten to tell me.
(chɔ̂ɔp ʔaahǎan thay)	(like Thai food)
kháw khoŋ ca chɔ̂ɔp ʔaahǎan thay. (mây)	He surely likes Thai food. (not)
kháw khoŋ ca mây chɔ̂ɔp ʔaahǎan thay.	He most likely doesn't like Thai food.
(sabaay)	(be well)
kháw khoŋ ca mây sabaay. (mii ŋən phɔɔ)	He must not be well. (have enough money)
kháw khoŋ ca mây mii ŋən phɔɔ.	He must not have enough money.

41.8 Conversation. 41.8

The teacher should ask each student his name, nationality, how long he has been here, where he lives and works, and how much longer he expects to be here.

41.9 Particles 41.9

thii, nɔ̀y.

When the speaker, for his own good or advantage, desires an action or reaction from the hearer that he considers to be an imposition, he can add politeness by minimizing the request: 'just once' (thii), or 'just a little' (nɔ̀y). Sentences with thii and nɔ̀y are commonly introduced by khɔ̌ɔ when the stated action is the speaker's (khɔ̌ɔ phûut ka kháw nɔ̀y, 'May I speak to him?'), and chûay when it is the hearer's (chûay phûut ka kháw nɔ̀y, 'Please speak to him.').

The students should practice the following sentences to acquire natural rhythm and tone of voice, and then use these and similar sentences to actually elicit interpersonal cooperation in the classroom situation.

khɔ̌ɔ phûut thii.	May I say something?
khɔ̌ɔ nâŋ thii.	May I sit down?
khɔ̌ɔ yʉʉn thii.	May I stand up?
khɔ̌ɔ thíŋ burìi thii.	May I throw my cigarette away?
khɔ̌ɔ pay hɔ̂ŋ náam thii.	May I go to the bathroom?
khɔ̌ɔ phûut ka kháw nɔ̀y.	May I speak to him?
khɔ̌ɔ thǎam ʔaray nɔ̀y.	May I ask you something?
khɔ̌ɔ sùup burìi nɔ̀y.	May I smoke?
khɔ̌ɔ yʉʉm naŋsʉ̌ʉ nɔ̀y.	May I borrow your book?
khɔ̌ɔ khǐan thîi kradaandam nɔ̀y.	May I write on the blackboard?
chûay cùt burìi thii.	Please give me a light.
chûay bɔɔk kháw thii.	Please tell him.
chûay thíŋ burìi thii.	Please throw my cigarette away.
chûay yók kâwʔîi hây thii.	Please lift the chair for me.
chûay khǐan kham wâa sâap hây thii.	Please write the word 'sâap' for me.
chûay bɔɔk kháw nɔ̀y.	Please tell him.
chûay sɔ̌ɔn phasǎa thay nɔ̀y.	Please teach me some Thai.
chûay sòŋ naŋsʉ̌ʉ hây nɔ̀y.	Please hand me that book.
chûay yók tóʔ hây nɔ̀y.	Please lift the table for me.
chûay chǎay fay hây nɔ̀y.	Please shine the light for me.

11

๔๑.๑๐ การเขียน

ซิ   ธุระ   เยอะแยะ โต๊ะ หัวเราะ ค่ะ   จ้ะ   จ๊ะ

เดี๋ยว	ริ	เละ	แฉะ
เกี๊ยะ	ครึ	เตะ	และ
ผัวะ	หึ	เลอะ	ปะ
เผียะ	ดุ	เปรอะ	พระ
จั๊วะ	ปุ๊	โละ	เพราะ
ติ	ยุ	โต๊ะ	เหมาะ

ซิ ธุระ เยอะแยะ โต๊ะ หัวเราะ ค่ะ จ้ะ จ๊ะ

sí thúráʔ   yɔ́ʔyéʔ   tóʔ   hǔarɔ́ʔ   khâ câ cá

The symbol for final ʔ is ะ. It is used with all vowels except iʔ, ʉʔ, and uʔ (which are written with the short vowel symbols without a final). Alone, this symbol stands for aʔ (see 38.10). With the symbol for aw, it stands for ɔʔ. With all other vowels, it follows the long vowel symbol.

These syllables are short, dead syllables and their tones behave accordingly (see 28.10). Falling tones are written with **máy ʔèek** in syllables having low initials and **máy thoo** in syllables having mid and high initials, just as they are in live syllables. Syllables with mid consonants require a special symbol for high tones (๊). Review 19.10 for the rising tone symbol used with mid consonants.

Practice reading and writing the following words.

เดี่ยว dǐaw	ริ ríʔ	เละ léʔ	แฉะ chèʔ
เกียะ kíaʔ	ครึ khrʉ́ʔ	เตะ tèʔ	และ léʔ
ผัวะ phùaʔ	หึ hʉ̀ʔ	เลอะ lɤ́ʔ	ปะ pàʔ
เผียะ phìaʔ	ดุ dùʔ	เปรอะ prɤ̀ʔ	พระ phráʔ
จั๊วะ cúaʔ	ปุ๊ púʔ	โละ lóʔ	เพราะ phrɔ́ʔ
ติ tìʔ	ยุ yúʔ	โต๊ะ tóʔ	เหมาะ mɔ̀ʔ

13

บทที่ ๔๒

๔๒.๑ คำศัพท์

มะพร้าว

ราคาหลาละเจ็ดสิบห้าบาท
ราคาที่คนขายบอกหลาละ ๓๕ บาท

ผ้านี่สีไม่ตก
ผ้าไหมไทยสีไม่ตก
ผ้าที่ดีที่สุดสีไม่ตก
ผ้าไหมไทยอย่างดีที่สุดสีไม่ตก

คิด
เกิน
เกินไป
แพงเกินไป

ฮาวาย
เสื้อฮาวาย
จอนซื้อผ้ามาตัดเสื้อ
จอนต้องการซื้อผ้ามาตัดเสื้อ
จอนต้องการซื้อผ้าไหมไทยมาตัดเสื้อ
จอนต้องการซื้อผ้าไหมไทยมาตัดเสื้อ
    ฮาวายแขนสั้น
จอนต้องการซื้อผ้าไหมไทยสองหลา
    มาตัดเสื้อฮาวายแขนสั้น

ยอม

จึง
เขาซื้อผ้าในราคาร้อยห้าสิบบาท
เขาต้องซื้อผ้าในราคา ๑๕๐ บาท
เขาจึงต้องซื้อผ้าในราคา ๑๕๐ บาท
เขาจึงต้องซื้อผ้าไหมนั้น
    ในราคา ๑๕๐ บาท
เขาจึงต้องซื้อผ้าไหมนั้นสองหลา
    ในราคา ๑๕๐ บาท

อื่น
คนอื่น
คนอื่นซื้อถูก
เขาซื้อแพงกว่าคนอื่นซื้อ
เขาไม่อยากซื้อแพงกว่าคนอื่น

เสีย

ค่า
จ้าง
ค่าจ้าง

เขาเห็นผ้าแล้ว
เขาเห็นผ้าไหมแล้ว
เขาเห็นผ้าไหมที่ต้องการแล้ว

ค่าจ้างตัดเสื้อ

ประมาณ

14

LESSON 42

42.1 Vocabulary and expansions.

maphráaw	Coconut.
phâa níi sǐi mây tòk.	In this cloth the color won't fade.
phâa mǎy thay sǐi mây tòk.	
phâa thîi dii thîisùt sǐi mây tòk.	
phâa mǎy thay yàaŋ dii thîisùt sǐi mây tòk.	
haawaay	Hawaii.
sûa haawaay	Sport shirt.
cɔɔn súu phâa maa tàt sûa.	John bought cloth to make a shirt.
cɔɔn tôŋkaan súu phâa maa tàt sûa.	
cɔɔn tôŋkaan súu phâa mǎy thay maa tàt sûa.	
cɔɔn tôŋkaan súu phâa mǎy thay maa tàt sûa haawaay khěɛn sân.	
cɔɔn tôŋkaan súu phâa mǎy thay sɔ̌ɔŋ lǎa maa tàt sûa haawaay khěɛn sân.	
ʔùun	Other.
khon ʔùun	Other people.
khon ʔùun súu thùuk.	Other people buy cheaply.
kháw súu phɛɛŋ kwàa khon ʔùun súu.	
kháw mây yàak súu phɛɛŋ kwàa khon ʔùun.	
kháw hěn phâa lɛ́ɛw.	He has seen the cloth already.
kháw hěn phâa mǎy lɛ́ɛw.	
kháw hěn phâa mǎy thîi tôŋkaan lɛ́ɛw.	
rakhaa lǎa la cèt sìp hâa bàat.	The price is 75 baht a yard.
rakhaa thîi khon khǎay bɔ̀ɔk lǎa la 75 bàat.	
khít	To think, figure out.
kəən	To exceed.
kəən pay	Too, excessively.
phɛɛŋ kəən pay	Too expensive.
yɔɔm	To be willing.
cuŋ	So, therefore, consequently.
kháw súu phâa nay rakhaa rɔ́ɔy hâa sìp bàat.	He bought the cloth for 150 baht.
kháw tôŋ súu phâa nay rakhaa 150 bàat.	
kháw cuŋ tôŋ súu phâa nay rakhaa 150 bàat.	
kháw cuŋ tôŋ súu phâa mǎy nán nay rakhaa 150 bàat.	
kháw cuŋ tôŋ súu phâa mǎy nán sɔ̌ɔŋ lǎa nay rakhaa 150 bàat.	
sǐa	To spend, waste, spoil.
khâa	Expenses, fee, cost, value.
câaŋ	To hire.
khâa câaŋ	Wages (for hiring someone).
khâa câaŋ tàt sûa	The cost of making a shirt.
pramaan	Approximately.
(More.)	

15

เขาจะต้องเสียอีกสี่สิบบาท	กระโปรง
เขาจะต้องเสียอีกประมาณ ๔๐ บาท	นุ่ง
เขาจะต้องเสียค่าจ้างตัดเสื้ออีกประมาณ ๔๐ บาท	นุ่งกระโปรง
แว่น	ผ้าซิ่น
แว่นตา	นุ่งผ้าซิ่น
แหวน	เต้นรำ

๔๒.๒ แบบฝึกหัดการสลับเสียงสูงต่ำ

มะนาวกับมะพร้าวอะไรจะใหญ่กว่ากัน
    มะพร้าวใหญ่กว่ามะนาว

มะนาวกับมะพร้าวอะไรจะเล็กกว่ากัน
    มะนาวเล็กกว่ามะพร้าว

หมา	–	ม้า	ไข่ไก่	–	ไข่เป็ด
โต๊ะ	–	หนังสือ	บุหรี่	–	ที่เขี่ยบุหรี่
ไข่	–	ไก่	เมืองไทย	–	อเมริกา
รถยนต์	–	สามล้อ	บ้าน	–	สถานีรถไฟ

๔๒.๓ โครงสร้างของประโยค

ซื้อมาตัดเสื้อ	ซื้อผ้าในราคา ๑๕๐ บาท
ซื้อมาทำโต๊ะ	ซื้อรถในราคาสองหมื่น
ซื้อมาเขียนหนังสือ	ซื้อผ้า ๑๕๐ บาท
	ซื้อรถสองหมื่นบาท
ไม่ยอมลดราคา	ค่าจ้างตัดเสื้อ
ไม่ยอมกินข้าว	ค่าจ้างแก้รถ
ไม่ยอมแพ้	ค่าจ้างทำสวน

16

kháw ca tôŋ sĭa ʔìik sìi sìp bàat.	He will have to spend 40 more baht.
kháw ca tôŋ sĭa ʔìik pramaan 40 bàat.	
kháw ca tôŋ sĭa khâa câaŋ tàt sûa ʔìik pramaan 40 bàat.	

wên	Lens, magnifying glass.
wên taa	Eyeglasses.
wɛ̌ɛn	A ring (for the finger).
kraprooŋ	A skirt.
nûŋ	To wear a lower garment.
nûŋ kraprooŋ	To wear (or put on) a skirt.
phâa sîn	Thai style skirt.
nûŋ phâa sîn	To wear (or put on) a Thai skirt.
tênram	To dance (Western style).

42.2 Tone manipulation.

Response drill.

manaaw ka maphráaw, ʔaray ca yày kwàa kan.	Which are larger, limes or coconuts?
maphráaw yày kwàa manaaw.	Coconuts are larger than limes.
manaaw ka maphráaw, ʔaray ca lék kwàa kan.	Which are smaller, limes or coconuts?
manaaw lék kwàa maphráaw.	Limes are smaller than coconuts.

Do all pairs below with both **yày** and **lék**. Later the teacher should choose pairs at random and the students should answer without books. The purpose is to get correct tones while the attention is primarily on the meaning.

mǎa – máa	Dogs – horses.	khày kày – khày pèt	Chicken eggs – duck eggs.
tóʔ – naŋsǔu	Tables – books.	burìi – thîi khìa burìi	Cigarettes – ash trays.
khày – kày	Eggs – chickens	muaŋ thay – ʔameerikaa	Thailand – America.
rótyon – sǎamlɔ́ɔ	Cars – samlors.	bâan – sathǎanii rótfay	Houses – railway stations.

42.3 Patterns.

súu maa tàt sûa.	He bought it to make a shirt.
súu maa tham tóʔ	He bought it to make a table.
súu maa khĭan naŋsǔu	He bought it to write in.
mây yɔɔm lót rakhaa.	He wouldn't reduce the price.
mây yɔɔm kin khâaw.	He wouldn't eat.
mây yɔɔm phɛ́ɛ.	He was unwilling to lose. He wouldn't give up.
súu phâa nay rakhaa 150 bàat.	He bought the cloth for 150 baht (or less).
súu rót nay rakhaa sɔ̌ɔŋ mùun.	He paid within 20,000 for the car.
súu phâa 150 bàat.	He bought the cloth for 150 baht.
súu rót sɔ̌ɔŋ mùun bàat.	He bought the car for 20,000 baht.
khâa câaŋ tàt sûa.	The cost of making a shirt.
khâa câaŋ kɛ̂ɛ rót.	The cost of repairing a car.
khâa câaŋ tham sǔan.	The cost of doing the gardening.

๔๒.๔ แบบฝึกหัดการฟังเสียงสูงต่ำ

ศรีอยุธยา	ซอยร่วมฤดี
สะพานควาย	อนุสาวรีย์ชัยสมรภูมิ
บางลำพู	อนุสาวรีย์ประชาธิปไตย
ซอยหลังสวน	

๔๒.๕ บทบรรยาย

     ผ้าไหมไทยอย่างดีที่สุดสีไม่ตก เวลาซักจะไม่หดและไม่ต้องซักแห้งด้วย คุณจอนต้องการซื้อผ้าไหมไทยสองหลามาตัดเสื้อฮาวายแขนสั้น แต่เขาไม่อยากซื้อ แพงกว่าคนอื่น เขาเห็นผ้าไหมที่ต้องการแล้วแต่ราคาที่คนขายบอกหลาละเจ็ดสิบ ห้าบาท เขาคิดว่าแพงเกินไปแต่คนขายไม่ยอมลดราคา เขาจึงต้องซื้อผ้าไหมนั้น สองหลาในราคาร้อยห้าสิบบาท และเขาจะต้องเสียค่าจ้างตัดเสื้ออีกประมาณสี่สิบ บาท

๔๒.๖ ความแตกต่างระหว่างเสียงสูงต่ำ

แว่นใส่ที่ตา	แหวนใส่ที่นิ้ว

แว่นใส่ที่ไหน	แว่นใส่ที่ตาใช่ไหม
ที่ตา แว่นใส่ที่ตา	ใช่ แว่นใส่ที่ตา
แหวนใส่ที่ไหน	แหวนใส่ที่นิ้วใช่ไหม
ที่นิ้ว แหวนใส่ที่นิ้ว	ใช่ แหวนใส่ที่นิ้ว
อะไรใส่ที่ตา	แว่นใส่ที่นิ้วใช่ไหม
แว่น แว่นใส่ที่ตา	ไม่ใช่ แว่นใส่ที่ตา
อะไรใส่ที่นิ้ว	แหวนใส่ที่ตาใช่ไหม
แหวน แหวนใส่ที่นิ้ว	ไม่ใช่ แหวนใส่ที่นิ้ว

Streets and places in Bangkok.

sii ʔayuthayaa	One of Bangkok's major streets.
saphaan khwaay	'Buffalo Bridge'. A district in Bangkok.
baaŋ lamphuu	A district in Bangkok.
sɔɔy laŋ suan	A Soi between Wireless and Rajdamri Roads.
sɔɔy ruam rɨdii	A Soi behind Wireless Road.
ʔanusawwarii chaysamɔɔraphuum	The Monument of Victory.
ʔanusawwarii prachaathippatay	The Monument of Democracy.

42.5 Narrative. 42.5

      phâa măy thay yàaŋ dii thîisùt sǐi mây tòk, weelaa sák ca mây hòt, lέʔ mây tôŋ sák hἔɛŋ dûay. khun cɔɔn tôŋkaan sɨ́ɨ phâa măy thay sɔ̌ɔŋ lǎa maa tàt sɨ̂a haawaay khἔɛn sân, tὲɛ kháw mây yàak sɨ́ɨ phɛɛŋ kwàa khon ʔɨ̀ɨn. kháw hěn phâa măy thîi tôŋkaan lέɛw, tὲɛ rakhaa thîi khon khǎay bɔ̀ɔk lǎa la cèt sìp hâa bàat. kháw khít wâa phɛɛŋ kəən pay, tὲɛ khon khǎay mây yɔɔm lót rakhaa. kháw cɨŋ tôŋ sɨ́ɨ phâa măy nán sɔ̌ɔŋ lǎa nay rakhaa rɔ́ɔy hâa sìp bàat. lέʔ kháw ca tôŋ sǐa khâa câaŋ tàt sɨ̂a ʔìik pramaan sìi sìp bàat.

42.6 Tone distinctions. 42.6

wên sày thîi taa.	You put eyeglasses on the eyes.
wἔɛn sày thîi níw.	You put rings on the fingers.

wên sày thîi năy.
    thîi taa. wên sày thîi taa.

wἔɛn sày thîi năy
    thîi níw. wἔɛn sày thîi níw.

ʔaray sày thîi taa.
    wên. wên sày thîi taa.

ʔaray sày thîi níw.
    wἔɛn. wἔɛn sày thîi níw.

wên sày thîi taa, chây máy.
    chây. wên sày thîi taa.

wἔɛn sày thîi níw, chây máy.
    chây. wἔɛn sày thîi níw.

wên sày thîi níw, chây máy.
    mây chây. wên sày thîi taa.

wἔɛn sày thîi taa, chây máy.
    mây chây. wἔɛn sày thîi níw.

๔๒.๗ คำถามบทบรรยาย

ผ้าไหมไทยอย่างดีสีตก	
ใช้ไหม	ไม่ใช่
เวลาซักแล้วไม่หดใช่ไหม	ใช่
ต้องซักแห้งใช่ไหม	ไม่ใช่
คุณจอนซื้อผ้าไหมมา	
ตัดเสื้อใช่ไหม	ใช่
คนขายบอกขายหลาละ	
ห้าสิบเจ็ดบาทใช่ไหม	ไม่ใช่
เขาบอกขายหลาละ	
เจ็ดสิบห้าบาทใช่ไหม	ใช่
คุณจอนคิดว่าราคานั้น	
แพงไปใช่ไหม	ใช่
คนขายยอมลดราคาใช่ไหม	ไม่ใช่
คุณจอนซื้อผ้าไหมสองหลา	
ใช่ไหม	ใช่
เขาซื้อหลาละเจ็ดสิบห้าบาท	
ใช่ไหม	ใช่
คุณจอนไม่ต้องเสียค่าจ้าง	
ตัดเสื้ออีกใช่ไหม	ไม่ใช่
เขาต้องเสียค่าจ้าง	
ประมาณสี่สิบบาทใช่ไหม	ใช่
ผ้าไหมไทยอย่างดีสีตกไหม	ไม่ตก
เวลาซักแล้วหดไหม	ไม่หด
ต้องซักแห้งไหม	ไม่ต้อง
คุณจอนต้องการตัดเสื้อ	
หรือกางเกง	เสื้อ
แขนสั้นหรือแขนยาว	แขนสั้น
คนขายยอมลดราคาไหม	ไม่ยอม

ผ้าไหมไทยอย่างดี	
สีตกใช้ไหม	ไม่ใช่ สีไม่ตก
ต้องซักแห้งใช้ไหม	ไม่ใช่ ซักน้ำก็ได้
คุณจอนซื้อผ้ามา	
ตัดกางเกงใช้ไหม	ไม่ใช่ ซื้อมาตัดเสื้อ
คนขายบอกขายหลาละ	
ห้าสิบเจ็ดบาทใช้ไหม	ไม่ใช่ บอกขายหลาละ
	เจ็ดสิบห้าบาท
คุณจอนคิดว่าราคานั้น	
ถูกไปใช้ไหม	ไม่ใช่
	เขาคิดว่าแพงไป
คุณจอนซื้อผ้าไหม	
สามหลาใช้ไหม	ไม่ใช่
	เขาซื้อสองหลา
เขาจะต้องเสียค่าตัดเสื้อ	
ห้าสิบบาทใช้ไหม	ไม่ใช่ เขาจะต้องเสีย
	ประมาณสี่สิบบาท
คุณจอนซื้ออะไร	ซื้อผ้า
ผ้าอะไร	ผ้าไหมไทย
ซื้อทำไม	ซื้อมาตัดเสื้อ
เสื้ออะไร	เสื้อฮาวาย
เขาต้องซื้อผ้ากี่หลา	สองหลา
เขาซื้อหลาละกี่บาท	เจ็ดสิบห้าบาท
แล้วเขาจะต้องเสียค่าจ้าง	
ตัดเสื้ออีกกี่บาท	ประมาณสี่สิบบาท

phâa mǎy thay yàaŋ dii sǐi tòk, chây máy.   mây châ⸴.

weelaa sák lɛ́ɛw mây hòt, chây máy.   chây.

tôŋ sák hɛ̂ɛŋ, chây máy.   mây chây.

khun cɔɔn súu phâa mǎy maa tàt sûa, chây máy.   chây.

khon khǎay bɔ̀ɔk khǎay lǎa la hâa sìp cèt bàat, chây máy.   mây chây.

kháw bɔ̀ɔk khǎay lǎa la cèt sìp hâa bàat, chây máy.   chây.

khun cɔɔn khít wâa rakhaa nán phɛɛŋ pay, chây máy.   chây.

khon khǎay yɔɔm lót rakhaa, chây máy.   mây chây.

khun cɔɔn súu phâa mǎy sɔ̌ɔŋ lǎa, chây máy.   chây.

kháw súu lǎa la cèt sìp hâa bàat, chây may.   chây.

khun cɔɔn mây tôŋ sǐa khâa câaŋ tàt sûa ʔìik, chây máy.   mây chây.

kháw ca tôŋ sǐa khâa câaŋ pramaan sìi sìp bàat, chây máy.   chây.

phâa mǎy thay yàaŋ dii sǐi tòk máy.   mây tòk.

weelaa sák lɛ́ɛw hòt máy.   mây hòt.

tôŋ sák hɛ̂ɛŋ máy.   mây tôŋ.

khun cɔɔn tôŋkaan tàt sûa rú kaŋkeeŋ..   sûa.

khɛ̌ɛn sân rú khɛ̌ɛn yaaw.   khɛ̌ɛn sân.

khon khǎay yɔɔm lót rakhaa máy.   mây yɔɔm.

phâa mǎy thay yàaŋ dii sǐi tòk, chây máy.   mây chây. sǐi mây tòk.

tôŋ sák hɛ̂ɛŋ, chây máy.   mây chây. sák náam kɔ̂ dây.

khun cɔɔn súu phâa maa tàt kaŋkeeŋ, chây máy.   máy chây. súu maa tàt sûa.

khon khǎay bɔ̀ɔk khǎay lǎa la hâa sìp cèt bàat, chây máy.   mây chây. bɔ̀ɔk khǎay lǎa la
                                                                        cèt sìp hâa bàat.

khun cɔɔn khít wâa rakhaa nán thùuk pay, chây máy.   mây chây.
                                                             kháw khít wâa phɛɛŋ pay.

khun cɔɔn súu phâa mǎy sǎam lǎa, chây máy.   mây chây. kháw súu sɔ̌ɔŋ lǎa.

kháw ca tôŋ sǐa khâa tàt sûa hâa sìp bàat, chây máy.   mây chây. kháw ca tôŋ sǐa
                                                             pramaan sìi sìp bàat.

khun cɔɔn súu ʔaray.   súu phâa.

phâa ʔaray.   phâa mǎy thay.

súu thammay.   súu maa tàt sûa.

sûa ʔaray.   sûa haawaay.

kháw tôŋ súu phâa kìi lǎa.   sɔ̌ɔŋ lǎa.

kháw súu lǎa la kìi bàat.   cèt sìp hâa bàat.

lɛ́ɛw kháw ca tôŋ sǐa khâa câaŋ tàt sûa ʔìik kìi bàat.   pramaan sìi sìp bàat.

๔๒.๘ การสนทนาโต้ตอบ

คุณพ่อสูง	ลูกชายเตี้ย
คุณพ่ออ้วน	ลูกชายผอม
คุณพ่อนุ่งกางเกงขายาว	ลูกชายนุ่งกางเกงขาสั้น
คุณพ่อกำลังสูบบุหรี่	ลูกชายกำลังอ่านหนังสือ
คุณแม่สูง	ลูกสาวเตี้ย
คุณแม่ผอม	ลูกสาวอ้วน
คุณแม่นุ่งผ้าซิ่น	ลูกสาวนุ่งกระโปรง
คุณแม่กำลังกินน้ำ	ลูกสาวกำลังเต้นรำ

khun phɔ̌ɔ sǔuŋ.	The father is tall.
khun phɔ̌ɔ ʔûan.	The father is fat.
khun phɔ̌ɔ nûŋ kaŋkeeŋ khǎa yaaw.	The father is wearing long pants.
khun phɔ̌ɔ kamlaŋ sùup burìi.	The father is smoking.
khun mɛ̂ɛ sǔuŋ.	The mother is tall.
khun mɛ̂ɛ phɔ̌ɔm.	The mother is thin.
khun mɛ̂ɛ nûŋ phâa sîn.	The mother is wearing a phasin.
khun mɛ̂ɛ kamlaŋ kin náam.	The mother is drinking.
lûuk chaay tîa.	The son is short.
lûuk chaay phɔ̌ɔm.	The son is thin.
lûuk chaay nûŋ kaŋkeeŋ khǎa sân.	The son is wearing short pants.
lûuk chaay kamlaŋ ʔàan naŋsɯ̌ɯ.	The son is reading.
lûuk sǎaw tîa.	The daughter is short.
lûuk sǎaw ʔûan.	The daughter is fat.
lûuk sǎaw nûŋ kraprooŋ.	The daughter is wearing a skirt.
lûuk sǎaw kamlaŋ tênram.	The daughter is dancing.

The teacher should ask the students questions about the picture. At least 764 simple questions can be asked. A few examples are given below.

The daughter is short and fat, right?
The one wearing the long pants is dancing, right?
What is the mother doing?
What is the one who is dancing wearing?
Who is tall and thin?
Is the one in the short pants fat or thin?
Is the father fat?

๔๒.๕ วลีท้ายประโยค

ที หน่อย ด้วย

เปิดไฟให้หน่อย แล้วก็เปิดพัดลมด้วย

เปิดประตูที	ช่วยเปิดประตูที
เปิดประตูหน่อย	ช่วยเปิดประตูหน่อย
เปิดประตูด้วย	ช่วยเปิดประตูด้วย
เอาหนังสือมาที	ช่วยเอาหนังสือมาที
เอาหนังสือมาหน่อย	ช่วยเอาหนังสือมาหน่อย
เอาหนังสือมาด้วย	ช่วยเอาหนังสือมาด้วย
รีดเสื้อให้ที	ช่วยรีดเสื้อให้ที
รีดเสื้อให้หน่อย	ช่วยรีดเสื้อให้หน่อย
รีดเสื้อให้ด้วย	ช่วยรีดเสื้อให้ด้วย

๔๒.๑๐ การเขียน

thii, nɔ̀y, dûay.

When the speaker desires an action from the hearer that he does not consider to be an imposition, he can make the request less abrupt by adding **dûay** (along with your other duties, while you're at it). Typical situations are: asking the bus driver to stop and let you off (cɔ̀ɔt dûay), asking the waiter to figure up the bill (khít taŋ dûay), and yelling for help when drowning (chûay dûay!).

The three words **thii, nɔ̀y**, and **dûay**, in addition to their literal meanings, show the degree of imposition the speaker feels, as indicated below.

thii: More than slight imposition (as when making requests to non-intimate equals or superiors).

nɔ̀y: Slight imposition (to intimate equals or inferiors).

dûay: No imposition.

But their literal meanings cannot be ignored. They are free to function as imposition indicators only when their literal meanings are *allowed* by the situation but not *required* by it. You cannot say **phûut chácháa thii** (unless you really mean 'just this once'), but must use **nɔ̀y** regardless of who the hearer is. And **dûay** does not necessarily imply that there is no imposition felt when it follows the second of two requests and thus really means 'also'.

pɔ̀ɔt fay hây nɔ̀y. lɛ́ɛw kɔ̂ pɔ̀ɔt phátlom dûay.

As with most things in language, choose first for meaning; but when more than one word is possible, choose for flavor.

Requests with all three of these words can be made more polite by adding **chûay**.

Practice saying the following requests.

pɔ̀ɔt pratuu thii.	chûay pɔ̀ɔt pratuu thii.
pɔ̀ɔt pratuu nɔ̀y.	chûay pɔ̀ɔt pratuu nɔ̀y.
pɔ̀ɔt pratuu dûay.	chûay pɔ̀ɔt pratuu dûay
ʔaw naŋsɯ̌ɯ maa thii.	chûay ʔaw naŋsɯ̌ɯ maa thii.
ʔaw naŋsɯ̌ɯ maa nɔ̀y.	chûay ʔaw naŋsɯ̌ɯ maa nɔ̀y.
ʔaw naŋsɯ̌ɯ maa dûay.	chûay ʔaw naŋsɯ̌ɯ maa dûay.
rîit sɯ̂a hây thii.	chûay rîit sɯ̂a hây thii.
rîit sɯ̂a hây nɔ̀y.	chûay rîit sɯ̂a hây nɔ̀y.
rîit sɯ̂a hây dûay.	chûay rîit sɯ̂a hây dûay.

Practice reading and writing lesson 1 of Book 1 in Thai. Notice that in the word **sawàt** the **karan** symbol silences a whole syllable. This is like writing **sawàt** in the transcription.

บทที่ ๔๓

๔๓.๑ คำศัพท์

หลอด	แรง
หลอดไฟ	เทียน
	แรงเทียน
	ฉาย
ถ้าจะ	ไฟฉาย
	ถ่าน
ติด	ถ่านไฟฉาย
เปิดไม่ติด	
	ก้อน
ไหนดูซิ	ถ่านไฟฉายสองก้อน
ไหนขอดูซิ	
ไหนขอผมดูซิ	ไข
ไหนขอผมดูหน่อยซิ	เทียนไข
จริง	ห่อ
จริง ๆ	เทียนไขห่อหนึ่ง
จริง ๆ ด้วย	
	ยี่ห้อ
ขาด	สิ
หลอดขาด	ลุก
	ลุกขึ้น
ฟิว	
ฟิวขาด	บท

26

LESSON 43

43.1 Vocabulary and expansions.

43.1

lɔ̀ɔt	A tube.
lɔ̀ɔt fay	An electric light bulb.
thâa ca	It appears, there is some evidence or reason to think so.
tìt	To be attached to.
pə̀ət mây tìt	It won't go on (turn on, doesn't connect).
nǎy duu sí.	Let me see it.
nǎy khɔ̌ɔ duu sí.	May I see it?
nǎy khɔ̌ɔ phǒm duu sí.	May I see it?
nǎy khɔ̌ɔ phǒm duu nɔ̀y sí.	Please let me have a look at it.
ciŋ	To be true.
ciŋciŋ	Really.
ciŋciŋ dûay	It is true, all right.
khàat	To be torn, broken, lacking.
lɔ̀ɔt khàat	The bulb is burned out.
fiw	A fuse.
fiw khàat	The fuse is burned out.
rɛɛŋ	Strength, power.
thian	A candle.
rɛɛŋ thian	Candle power, watt.
chǎay	To shine a light.
fay chǎay	A flashlight.
thàan	Charcoal.
thàan fay chǎay	A flashlight battery.
kɔ̂ɔn	A lump, a hunk; classifier for things like rocks, cubes of sugar, cakes of soap, flashlight batteries.
thàan fay chǎay sɔ̌ɔŋ kɔ̂ɔn	Two flashlight batteries.
khǎy	Animal fat, tallow.
thian khǎy	A candle made of tallow.
hɔ̀ɔ	To wrap; classifier for things wrapped up.
thian khǎy hɔ̀ɔ nùŋ	A package af candles.
yîihɔ̂ɔ	Brand, make, trademark.
sì	A particle used to suggest an action.
lúk	To rise.
lúk khɯ̂n	To get up.
bòt	A lesson in a textbook.

27

๔๓.๒ แบบฝึกหัดการสลับเสียงสูงต่ำ

ช่วยน้องหน่อยนะพี่
    พี่ช่วยไม่ได้หรอกน้อง

รับปู่หน่อยนะหลาน
    หลานรับไม่ได้หรอกปู่

บอกป้าหน่อยนะลูก
    ลูกบอกไม่ได้หรอกป้า

ถามแม่หน่อยนะตุ่ม
    ตุ่มถามไม่ได้หรอกแม่

ช่วยลุงหน่อยนะแอ๊ด
    แอ๊ดช่วยไม่ได้หรอกลุง

รับพี่หน่อยนะน้อง
    น้องรับไม่ได้หรอกพี่

บอกปู่หน่อยนะตุ่ม
    ตุ่มบอกไม่ได้หรอกปู่

ถามลุงหน่อยนะหลาน
    หลานถามไม่ได้หรอกลุง

ช่วยน้าหน่อยนะแดง
    แดงช่วยไม่ได้หรอกน้า

บอกศรีหน่อยนะลุง
    ลุงบอกไม่ได้หรอกศรี

๔๓.๓ โครงสร้างของประโยค

ถ้าจะเสีย
อาจจะเสีย
คงจะเสีย

ยี่สิบห้าแรงสองหลอด
หกสิบแรงสี่หลอด
ร้อยแรงหลอดหนึ่ง

เปิดไม่ติด
สตาร์ทไม่ติด

ยังไม่ต้องไปก็ได้
ยังไม่ต้องให้ก็ได้
ยังไม่ต้องปิดก็ได้
ยังไม่ต้องซ่อก็ได้

หลอดขาดแล้ว
ฟิวขาดแล้ว
เสื้อขาดแล้ว

43.2 Tone manipulation.

Response drill.

chûay nɔ́ɔŋ nɔ̀y ná, phîi.
   phîi chûay mây dây lɔk, nɔ́ɔŋ.

   Please help me, Older One.
      I can't help you, Younger One.

ráp pùu nɔ̀y ná, lǎan.
   lǎan ráp mây dày lɔk, pùu.

   Please pick me up, Grandson.
      I can't pick you up, Grandpa.

bɔ̀ɔk pǎa nɔ̀y ná, lûuk.
   lûuk bɔ̀ɔk mây dây lɔk, pǎa.

   Please tell me, Son.
      I can't tell you, Papá.

thǎam mɛ̂ɛ nɔ̀y ná, tùm.
   tùm thǎam mây dây lɔk, mɛ̂ɛ.

   Please ask me, Toom.
      I can't ask you, Mother.

chûay luŋ nɔ̀y ná, ʔɛ́ɛt
   ʔɛ́ɛt chûay mây dây lɔk, luŋ

   Please help me, At.
      I can't help you, Uncle.

ráp phîi nɔ̀y ná, nɔ́ɔŋ.
   nɔ́ɔŋ ráp mây dây lɔk, phîi.

   Please pick me up, Younger One.
      I can't pick you up, Older One.

bɔ̀ɔk pùu nɔ̀y ná, tùm.
   tùm bɔ̀ɔk mây dây lɔk, pùu.

   Please tell me, Toom.
      I can't tell you, Grandpa.

thǎam luŋ nɔ̀y na, lǎan.
   lǎan thǎam mây dây lɔk, luŋ

   Please ask me, Niece.
      I can't ask you, Uncle.

chûay náa nɔ̀y na, dɛɛŋ.
   dɛɛŋ chûay mây dây lɔk, náa.

   Please help me, Daeng.
      I can't help you, Nah.

bɔ̀ɔk sǐi nɔ̀y ná, luŋ
   luŋ bɔ̀ɔk mây dây lɔk, sǐi.

   Please tell me, Uncle.
      I can't tell you, Sri.

43.3 Patterns.

thâa ca sǐa.
ʔàat ca sǐa.
khoŋ cà sǐa.

It appears to be out of order.
It might be out of order.
It is most likely out of order.

pàat mây tìt.
satáat mây tìt.

It won't go on.
It won't start (referring to a car).

lɔ̀ɔt khàat lɛ́ɛw.
fiw khàat lɛ́ɛw.
sɯ̂a khàat lɛ́ɛw.

The bulb is burned out.
The fuse is burned out.
The shirt is torn.

yîi sìp hâa rɛɛŋ sɔ̌ɔŋ lɔ̀ɔt.
hòk sìp rɛɛŋ sìi lɔ̀ɔt.
rɔ́ɔy rɛɛŋ lɔ̀ɔt nɯŋ.

Two 25 watt bulbs.
Four 60 watt bulbs.
One 100 watt bulb.

yaŋ mây tôŋ pay kɔ̂ dây.
yaŋ mây tôŋ hây kɔ̂ dây.
yaŋ mây tôŋ pit kɔ̂ dây
yaŋ mây tôŋ sɯ́ɯ kɔ̂ dây.

You don't have to go yet.
You don't have to give it to me yet.
You don't have to turn it off yet.
You don't have to buy any yet.

๔๓.๔ แบบฝึกหัดการฟังเสียงสูงต่ำ

ผ้าห่ม	ผ้าเช็ดฝุ่น
ผ้าปูที่นอน	กระบอกฉีดยุง
ไม้กวาด	กระดาษชำระ
ผ้าม่าน	พรมปูพื้น

๔๓.๕ บทสนทนา

ก. หลอดไฟนี่ถ้าจะเสีย เปิดไม่ติด

    ข. ไหนขอผมดูหน่อยซิฮะ
    จริง ๆ ด้วยฮะ
    หลอดขาดแล้ว ไม่เป็นไรฮะ
    เดี๋ยวจะออกไปซื้อให้ใหม่
    เอากี่แรงเทียนล่ะฮะ

ก. เอายี่สิบห้าแรงหลอดหนึ่ง
หกสิบแรงสองหลอด

อ้อ ช่วยซื้อถ่านไฟฉายให้สามก้อน
แล้วก็เทียนไขสักห่อหนึ่งด้วย

    ข. เอาถ่านไฟฉายยี่ห้ออะไรฮะ

ก. อะไรก็ได้ เอาเงินไปด้วยสิ นี่ร้อยบาท

ข. ยังไม่ต้องให้เดี๋ยวนี้ก็ได้ฮะ
เพราะยังไม่ทราบว่าทั้งหมด
เท่าไหร่

๔๓.๖ ความแตกต่างระหว่างเสียงสูงต่ำ

โต๊ะอยู่ที่นี่ ประตูอยู่ที่โน่น	
โต๊ะอยู่ที่ไหน	อะไรอยู่ที่นี่
ที่นี่ โต๊ะอยู่ที่นี่	โต๊ะ โต๊ะอยู่ที่นี่
ประตูอยู่ที่ไหน	อะไรอยู่ที่โน่น
ที่โน่น ประตูอยู่ที่โน่น	ประตู ประตูอยู่ที่โน่น
โต๊ะอยู่ใกล้กว่าประตูใช่ไหม	โต๊ะอยู่ไกลกว่าประตูใช่ไหม
ใช่ โต๊ะอยู่ใกล้กว่าประตู	ไม่ใช่ โต๊ะอยู่ไกลกว่าประตู
ประตูอยู่ไกลกว่าโต๊ะใช่ไหม	ประตูอยู่ไกลกว่าโต๊ะใช่ไหม
ใช่ ประตูอยู่ไกลกว่าโต๊ะ	ไม่ใช่ ประตูอยู่ไกลกว่าโต๊ะ
อะไรอยู่ใกล้กว่ากัน	อะไรอยู่ไกลกว่ากัน
โต๊ะ โต๊ะอยู่ใกล้กว่าประตู	ประตู ประตูอยู่ไกลกว่าโต๊ะ

43.4 Tone identification.

Household things.

phaa hom	Blankets.	phaa chet fun	A dust cloth.
phaa puu thii nɔɔn	Bed sheets.	krabɔɔk chiit yuŋ	A flit gun.
may kwaat	Broom.	kradaat chamraʔ	Toilet paper.
phaa maan	Curtains.	phrom puu phʉʉn	A rug.

43.5 Dialog.

A. lɔ̀ɔt fay níi thâa ca sǐa.
  pə̀ət mây tìt.

  B. nǎy khɔ̌ɔ phǒm duu nɔ̀y sí háʔ.
  ciŋciŋ dûay háʔ.
  lɔ̀ɔt khàat lέεw.
  mây pen ray háʔ.
  dǐaw ca ʔɔ̀ɔk pay sʉ́ʉ hây mày.
  ʔaw kìi rεεŋ thian la háʔ.

A. ʔaw yii sìp hâa rεεŋ lɔ̀ɔt nʉŋ
  hòk sìp rεεŋ sɔ̌ɔŋ lɔ̀ɔt.
  ʔɔ̂ɔ, chûay sʉ́ʉ thàan fay chǎay
  hây sǎam kɔ̂ɔn,
  lέεw kɔ̂ thian khǎy sák hɔ̀ɔ nʉŋ dûay.

  B. ʔaw thàan fay chǎay yîihɔ̂ɔ ʔaray háʔ.

A. ʔaray kɔ̂ dây.
  ʔaw ŋən pay dûay sì.
  níi rɔ́ɔy bàat.

  B. yaŋ mây tɔ̂ŋ hây dǐawníi kɔ̂ dây háʔ.
  phrɔ́ʔ yaŋ mây sâap wâa tháŋmòt
  thâwrày.

This light bulb seems to be burned out.
It won't go on.

    Here, let me have a look at it.
    It's true, all right.
    The bulb is burned out.
    Never mind.
    I'll go buy you a new one (in a while).
    How many watts?

I want one 25 watt bulb,
and two 60 watt ones.
Oh, and buy me three flashlight batteries
and a package of candles.

    What brand of batteries do you want?

Any kind will do.
Take some money with you.
Here's 100 baht.

    You don't have to give it to me now.
    Because I don't know yet how much it
    will be altogether.

43.6 Tone distinctions.

tóʔ yùu thîi níi.
pràtuu yùu thîi nôon.

tóʔ yùu thîi nǎy.
  thîi níi.   tóʔ yùu thîi níi.

pratuu yùu thîi nǎy.
  thîi nôon.   pratuu yùu thîi nôon.

tóʔ yùu klây kwàa pratuu, chây máy.
  chây.   tóʔ yùu klây kwàa pratuu.

pratuu yùu klay kwàa tóʔ, chây máy.
  chây.   pratuu yùu klay kwàa tóʔ.

ʔaray yùu klây kwàa kan.
  tóʔ.   tóʔ yùu klây kwàa pratuu.

ʔaray yùu thîi níi.
  tóʔ.   tóʔ yùu thîi níi.

ʔaray yùu thîi nôon.
  pratuu.   pratuu yùu thîi nôon.

tóʔ yùu klay kwàa pratuu, chây máy.
  mây chây.   tóʔ yùu klây kwàa pratuu.

pratuu yùu klây kwàa tóʔ, chây máy.
  mây chây.   pratuu yùu klay kwàa tóʔ.

ʔaray yùu klay kwàa kan.
  pratuu.   pratuu yùu klay kwàa tóʔ.

๔๓.๗ แบบฝึกหัดไวยากรณ์

ก.

หลอดไฟนี่ถ้าจะเสีย   (โทรศัพท์)   นมนี่คงจะเสีย   (วิทยุ)

โทรศัพท์นี่ถ้าจะเสีย   (อาจ)   วิทยุนี่คงจะเสีย   (ถ้า)

โทรศัพท์นี่อาจจะเสีย   (นม)   วิทยุนี่ถ้าจะเสีย   (มะนาว)

นมนี่อาจจะเสีย   (คง)   มะนาวนี่ถ้าจะเสีย

ข.

เอาอย่างใหญ่หรืออย่างเล็ก   มีกาแฟหรือน้ำชา

     อย่างใหญ่ก็ได้ อย่างเล็กก็ได้   กาแฟก็มี น้ำชาก็มี

มีอย่างใหญ่หรืออย่างเล็ก   ไปดูหนังหรือไปซื้อของ

     อย่างใหญ่ก็มี อย่างเล็กก็มี   ไปดูหนังก็ได้ ไปซื้อของก็ได้

เอากาแฟหรือน้ำชา   จะไปเดี๋ยวนี้หรือจะกินข้าวก่อน

     กาแฟก็ได้ น้ำชาก็ได้   ไปเดี๋ยวนี้ก็ได้ กินข้าวก่อนก็ได้

ค.

เขาอาจจะอยู่ที่อ๊อฟฟิต   (ถ้า)   เขาถ้าจะไม่อยู่ที่อ๊อฟฟิต (กลับบ้านแล้ว)

เขาถ้าจะอยู่ที่อ๊อฟฟิต   (คง)   เขาถ้าจะกลับบ้านแล้ว   (คง)

เขาคงจะอยู่ที่อ๊อฟฟิต   (ไม่)   เขาคงจะกลับบ้านแล้ว   (อาจ)

เขาคงจะไม่อยู่ที่อ๊อฟฟิต   (อาจ)   เขาอาจจะกลับบ้านแล้ว

เขาอาจจะไม่อยู่ที่อ๊อฟฟิต   (ถ้า)

a. Substitution drill.

lɔɔt fay nîi thâa ca sǐa. (thoorasàp)   This light seems to be burned out. (phone)

thoorasàp nîi thâa ca sǐa. (ʔàat)   This phone seems to be out of order. (might)

thoorasàp nîi ʔàat ca sǐa. (nom)   This phone might be out of order. (milk)

nom nîi ʔàat ca sǐa. (khoŋ)   This milk might be sour. (most likely)

nom nîi khoŋ ca sǐa. (wítthayúʔ)   This milk is most likely sour. (radio)

wítthayúʔ nîi khoŋ ca sǐa.   This radio is most likely out of order.

(thâa)   (seems to be)

wítthayúʔ nîi thâa ca sǐa. (manaaw)   This radio seems to be out of order. (lime)

manaaw nîi thâa ca sǐa.   This lime seems to be spoiled.

b. Response drill.

ʔaw yàaŋ yày rɨ yàaŋ lék.   Do you want the large or small kind?
    yàaŋ yày kɔ̂ dây. yàaŋ lék kɔ̂ dây.   Either kind is all right.

mii yàaŋ yày rɨ yàaŋ lék.   Do you have the large or small kind?
    yàaŋ yày kɔ̂ mii. yàaŋ lék kɔ̂ mii.   We have both kinds.

ʔaw kaafɛɛ rɨ nám chaa.   Do you want coffee or tea?
    kaafɛɛ kɔ̂ dây. nám chaa kɔ̂ dây.   Either one will be all right.

mii kaafɛɛ rɨ nám chaa.   Do you have coffee or tea?
    kaafɛɛ kɔ̂ mii. nám chaa kɔ̂ mii.   We have coffee. And we have tea, too.

pay duu nǎŋ rɨ pay sɨɨ khɔ̌ɔŋ.   Do you want to see a show or go shopping?
    pay duu nǎŋ kɔ̂ dây.   Either one is all right with me.
    pay sɨɨ khɔ̌ɔŋ kɔ̂ dây.

ca pay dǐawníi rɨ ca kin khâaw kɔ̀ɔn.   Do you want to go now or eat first?
    pay dǐawníi kɔ̂ dây.   It is all right to go now.
    kin khâaw kɔ̀ɔn kɔ̂ dây.   And it is all right if we eat first.

c. Substitution drill.

kháw ʔàat ca yùu thîi ʔɔpfít. (thâa)   He might be at the office. (probably)

kháw thâa ca yùu thîi ʔɔpfít. (khoŋ)   He is probably at the office. (most likely)

kháw khoŋ ca yùu thîi ʔɔpfít. (mây)   He is most likely at the office. (not)

kháw khoŋ ca mây yùu thîi ʔɔpfít. (ʔàat)   He is most likely not at the office. (might)

kháw ʔàat ca mây yùu thîi ʔɔpfít. (thâa)   He might not be at the office. (probably)

kháw thâa ca mây yùu thîi ʔɔpfít.   He is probably not at the office.

(klàp bâan lɛ́ɛw)   (already gone home)

kháw thâa ca klàp bâan lɛ́ɛw. (khoŋ)   He has probably gone home. (most likely)

kháw khoŋ ca klàp bâan lɛ́ɛw. (ʔàat)   He has most likely gone home. (might)

kháw ʔàat ca klàp bâan lɛ́ɛw.   He might have gone home.

๔๓.๘ การสนทนาโต้ตอบ

๔๓.๙ วลีท้ายประโยค
ซี่

ร้อนไหม   บ้านคุณจอนอยู่ที่ไหน
    ไม่ร้อน   ไม่ทราบ
ไม่ร้อนก็ปิดพัดลมซี่   ก็ถามเขาซี่

มืดไหม   บทที่สี่สิบสี่อยู่หน้าอะไร
    มืด   ไม่ทราบ
มืดก็เปิดไฟซี่   ก็เปิดดูซี่

หนังสือเล่มนี้มีกี่หน้า   นั่นเรียกว่าอะไร
    ไม่ทราบ   ไม่ทราบ
ไม่ทราบก็เปิดดูซี่   ก็ถามซี่
                                                    นั่นเรียกว่าอะไร
                                              เรียกว่าพัดลม

๔๓.๑๐ การเขียน
หรือ   โทษ   ใหญ่   เทอม

34

43.8 Conversation.

The teacher should ask each student about his daily schedule from the time he gets up in the morning until he goes to bed at night.

43.9 Particles.

43.9

sî.

Speaker urges hearer to do something that should obviously be done. (The particles sí and sî both change to si when followed by khráp (khá, cá). Practice using them without the polite particles first so that the difference can be learned.)

After listening and repeating many times to get the rhythm and tone of voice, the student should first take the second part of the following response drill and then the first.

rɔ́ɔn máy.	Is it (too) hot (for you)?
mây rɔ́ɔn.	No.
mây rɔ́ɔn kɔ̂ pìt phátlom sî.	Then turn off the fan!
mûut máy.	Is it too dark
mûut.	Yes.
mûut kɔ̂ pə̀ət fay sî.	Then turn on the light!
naŋsɯ̆ɯ lêm níi mii kìi nâa.	How many pages does this book have?
mây sâap.	I don't know.
mây sâap kɔ̂ pə̀ət duu sî.	Well open it and see!
bâan khun cɔɔn yùu thîi nǎy.	Where does John live?
mây sâap.	I don't know.
kɔ̂ thǎam kháw sî.	Well ask him!
bòt thîi sìi sìp sìi yùu nâa ʔaray.	What page is lesson 44 on?
mây sâap.	I don't know.
kɔ̂ pə̀ət duu sî.	Well open your book and see!
nân rîak wâa ʔaray.	What is that called?
mây sâap.	I don't know.
kɔ̂ thǎam sî.	Well ask (me, or the teacher)!
nân rîak wâa ʔaray.	What is that called?
rîak wâa phátlom.	It is called a phátlom.

43.10 Writing.

43.10

Practice reading and writing lesson 2 of Book 1 in Thai. Notice the following irregularities that occur in it.

lɤ̆ə   This is written as if it were rɯ̆ɯ.

thôot   The final consonant is another high s (there are three altogether). It corresponds to the Sanskrit s. In final position, of course, it is pronounced like t.

yày   The initial consonant is an irregular symbol for y.

thəəm   In words borrowed from English, əə is usually written like this even when there is a final consonant.

35

บทที่ ๔๔

๔๔.๑ คำศัพท์

ก

เอง
เมื่อกี้
เมื่อกี้นี้
เมื่อกี้นี้เอง

ฟ้า
ไฟฟ้า

ขนาด

หลอดไฟฟ้าขาด
หลอดไฟฟ้าที่บ้านคุณจอนขาด
หลอดไฟฟ้าที่บ้านคุณจอนขาดหลอดหนึ่ง
หลอดไฟฟ้าขนาดหกสิบแรงเทียนที่บ้าน
    คุณจอนขาดหลอดหนึ่ง
เขาจึงซื้อใหม่
เขาจึงไปซื้อใหม่
เขาจึงให้คนสวนไปซื้อใหม่
เขาจึงให้คนสวนไปซื้อให้ใหม่

ไว้
ซื้อไว้
เขาให้คนสวนซื้อไว้
เขาให้คนสวนซื้อหลอดไว้
เขาให้คนสวนซื้อหลอดขนาดหกสิบ
    แรงเทียนไว้
เขาให้คนสวนซื้อหลอดขนาดหกสิบ
    แรงเทียนไว้สองหลอด

เผื่อ

เผื่อว่าไฟเสีย
ซื้อไว้เผื่อว่าไฟเสีย
ซื้อถ่านไฟฉายไว้เผื่อว่าไฟเสีย
ซื้อถ่านไฟฉายกับเทียนไขไว้
    เผื่อว่าไฟเสีย
ให้ซื้อถ่านไฟฉายกับเทียนไขไว้
    เผื่อว่าไฟเสีย
และให้ซื้อถ่านไฟฉายกับเทียนไขไว้ด้วย
    เผื่อว่าไฟเสีย

เอาเงินไปด้วย
ไม่ได้เอาเงินไปด้วยเลย
คนสวนไม่ได้เอาเงินไปด้วยเลย

เจ้า
เจ้าของ
เจ้าของร้าน

เก็บ

เฆี่ยน

หนังสือพิมพ์

เล่น
แมว
เล่นกับแมว

ลอง

LESSON 44

44.1 Vocabulary and expansions.

44.1

kíi	A moment ago
ʔeeŋ	Self, by oneself, just (after demonstratives).
mûa kíi	A moment ago.
mûa kíi níi	This preceding moment.
mûa kíi níi ʔeeŋ	Just this preceding moment, just now.
fáa	Sky.
fay fáa	Electricity.
khanàat	Size.
lɔɔt fay fáa khàat.	The light bulb is burned out.

lɔɔt fay fáa thîi bâan khun cɔɔn khàat.

lɔɔt fay fáa thîi bâan khun cɔɔn khàat lɔɔt nɯŋ.

lɔɔt fay fáa khanàat hòk sìp rɛɛŋ thian thîi bâan khun cɔɔn khàat lɔɔt nɯŋ.

kháw cɯŋ sɯ́ɯ mày.	So he bought a new one.

kháw cɯŋ pay sɯ́ɯ mày.

kháw cɯŋ hây khon sŭan pay sɯ́ɯ mày.

kháw cɯŋ hây khon sŭan pay sɯ́ɯ hây mày.

wáy	For future use or reference.
sɯ́ɯ wáy	To buy so as to have on hand for later use.
kháw hây khon sŭan sɯ́ɯ wáy.	He had the gardener buy something for later use.
kháw hây khon sŭan sɯ́ɯ lɔɔt wáy.	

kháw hây khon sŭan sɯ́ɯ lɔɔt khanàat hòk sìp rɛɛŋ thian wáy.

kháw hây khon sŭan sɯ́ɯ lɔɔt khanàat hòk sìp rɛɛŋ thian wáy sɔ̆ɔŋ lɔɔt.

phɯ̀a	In case.
phɯ̀a wâa fay sĭa.	In case the electricity goes off.
sɯ́ɯ wáy phɯ̀a wâa fay sĭa.	Buy and have on hand in case the electricity fails.

sɯ́ɯ thàan fay chăay wáy phɯ̀a wâa fay sĭa.

sɯ́ɯ thàan fay chăay kàp thian khăy wáy phɯ̀a wâa fay sĭa.

hây sɯ́ɯ thàan fay chăay kàp thian khăy wáy phɯ̀a wâa fay sĭa.

lɛ́ʔ hây sɯ́ɯ thàan fay chăay kàp thian khăy wáy dûay phɯ̀a wâa fay sĭa.

ʔaw ŋən pay dûay.	Take some money along with you.
mây dây ʔaw ŋən pay dûay ləəy.	He didn't take any money with him at all.

khon sŭan mây dây ʔaw ŋən pay dûay ləəy.

câw	Prince, ruler.
câw khɔ̆ɔŋ	Owner.
câw khɔ̆ɔŋ ráan	Shop owner.
kèp	To collect, keep, store.
khîan	To whip, beat.
naŋsɯ̆ɯ phim	Newspaper.
lên	To play.
mɛɛw	Cat.
lên kàp mɛɛw	To play with a cat.
lɔɔŋ	To try out.

37

๔๔.๒ แบบฝึกหัดการสลับเสียงสูงต่ำ

หุงข้าวแล้วหรือยังแดง
 ข้าวหรือฮะ หุงแล้วฮ่ะ
 หุงเมอกนเอง

กางมุ้งแล้วหรือยังศรี
 มุ้งหรือฮะ กางแล้วฮ่ะ
 กางเมอกนเอง

ซ้อถ่านแล้วหรือยังต้อย
 ถ่านหรือฮะ ซ้อแล้วฮ่ะ
 ซ้อเมอกนเอง

ถูพื้นแล้วหรือยังตุ่ม
 พื้นหรือฮะ ถูแล้วฮ่ะ
 ถูเมอกนเอง

ทอดหมูแล้วหรือยังหน่อย
 หมูหรือฮะ ทอดแล้วฮ่ะ
 ทอดเมอกนเอง

รีดเสื้อแล้วหรือยังต้อย
 เสื้อหรือฮะ รีดแล้วฮ่ะ
 รีดเมอกนเอง

ปิดไฟแล้วหรือยังแอ๊ด
 ไฟหรือฮะ ปิดแล้วฮ่ะ
 ปิดเมอกนเอง

ซ้อไฟฉายแล้วหรือยังน้อย
 ไฟฉายหรือฮะ ซ้อแล้วฮ่ะ
 ซ้อเมอกนเอง

๔๔.๓ โครงสร้างของประโยค

ซ้อหลอดไฟไว้
หุงข้าวไว้
กางมุ้งไว้
เก็บหนังสือไว้

เสื้อเชิ้ต
เสื้อฮาวาย
เสื้อนอก
เสื้อฝน
เสื้อหนาว
เสื้อสเว็ตเตอร์

เจ้าของร้าน
เจ้าของบ้าน
เจ้าของวิทยุ
เจ้าของภาษาอังกฤษ

ซ้อไฟฉายเผื่อว่าไฟเสีย
ใส่เสื้อฝนเผื่อว่าฝนตก
หุงข้าวมาก ๆ เผื่อว่าคนอื่นมา

44.2 Tone manipulation.

Response drill.

hŭŋ khâaw lɛ́ɛw rɨ́ yaŋ, dɛɛŋ.	Have you cooked the rice yet, Daeng?
khâaw lɔ̆há. hŭŋ lɛ́ɛw hâ.	The rice? Yes, I've cooked it.
hŭŋ mɨ̂a kíi níi ʔeeŋ.	I cooked it just a minute ago.
sɨ́ɨ thàan lɛ́ɛw rɨ́ yaŋ, tôy.	Have you bought the charcoal yet, Toy?
thàan lɔ̆há. sɨ́ɨ lɛ́ɛw hâ.	The charcoal? Yes, I've bought it.
sɨ́ɨ mɨ̂a kíi níi ʔeeŋ.	I bought it just a minute ago.
thɔ̂ɔt mŭu lɛ́ɛw rɨ́ yaŋ, nɔ̀y.	Have you fried the pork yet, Noy?
mŭu lɔ̆há. thɔ̂ɔt lɛ́ɛw hâ.	The pork? Yes, I've fried it.
thɔ̂ɔt mɨ̂a kíi níi ʔeeŋ.	I fried it just a minute ago.
pìt fay lɛ́ɛw rɨ́ yaŋ, ʔɛ́ɛt.	Have you turned the light off yet, At?
fay lɔ̆há. pìt lɛ́ɛw hâ.	The light? Yes, I've turned it off.
pìt mɨ̂a kíi níi ʔeeŋ.	I turned it off just a minute ago.
kaaŋ múŋ lɛ́ɛw rɨ́ yaŋ, sǐi.	Have you put up the mosquito net yet, Sri?
múŋ lɔ̆há. kaaŋ lɛ́ɛw hâ.	The mosquito net? Yes, I've put it up.
kaaŋ mɨ̂a kíi níi ʔeeŋ.	I put it up just a minute ago.
thŭu phɨ́ɨn lɛ́ɛw rɨ́ yaŋ, tùm.	Have you scrubbed the floor yet, Toom?
phɨ́ɨn lɔ̆há. thŭu lɛ́ɛw hâ.	The floor? Yes, I've scrubbed it.
thŭu mɨ̂a kíi níi ʔeeŋ.	I scrubbed it just a minute ago.
rîit sɨ̂a lɛ́ɛw rɨ́ yaŋ, tôy.	Have you ironed the shirt yet, Toy?
sɨ̂a lɔ̆há. rîit lɛ́ɛw hâ.	The shirt? Yes, I've ironed it.
rîit mɨ̂a kíi níi ʔeeŋ.	I ironed it just a minute ago.
sɨ́ɨ fay chǎay lɛ́ɛw rɨ́ yaŋ, nɔ́ɔy.	Have you bought the flashlight yet, Noy?
fay chǎay lɔ̆há. sɨ́ɨ lɛ́ɛw hâ.	The flashlight? Yes, I've bought it.
sɨ́ɨ mɨ̂a kíi níi ʔeeŋ.	I bought it just a minute ago.

44.3 Patterns.

sɨ́ɨ lɔ̀ɔt fay wáy.	To buy light bulbs for later use.
hŭŋ khâaw wáy.	To cook the rice for later use.
kaaŋ múŋ wáy.	To put up the mosquito net for later use.
kèp naŋsɨ́ɨ wáy.	To put away the book for later use.
câwkhɔ̆ɔŋ ráan.	The owner of the store.
câwkhɔ̆ɔŋ bâan.	The owner of the house, landlord.
câwkhɔ̆ɔŋ wítthayú.	The owner of the radio.
câwkhɔ̆ɔŋ phasǎa ʔaŋkrìt.	A native speaker of English.
sɨ̂a chɔ̂ət.	A dress shirt.
sɨ̂a haawaay.	A sport shirt.
sɨ̂a nɔ̂ɔk.	A suit coat or sport coat.
sɨ̂a fŏn.	A raincoat.
sɨ̂a nǎaw.	A coat (for keeping warm).
sɨ̂a sawéttɔ̂ə.	A sweater.
sɨ́ɨ fay chǎay phɨ̀a wâa fay sǐa.	Buy a flashlight in case the electricity goes off.
sày sɨ̂a fŏn phɨ̀a wâa fŏn tòk.	Wear a raincoat in case it rains.
hŭŋ khâaw mâkmâak phɨ̀a wâa khon ʔɨ̀ɨn maa.	Cook a lot of rice in case others come.

๔๔.๔ แบบฝึกหัดการฟังเสียงสูงต่ำ

โต๊ะเครื่องแป้ง   ผ้าปูโต๊ะ

อ่างล้างหน้า   ตะกร้าผง

ไม้จิ้มฟัน   จักรเย็บผ้า

ปลอกหมอน   ผ้าเช็ดตัว

๔๔.๕ บทบรรยาย

       หลอดไฟฟ้าขนาดหกสิบแรงเทียนที่บ้านคุณจอนขาดหลอดหนึ่ง เขาจึงให้คนสวนไปซื้อให้ใหม่ แล้วเขาให้คนสวนซื้อหลอดขนาดหกสิบแรงเทียนและยี่สิบห้าแรงเทียนไว้อีกอย่างละหลอด และให้ซื้อถ่านไฟฉายสามก้อนกับเทียนไขไว้ด้วยเผื่อว่าไฟเสียคนสวนไม่ได้เอาเงินไปด้วยเลย เพราะเจ้าของร้านจะเก็บทีหลัง

๔๔.๖ ความแตกต่างของเสียงสูงต่ำ

ผู้หญิงเขียนหมา   ผู้ชายเฆี่ยนหมา

ผู้หญิงทำอะไร   ผู้หญิงเขียนหมาใช่ไหม

     เขียนหมา ผู้หญิงเขียนหมา   ใช่ ผู้หญิงเขียนหมา

ผู้ชายทำอะไร   ผู้ชายเฆี่ยนหมาใช่ไหม

     เฆี่ยนหมา ผู้ชายเฆี่ยนหมา   ใช่ ผู้ชายเฆี่ยนหมา

ใครเขียนหมา   ผู้หญิงเฆี่ยนหมาใช่ไหม

     ผู้หญิง ผู้หญิงเขียนหมา   ไม่ใช่ ผู้หญิงเขียนหมา

ใครเฆี่ยนหมา   ผู้ชายเขียนหมาใช่ไหม

     ผู้ชาย ผู้ชายเฆี่ยนหมา   ไม่ใช่ ผู้ชายเฆี่ยนหมา

๔๔.๗ คำถามบทบรรยาย

หลอดไฟฟ้าที่บ้านคุณจอนขาด

     หลอดหนึ่งใช่ไหม   ใช่

เขาให้คนสวนไปแก้ใช่ไหม   ไม่ใช่

เขาให้คนสวนไปซื้อให้ใหม่

     ใช่ไหม   ใช่

คนสวนซื้อหลอดไฟขนาด

     ร้อยแรงเทียนใช่ไหม   ไม่ใช่

เขาซื้อหลอดไฟหกสิบแรงเทียน

     สองหลอดใช่ไหม   ใช่

แล้วก็หลอดไฟยี่สิบห้าแรงเทียน

     หนึ่งหลอดใช่ไหม   ใช่

เขาไปซื้อหลอดไฟอย่างเดียว

     ใช่ไหม   ไม่ใช่

เขาซื้อหลายอย่างใช่ไหม   ใช่

คุณจอนให้คนสวนไปซื้อเตียง

     ใช่ไหม   ไม่ใช่

44.4 Tone identification.

Household things.

to? khrɯaŋ pɛɛŋ	Dressing table.	phaa puu to?	Tablecloth.
?aaŋ laaŋ naa	Wash basin.	takraa phoŋ	Waste basket.
may cim fan	Toothpick.	cak yep phaa	Sewing machine.
plɔɔk mɔɔn	Pillow case.	phaa chet tua	Towel.

44.5 Narrative.

lɔɔt fay fáa khanàat hòk sìp rɛɛŋ thian thîi bâan khun cɔɔn khàat lɔɔt nɯŋ, kháw cɯŋ hây khon sǔan pay sɯ́ɯ hây mày. lɛ́ɛw kháw hây khon sǔan sɯ́ɯ lɔɔt khanàat hòk sìp rɛɛŋ thian lɛ́? yîi sìp hâa rɛɛŋ thian wáy ?ìik yàaŋ la lɔɔt. lɛ́? hây sɯ́ɯ thàan fay chǎay sǎam kôon kàp thian khǎy wáy dûay phɯ̀a wâa fay sǐa. khon sǔan mây dây ?aw ŋən pay dûay ləəy, phrɔ́? câwkhɔ̌ɔŋ ráan ca kèp thii lǎŋ.

44.6 Tone distinctions.

phûu yǐŋ khǐan mǎa.	The girl drew a dog.
phûu chaay khîan mǎa.	The boy whipped the dog.

phûu yǐŋ tham ?aray.
    khǐan mǎa. phûu yǐŋ khǐan mǎa.
phûu chaay tham ?aray.
    khîan mǎa. phûu chaay khîan mǎa.

phûu yǐŋ khǐan mǎa, chây máy.
    chây. phûu yǐŋ khǐan mǎa.
phûu chaay khîan mǎa, chây máy.
    chây. phûu chaay khîan mǎa.

khray khǐan mǎa.
    phûu yǐŋ. phûu yǐŋ khǐan mǎa.
khray khîan mǎa.
    phûu chaay. phûu chaay khîan mǎa.

phûu yǐŋ khǐan mǎa, chây máy.
    mây chây. phûu yǐŋ khǐan mǎa.
phûu chaay khîan mǎa, chây máy.
    mây chây. phûu chaay khîan mǎa.

44.7 Questions on the narrative.

lɔɔt fay fáa thîi bâan khun cɔɔn khàat lɔɔt nɯŋ, chây máy.	chây.
kháw hây khon sǔan pay kɛ̂ɛ, chây máy.	mây chây.
kháw hây khon sǔan pay sɯ́ɯ hây mày, chây máy.	chây.
khon sǔan sɯ́ɯ lɔɔt fay khanàat rɔ́ɔy rɛɛŋ thian, chây máy.	mây chây.
kháw sɯ́ɯ lɔɔt fay hòk sìp rɛɛŋ thian sɔ̌ɔŋ lɔɔt, chây máy.	chây.
lɛ́ɛw kô lɔɔt fay yîi sìp hâa rɛɛŋ thian nɯ̀ŋ lɔɔt, chây máy.	chây.
kháw pay sɯ́ɯ lɔɔt fay yàaŋ diaw, chây máy.	mây chây.
kháw sɯ́ɯ lǎay yàaŋ, chây máy.	chây.
khun cɔɔn hây khon sǔan pay sɯ́ɯ tiaŋ, chây máy.	mây chây.

(More.)

เขาให้คนสวนซื้อเทียนใช่ไหม	ใช่
แล้วก็ให้ซื้อไฟฉายด้วยใช่ไหม	ไม่ใช่
ให้ซื้อถ่านไฟฉายใช่ไหม	ใช่
คนสวนเอาเงินไปด้วยใช่ไหม	ไม่ใช่
คนสวนไม่ได้เอาเงินไปด้วยใช่ไหม	ใช่
เจ้าของร้านจะเก็บทีหลังใช่ไหม	ใช่
คุณจอนให้คนสวนแก้หลอดไฟใช่ไหม	ไม่ใช่ เขาให้ไปซื้อใหม่
หลอดไฟร้อยแรงเทียนใช่ไหม	ไม่ใช่ หกสิบแรงเทียน
	และยี่สิบห้าแรงเทียน
แล้วก็ให้คนสวนซื้อไฟฉายด้วย	
ใช่ไหม	ไม่ใช่ ให้ซื้อถ่านไฟฉาย
แล้วก็เทียนไขด้วยใช่ไหม	ใช่
ซื้อเทียนมาใช้ทุกวันใช่ไหม	ไม่ใช่ ซื้อไว้เผื่อว่าไฟเสีย
คุณจอนจะเอาเงินไปให้เจ้าของร้าน	
ทีหลังใช่ไหม	ไม่ใช่ เจ้าของร้านจะมาเก็บ
หลอดไฟที่บ้านใครขาด	บ้านคุณจอน
ขาดกี่หลอด	หลอดเดียว
เขาให้ใครไปซื้อใหม่	คนสวน
ไปซื้ออะไร	หลอดไฟ ถ่านไฟฉาย แล้วก็เทียนไข
ซื้อให้ใคร	ซื้อให้คุณจอน
ซื้อทำไม	ซื้อไว้ใช้
ทำไมต้องซื้อเทียนไข	เผื่อว่าไฟเสีย
คนสวนไปซื้อของเอาเงินไปด้วย	
หรือเปล่า	เปล่า
ทำไมเขาไม่ได้เอาเงินไป	เพราะเจ้าของร้านจะเก็บเงินทีหลัง
คนสวนไปซื้อของกี่อย่าง	สามอย่าง
อะไรบ้าง	หลอดไฟ ถ่านไฟฉายกับเทียนไข
หลอดไฟกี่หลอด	สามหลอด
ถ่านไฟฉายกี่ก้อน	สามก้อน
แล้วก็เทียนไขกี่ห่อ	ห่อเดียว

kháw hây khon sǔan súɯ thian, chây máy.
lɛ́ɛw kô hây súɯ fay chǎay dûay, chây máy.
hây súɯ thàan fay chǎay, chây máy.
khon sǔan ʔaw ŋən pay dûay, chây máy.
khon sǔan mây dây ʔaw ŋən pay dûay, chây máy.
câwkhɔ̌ɔŋ ráan ca kèp thii lǎŋ, chây máy.

khun cɔɔn hây khon sǔan kɛ̂ɛ lɔ̀ɔt fay,
chây máy.

lɔ̀ɔt fay rɔ́ɔy rɛɛŋ thian,
chây máy.

lɛ́ɛw kô hây khon sǔan súɯ fay chǎay dûay,
chây mây.

lɛ́ɛw kô thian khǎy dûay, chây máy.

súɯ thian maa cháy thúk wan,
chây máy.

khun cɔɔn ca ʔaw ŋən pay hây câwkhɔ̌ɔŋ ráan
thii lǎŋ, chây máy.

lɔ̀ɔt fay thîi bâan khray khàat.
khàat kìi lɔ̀ɔt.
kháw hây khray pay súɯ mày.

pay súɯ ʔaray.

súɯ hây khray.
súɯ thammay.
thammay tôŋ súɯ thian khǎy.

khon sǔan pay súɯ khɔ̌ɔŋ,
ʔaw ŋən pay dûay rɯ́ plàaw.

thammay kháw mây dây ʔaw ŋən pay.

khon sǔan pay súɯ khɔ̌ɔŋ kìi yàaŋ.

ʔaray bâaŋ.

lɔ̀ɔt fay kìi lɔ̀ɔt.
thàan fay chǎay kìi kôɔn.
lɛ́ɛw kô thian khǎy kìi hɔ̀ɔ.

chây.
mây chây.
chây.
mây chây.
chây.
chây.

mây chây.
kháw hây pay súɯ mày.

mây chây.   hòk sìp rɛɛŋ thian
lɛ́ʔ yîi sìp hâa rɛɛŋ thian.

mây chây.
hây súɯ thàan fay chǎay.

chây.

mây chây.
súɯ wáy phɯ̀a wâa fay sǐa.

mây chây.
câwkhɔ̌ɔŋ ráan ca maa kèp.

bâan khun cɔɔn.
lɔ̀ɔt diaw.
khon sǔan.

lɔ̀ɔt fay, thàan fay chǎay,
lɛ́ɛw kô thian khǎy.

súɯ hây khun cɔɔn.
súɯ wáy cháy.
phɯ̀a wâa fay sǐa.

plàaw.

phrɔ́ʔ câwkhɔ̌ɔŋ ráan
ca kèp ŋən thii lǎŋ.

sǎam yàaŋ.

lɔ̀ɔt fay, thàan fay chǎay,
kàp thian khǎy.

sǎam lɔ̀ɔt.
sǎam kôɔn.
hɔ̀ɔ diaw.

43

๔๔.๘   การสนทนาโต้ตอบ

คุณพ่อนั่งที่หน้าต่าง   ลูกชายนั่งที่โต๊ะ
คุณพ่อกำลังอ่านหนังสือพิมพ์   ลูกชายกำลังเล่นกับแมว
คุณพ่อนุ่งกางเกงขายาว   ลูกชายนุ่งกางเกงขาสั้น

คุณแม่นั่งที่เก้าอี้   ลูกสาวนั่งที่พื้น
คุณแม่กำลังอ่านหนังสือ   ลูกสาวกำลังเล่นกับหมา
คุณแม่นุ่งผ้าซิ่น   ลูกสาวนุ่งกระโปรง

คนที่อยู่ที่หน้าต่างกำลังเล่นกับแมวใช่ไหม

44.8   Conversation.

khun phɔ̂ɔ nâŋ thîi nâatàaŋ. The father is sitting at the window.

khun phɔ̂ɔ kamlaŋ ʔàan naŋsɯ̆ɯ phim. The father is reading a newspaper.

khun phɔ̂ɔ nûŋ kaŋkeeŋ khǎa yaaw. The father is wearing long pants.

khun mɛ̂ɛ nâŋ thîi kâwʔîi. The mother is sitting on a chair.

khun mɛ̂ɛ kamlaŋ ʔàan naŋsɯ̆ɯ. The mother is reading a book.

khun mɛ̂ɛ nûŋ phâasîn. The mother is wearing a phasin.

lûuk chaay nâŋ thîi tóʔ. The son is sitting on the table.

lûuk chaay kamlaŋ lên kàp mɛɛw. The son is playing with a cat.

lûuk chaay nûŋ kaŋkeeŋ khǎa sân. The son is wearing short pants.

lûuk sǎaw nâŋ thîi phɯ́ɯn. The daughter is sitting on the floor.

lûuk sǎaw kamlaŋ lên kàp mǎa. The daughter is playing with a dog.

lûuk sǎaw nûŋ kraprooŋ. The daughter is wearing a skirt.

The teacher should ask the students questions about the picture. In addition to the obvious questions like 'Who is reading a book?' and 'Where is the father sitting?' there are hundreds of **chây máy** questions with and without **khon thîi** constructions. For example:

khon thîi yùu thîi nâatàaŋ kamlaŋ lên kàp mɛɛw, chây máy.

๔๔.๙ วลีท้ายประโยค
ซิ

ไหนลองพูดคำว่า งู ซิ พูดถูกหรือเปล่า
    งู
ถูกแล้ว

ไหนลองเขียนคำว่า เงิน ซิ เขียนถูกหรือเปล่า
    (เขียน...เงิน)
ถูกแล้ว

ไหนลองอ่านคำนี้ซิ (มือ) อ่านถูกหรือเปล่า
    มือ
ถูกแล้ว

อ้าปากซิ   หันหน้าไปทางขวาซิ
หุบปากซิ   ยกมือซ้ายซิ
ปิดปากซิ   หายใจเข้าซิ
หลับตาซิ   หายใจออกซิ
ลืมตาซิ   เปิดหนังสือซิ
ปิดตาซิ

๔๔.๑๐ การเขียน
    ขอบคุณ

46

sí.

Speaker requests or suggests an action in order to find out something.

nǎy lɔɔŋ phûut kham wâa ŋuu sí.	Try saying the word **ŋuu.**
phûut thùuk rɤ́ plàaw.	Let's see if you get it right.
ŋuu.	**ŋuu.**
thùuk lɛ́ɛw.	That's right.
nǎy lɔɔŋ khǐan kham wâa ŋən sí.	Try writting the word **ŋən.**
khǐan thùuk rɤ́ plàaw.	Let's see if you get it right.
(khǐan ŋ-ə-n.)	(He writes ŋ-ə-n.)
thùuk lɛ́ɛw.	That's right.
nǎy lɔɔŋ ʔàan kham níi sí (mɯɯ).	Try reading this word (**mɯɯ**).
ʔàan thùuk rɤ́ plàaw.	Let's see if you get it right.
mɯɯ.	**mɯɯ.**
thùuk lɛ́ɛw.	That's right.

The orders given by a doctor while examining a patient ('Open your mouth', for example) are typical of the use of **sí.** His purpose is to find out if anything is wrong. Similar orders can be used for classroom drill: the teacher orders and the student performs. The purpose of the orders here, however, is to find out if the student understands the new words being used. Treat this drill as a test of oral comprehension, otherwise the use of **sí** is inappropriate. The student needn't learn to use all of the new words; understanding takes much less practice than speaking. Even complete accuracy in understanding isn't required. In fact, a few mistakes will tend to keep the testing situation in mind.

ʔâa pàak sí.	Open your mouth.
hùp pàak sí.	Close your mouth.
pìt pàak sí.	Cover your mouth.
làp taa sí.	Close your eyes.
lɯɯm taa sí.	Open your eyes.
pìt taa sí.	Cover your eyes.
hǎn nâa pay thaaŋ khwǎa sí.	Turn your face to the right.
yók mɯɯ sáay sí.	Raise your left hand.
hǎay cay khâw sí.	Breath in.
hǎay cay ʔɔ̀ɔk sí.	Breath out.
pɤ̀ɤt naŋsɯ̌ɯ sí.	Open your book.

Practice reading and writing lesson 3 of Book 1 in Thai. Notice the following irregularity.

khɔ̀ɔpkhun The final consonant is an irregular **n.** It corresponds to the Sanskrit 'n.

บทที่ ๔๕

๔๕. ก

๔๕. ข เรียงความ

อากาศในประเทศไทย

ประเทศไทยเป็นประเทศร้อน หน้าร้อนอากาศร้อนมาก โดยเฉพาะในเดือน
เมษายนซึ่งเป็นเดือนที่ร้อนที่สุดของปี เดือนนี้คนส่วนมากชอบไปตากอากาศตาม
ชายทะเล เช่น ที่พัทยา บางแสน เป็นต้น

ต่อจากหน้าร้อนก็ถึงหน้าฝน ซึ่งจะเริ่มตั้งแต่กลางเดือนพฤษภาคมเป็น
ต้นไปเป็นเวลาประมาณหกเดือน ในระยะนี้ฝนตกมากซึ่งเป็นประโยชน์ในการ
ทำนา

ต่อจากหน้าฝนก็ถึงหน้าหนาว ซึ่งจะเริ่มราว ๆ เดือนพฤศจิกายนไปจนถึง
เดือนมกราคม หน้าหนาวในเมืองไทย อากาศจะไม่ค่อยหนาว ส่วนมากจะหนาวจัด
อยู่สองสามวันเท่านั้น ไม่มีหิมะตกเลย

อากาศ	ตากอากาศ	ระยะ
ประเทศ	ตาม	ประโยชน์
หน้า	ทะเล	นา
หน้าร้อน	ชายทะเล	จน
หน้าฝน	เช่น	จนถึง
หน้าหนาว	ต้น	ไม่ค่อย
โดยเฉพาะ	ต่อจาก	จัด
ซึ่ง	เริ่ม	หิมะ
ส่วน		
ส่วนมาก		

48

LESSON 45

(Review)

45.a Review sections 2, 5, 6, 7, and 9 of lessons 41 – 44.

45.b Reading selection.

In the four review lessons of Book 3, short reading selections have been added. These are not intended as review material. They introduce not only new words, but even a new style: written Thai. They have been placed in the review lessons as a means of keeping classes of differing speeds on the same schedule. Slow classes can (and should) skip them completely. Later lessons do not depend on their vocabulary or patterns. They are completely separate from the content and purpose of the book, which is strictly spoken Thai. For classes that have time left over after review, however, the reading selections offer passive exposure to new vocabulary as well as a diversion from the strictly oral approach. And for those students who have been following the writing sections of each lesson throughout the course and intend to go on with written Thai, they provide an introduction or bridge to such courses.

ʔaakàat nay prathêet thay

prathêet thay pen prathêet rɔ́ɔn. nâa rɔ́ɔn ʔaakàat rɔ́ɔn mâak. dooy chaphɔ́ʔ nay dʉan meesǎayon, sʉ̌ŋ pen dʉan thîi rɔ́ɔn thîisùt khɔ̌ŋ pii. dʉan níi khon sùan mâak chɔ̂ɔp pay tàak ʔaakàat taam chaay thalee, chên thîi phátthayaa, baaŋ sɛ̌ɛn pen tôn.

tɔ̀ɔ càak nâa rɔ́ɔn kɔ̂ thʉ̌ŋ nâa fǒn, sʉ̌ŋ ca rɔ̂əm tâŋtɛ̀ɛ klaaŋ dʉan phrɯ́tsaphaakhom pen tôn pay. pen weelaa pramaan hòk dʉan. nay rayáʔ níi fǒn tòk mâak, sʉ̌ŋ pen prayòot nay kaan tham naa.

tɔ̀ɔ càak nâa fǒn kɔ̂ thʉ̌ŋ nâa nǎaw, sʉ̌ŋ ca rɔ̂əm rawraaw dʉan phrɯ́tsacikaayon pay con thʉ̌ŋ dʉan mókkaraakhom. nâa nǎaw nay mʉaŋ thay ʔaakàat ca mây khɔ̂y nǎaw. sùan mâak ca nǎaw càt yùu sɔ̌ɔŋ sǎam wan thâwnán. mây mii hìmáʔ tòk ləəy.

ʔaakàat	Weather, the space above the ground.
prathêet	Country.
nâa	Season.
nâa rɔ́ɔn	Hot season.
nâa fǒn	Rainy season.
nâa nǎaw	Cold season.
dooy chaphɔ́ʔ	Especially.
sʉ̌ŋ	Relative pronoun (that, which).
sùan	A part.
sùan mâak	For the most part, the majority.
tàak ʔaakàat	To expose oneself to the weather. To take an airing or vacation.
taam	Along, at the various . . . .
thalee	Sea.
chaay thalee	Seashore.
chên	As, like, for example.
tôn	A beginning.
tɔ̀ɔ càak	Continuing on from.
rɔ̂əm	To begin.
rayáʔ	A stretch of distance or time.
prayòot	Use, usefulness.
naa	Rice fields.
con, con thʉ̌ŋ	Until.
mây khɔ̂y . . .	Not so. . . , not very . . . .
càt	Strong, intense, extreme.
hìmáʔ	Snow.

บทที่ ๔๖

๔๖.๑ คำศัพท์

ตาก	ขโมย
หมอน	
ตากหมอน	ค่อย
	ไม่ค่อย
ล้าง	ไม่ค่อยดี
หญ้า	ระวัง
ตัดหญ้า	
	ออก
ตั้งแต่	ออกไป
ตั้งแต่เมื่อไหร่	ออกเงิน
เช่า	คนใช้
บ้านเช่า	
	เสื่อ
แฟล็ต	เสื้อ
ปลอดภัย	กรง
เฝ้า	
ยาม	ง่าย
มียามเฝ้า	มอเตอร์ไซ
กลางวัน	เคย
กลางคืน	
ทั้งกลางวันกลางคืน	ตื่น
	สวย

50

LESSON 46

46.1 Vocabulary and expansions.

tàak	To expose (to sun, air, or wind).
mɔ̌ɔn	Pillow.
tàak mɔ̌ɔn	To air a pillow.
láaŋ	To wash (not used with 'hair' or 'clothes').
yâa	Grass.
tàt yâa	To cut the grass, mow the lawn.
tâŋtɛ̀ɛ	Since.
tâŋtɛ̀ɛ mɨarày	Since when?
châw	To rent.
bâan châw	A house for rent.
flɛ̀t	A flat, an apartment, a court. (The words ʔapháatmén and khɔ̀ɔt are also used.)
plɔ̀ɔtpʰay	To be safe.
fâw	To guard, watch, keep an eye on.
yaam	A guard, a night watchman.
mii yaam fâw	There is a watchman on duty.
klaaŋwan	Daytime.
klaaŋkʰɨɨn	Nighttime.
tʰáŋ klaaŋwan klaaŋkʰɨɨn	Night and day.
khamooy	A thief, to steal.
khɔ̂y	Gradually, little by little.
mây khɔ̂y	Not very.
mây khɔ̂y dii	Not very good.
rawaŋ	To be careful.
ʔɔ̀ɔk	To 'out'.
ʔɔ̀ɔk pay	To go out.
ʔɔ̀ɔk ŋən	To pay out money.
khon cháay	Servant (a person for use).
sɨ̀a	A mat.
sɨ̌a	A tiger.
kroŋ	A cage.
ŋâay	To be easy.
mɔɔtəəsay	Motorcycle.
khəəy	Having experienced (anywhere from once to regularly). The following three English meanings are all included in the meaning of **khəəy**: a) at least once (to have ever), b) regularly at some time in the past (used to), 3) almost all the time (to be used to, usually). These distinctions can be made when necessary by adding other words.
tɨ̀ɨn	To wake up
sǔay	**To be pretty.**

๔๖.๒ แบบฝึกหัดการสลับเสียงสูงต่ำ

ทำแกงที่ร้าน	(ครัว)	รีดเสื้อที่สนาม	(ห้อง)
ทำแกงที่ครัว	(ซื้อไข่)	รีดเสื้อที่ห้อง	(ตากหมอน)
ซื้อไข่ที่ครัว	(ร้าน)	ตากหมอนที่ห้อง	(หน้าต่าง)
ซื้อไข่ที่ร้าน	(กางมุ้ง)	ตากหมอนที่หน้าต่าง	(ทอดหมู)
กางมุ้งที่ร้าน	(ห้องนอน)	ทอดหมูที่หน้าต่าง	(ครัว)
กางมุ้งที่ห้องนอน	(ขายขวด)	ทอดหมูที่ครัว	(ถูพื้น)
ขายขวดที่ห้องนอน	(ถนน)	ถูพื้นที่ครัว	(บ้าน)
ขายขวดที่ถนน	(ตัดหญ้า)	ถูพื้นที่บ้าน	(ล้างจาน)
ตัดหญ้าที่ถนน	(สนาม)	ล้างจานที่บ้าน	(ครัว)
ตัดหญ้าที่สนาม	(รีดเสื้อ)	ล้างจานที่ครัว	

Substitution drill.

tham kɛɛŋ thîi ráan. (khrua)	Make the curry at the shop. (kitchen)
tham kɛɛŋ thîi khrua. (súu khày)	Make the curry in the kitchen. (buy eggs)
súu khày thîi khrua. (ráan)	Buy the eggs in the kitchen. (shop)
súu khày thîi ráan. (kaaŋ múŋ)	Buy the eggs at the shop. (put up the mosquito net)
kaaŋ múŋ thîi ráan. (hɔ̂ŋ nɔɔn)	Put up the mosquito net at the shop. (bedroom)
kaaŋ múŋ thîi hɔ̂ŋ nɔɔn. (khǎay khùat)	Put up the mosquito net in the bedroom. (sell bottles)
khǎay khùat thîi hɔ̂ŋ nɔɔn. (thanǒn)	Sell bottles in the bedroom. (street)
khǎay khùat thîi thanǒn. (tàt yâa)	Sell bottles in the street. (cut grass)
tàt yâa thîi thanǒn. (sanǎam)	Cut the grass in the street. (yard)
tàt yâa thîi sanǎam. (rîit sûa)	Cut the grass in the yard. (iron the shirt)
rîit sûa thîi sanǎam. (hɔ̂ŋ)	Iron the shirt in the yard. (room)
rîit sûa thîi hɔ̂ŋ. (tàak mɔ̌ɔn)	Iron the shirt in the room. (air the pillows)
tàak mɔ̌ɔn thîi hɔ̂ŋ. (nâatàaŋ)	Air the pillows in the room. (window)
tàak mɔ̌ɔn thîi nâatàaŋ. (thɔ̂ɔt mǔu)	Air the pillows at the window. (fry pork)
thɔ̂ɔt mǔu thîi nâatàaŋ. (khrua)	Fry the pork at the window. (kitchen)
thɔ̂ɔt mǔu thîi khrua. (thǔu phʉ́ʉn)	Fry the pork in the kitchen. (scrub the floor)
thǔu phʉ́ʉn thîi khrua. (bâan)	Scrub the floor in the kitchen. (house)
thǔu phʉ́ʉn thîi bâan. (láaŋ caan)	Scrub the floors in the house. (wash the dishes)
láaŋ caan thîi bâan. (khrua)	Wash the dishes in the house. (kitchen)
láaŋ caan thîi khrua.	Wash the dishes in the kitchen.

๔๖.๓   โครงสร้างของประโยค

เกือบเดือนหนึ่ง	คนสวน
เกือบอาทิตย์หนึ่ง	คนใช้
เกือบปีหนึ่ง	คนขายของ
เกือบชั่วโมงหนึ่ง	

ไหนจะดีกว่ากัน	เขาทำเอง
ไหนจะถูกกว่ากัน	เขาจ้างเอง
อะไรจะดีกว่ากัน	เขาล้างจานเอง
อะไรจะใหญ่กว่ากัน	

มีคนมาหา	ฉันเองก็ไม่รู้
มียามเฝ้า	คุณเองเป็นคนบอก
มีเด็กเล่น	ใครบอก คุณสวัสดิ์เอง

ไม่ค่อยมี	
ไม่ค่อยชอบ	เมื่อกันเอง
ไม่ค่อยดี	วันนั้นเอง
ไม่ค่อยปลอดภัย	เป็นธรรมดาอยู่เองที่...

ค่าน้ำ	
ค่าไฟ	คนใช้คนเดียว
ค่าแรง	คนใช้คนหนึ่ง
ค่าของ	คนใช้หนึ่งคน

๔๖.๔   แบบฝึกหัดการฟังเสียงสูงต่ำ

ส้มเขียวหวาน	กล้วยหอม
สับปะรด	มังคุด
แตงโม	ลำใย
มะละกอ	น้อยหน่า

46.3 Patterns.

kùap dɯan nɯŋ.	Almost a month.
kùap ʔathít nɯŋ.	Almost a week.
kùap pii nɯŋ.	Almost a year.
kùap chûamooŋ nɯŋ	Almost an hour.
nǎy ca dii kwàa kan.	Which is better?
nǎy ca thùuk kwàa kan.	Which is cheaper?
ʔaray ca dii kwàa kan.	Which is better?
ʔaray ca yày kwàa kan.	Which is bigger?
mii khon maa hǎa.	Someone has come to see you.
mii yaam fâw.	There is a guard watching it.
mii dèk lên.	There are children ‚playing.
mây khɔ̂y mii.	There isn't very much.
mây khɔ̂y chɔ̂ɔp.	I don't like it very much.
mây khɔ̂y dii.	It isn't very good.
mây khɔ̂y plɔ̀ɔtphay.	It isn't very safe.
khâa náam.	The water bill.
khâa fay.	The electricity bill.
khâa rɛɛŋ.	The cost for labor (strength).
khâa khɔ̌ɔŋ.	The cost for parts (as opposed to labor in figuring car repair costs).
khon sǔan.	A gardener.
khon cháay.	Servants.
khon khǎay khɔ̌ɔŋ.	A sales clerk.
kháw tham ʔeeŋ.	He did it himself.
kháw câaŋ ʔeeŋ.	He hired her himself.
kháw láaŋ caan ʔeeŋ.	He washed the dishes himself.
chán ʔeeŋ kɔ̂ mây rúu.	I myself don't know. Even I don't know.
khun ʔeeŋ pen khon bɔ̀ɔk.	It was you yourself who told me.
khray bɔ̀ɔk. khun sawàt ʔeeŋ.	Who told you? Sawat himself.
mɯ̂a kíi níi ʔeeŋ.	Just a minute ago.
wan nán ʔeeŋ.	On that very day.
pen thammadaa yùu ʔeeŋ thîi… .	It's only natural that… .
khon cháay khon diaw.	A single servant.
khon cháay khon nɯŋ.	A servant.
khon cháay nɯ̀ŋ khon.	One servant.

46.4 Tone identification.
Fruits.

som khiaw waan	The common green orange of Thailand.	kluay hɔɔm	Fragrant bananas. The kind usually referred to by the English word.
sapparot	Pineapple.	maŋkhut	Mangosteen.
tɛɛŋ moo	Watermelon.	lamyay	Lamyai.
malakɔɔ	Papaya.	nɔɔynaa	Custard apple.

๔๖.๕ บทสนทนา

ก. คุณมาถึงกรุงเทพฯ ตั้งแต่เมื่อไหร่

ข. เกือบเดือนหนึ่งแล้ว ผม
กำลังหาบ้านเช่า
อยู่บ้านกับอยู่แฟล็ตไหน
จะดีกว่ากัน

ก. ผมว่าอยู่แฟล็ตดีกว่า เพราะว่า
ปลอดภัยกว่า แล้วก็ถูกกว่าด้วย

ข. ปลอดภัยกว่ายังไง

ก. ก็ที่แฟล็ตมียามเฝ้าทั้งกลางวันกลาง
คืน ขโมยไม่ค่อยมี ไม่ต้องระวังมาก

ข. แล้วทำไมถูกกว่าล่ะ

ก. ก็ค่าน้ำก็ไม่ต้องออก คนสวนก็ไม่
ต้องจ้างเอง มีคนใช้คนเดียวก็พอ

๔๖.๖ ความแตกต่างระหว่างเสียงสูงต่ำ

เสื้ออยู่บนโต๊ะ   เสื้ออยู่ที่เก้าอี้   เสื้ออยู่ในกรง

เสื้ออยู่ที่ไหน
   บนโต๊ะ เสื้ออยู่บนโต๊ะ

เสื้ออยู่ที่ไหน
   ที่เก้าอี้ เสื้ออยู่ที่เก้าอี้

เสื้ออยู่ที่ไหน
   ในกรง เสื้ออยู่ในกรง

อะไรอยู่บนโต๊ะ
   เสื้อ เสื้ออยู่บนโต๊ะ

อะไรอยู่ที่เก้าอี้
   เสื้อ เสื้ออยู่ที่เก้าอี้

อะไรอยู่ในกรง
   เสื้อ เสื้ออยู่ในกรง

เสื้ออยู่บนโต๊ะใช่ไหม
   ใช่ เสื้ออยู่บนโต๊ะ

เสื้ออยู่ที่เก้าอี้ใช่ไหม
   ใช่ เสื้ออยู่ที่เก้าอี้

เสื้ออยู่ในกรงใช่ไหม
   ใช่ เสื้ออยู่ในกรง

เสื้ออยู่ที่เก้าอี้ใช่ไหม
   ไม่ใช่ เสื้ออยู่บนโต๊ะ

เสื้ออยู่ในกรงใช่ไหม
   ไม่ใช่ เสื้ออยู่ที่เก้าอี้

เสื้ออยู่บนโต๊ะใช่ไหม
   ไม่ใช่ เสื้ออยู่ในกรง

46.5 Dialog.   46.5

A. khun maa thਉ̆ŋ kruŋthêep tâŋtɛ̀ɛ   When did you arrive in Bangkok?
    mਉ̂arày.

  B. kਉ̀ap dਉan nਉŋ lɛ́ɛw.   It has been almost one month now.
     phǒm kamlaŋ hǎa bâan châw.   I'm looking for a house to rent.
     yùu bâan ka yùu flɛ̀t,   Do you think it's better to live
     nǎy ca dii kwàa kan.   in a house or an apartment?

A. phǒm wâa yùu flɛ̀t dii kwàa,   I'd say it's better to live in an apartment,
    phrɔ́ʔ wâa plɔ̀ɔtphay kwàa,   because it's safer
    lɛ́ɛw kɔ̂ thùuk kwàa dûay.   and cheaper.

  B. plɔ̀ɔtphay kwàa yaŋŋay.   How is it safer?

A. kɔ̂*, thîi flɛ̀t mii yaam fâw   Well, apartments have watchmen
    tháŋ klaaŋwan klaaŋkhਉਉn.   both day and night.
    khamooy mây khôy mii.   There are hardly any thieves.
    mây tôŋ rawaŋ mâak.   You don't have to be so careful.

  B. lɛ́ɛw thammay thùuk kwàa lâ.   And why is it cheaper?

A. kɔ̂, khâa náam kɔ̂ mây tôŋ ʔɔ̀ɔk.   Well, you don't have to pay the water bill.
    khon sǔan kɔ̂ mây tôŋ câaŋ ʔeeŋ.   And you don't have to hire your own gardener;
    mii khon cháay khon diaw kɔ̂ phɔɔ.   one servant is enough.

*kɔ̂ serves to link its clause or sentence to something else. In the last sentence of the dialog,
kɔ̂ links the three clauses (kɔ̂ mây tôŋ ʔɔ̀ɔk, kɔ̂ mây tôŋ câaŋ ʔeeŋ, kɔ̂ phɔɔ) together as part
of a series. The other two uses of kɔ̂ (kɔ̂, thîi flɛ̀t . . ., kɔ̂, khâa náam . . .) link their
sentences to the preceding questions; that is, they show that an answer is forthcoming.   It
is especially useful when the answerer needs time to think: 'I have heard your question and
am preparing an answer'. If the answerer doesn't give such a signal and prepares his answer
in silence, the questioner will think that he hasn't heard. (Compare the similar use of 'Well,'
in English.)

46.6 Tone distinctions.   46.6

sਉ̀a yùu bon tóʔ.   The mat is on the table.
sਉ̂a yùu thîi kâwʔii.   The shirt is on the chair.
sǔa yùu nay kroŋ.   The tiger is in the cage.

(See pictures on following page.)

sਉ̀a yùu thîi nǎy.   sਉ̀a yùu bon tóʔ, chây máy.
  bon tóʔ. sਉ̀a yùu bon tóʔ.   chây. sਉ̀a yùu bon tóʔ.
sਉ̂a yùu thîi nǎy.   sਉ̂a yùu thîi kâwʔii, chây máy.
  thîi kâwʔii. sਉ̂a yùu thîi kâwʔii.   chây. sਉ̂a yùu thîi kâwʔii.
sǔa yùu thîi nǎy.   sǔa yùu nay kroŋ, chây máy.
  nay kroŋ. sǔa yùu nay kroŋ.   chây. sǔa yùu nay kroŋ.

ʔaray yùu bon tóʔ.   sਉ̂a yùu thîi kâwʔii, chây máy.
  sਉ̀a. sਉ̀a yùu bon tóʔ.   mây chây. sਉ̀a yùu bon tóʔ.
ʔaray yùu thîi kâwʔii.   sǔa yùu nay kroŋ, chây máy.
  sਉ̂a. sਉ̂a yùu thîi kâwʔii.   mây chây. sਉ̂a yùu thîi kâwʔii.
ʔaray yùu nay kroŋ.   sਉ̀a yùu bon tóʔ, chây máy.
  sǔa. sǔa yùu nay kroŋ.   mây chây. sǔa yùu nay kroŋ.

๔๖.๗ แบบฝึกหัดไวยากรณ์

ก.

อยู่บ้านกับอยู่แฟล็ตไหนจะดีกว่ากัน   (ปลอดภัย)
        ฉันว่าอยู่แฟล็ตดีกว่า เพราะว่าปลอดภัยกว่า

ไปแท๊กซี่กับเดินไปไหนจะดีกว่ากัน   (เร็ว)
        ฉันว่าไปแท๊กซี่ดีกว่าเพราะว่าเร็วกว่า

ไปแท๊กซี่กับเดินไปไหนจะดีกว่ากัน   (ปลอดภัย)
        ฉันว่าเดินไปดีกว่าเพราะว่าปลอดภัยกว่า

พูดภาษาไทยกับพูดภาษาอังกฤษไหนจะดีกว่ากัน (ง่าย)
        ฉันว่าพูดภาษาอังกฤษดีกว่าเพราะว่าง่ายกว่า

ขับรถยนต์กับขับรถมอเตอร์ไซไหนจะดีกว่ากัน
(ถูก ปลอดภัย สบาย ง่าย)

กินอาหารไทยกับกินอาหารฝรั่งไหนจะดีกว่ากัน
(อร่อย ถูก ทำง่าย)

อยู่เมืองไทยกับอยู่เมืองนอกไหนจะดีกว่ากัน
(ถูก สบาย เย็น ร้อน)

ทำงานกลางวันกับทำงานกลางคืนไหนจะดีกว่ากัน
(เย็น ง่าย สบาย)

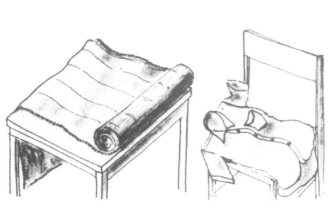

46.7 Grammar drills.

a. Response drill.

yùu bâan kàp yùu flèt,
năy ca dii kwàa kan. (plɔ̀ɔtphay)
   chán wâa yùu flèt dii kwàa,
   phrɔ́ʔ wâa plɔ̀ɔtphay kwàa.

Living in a house and living in an apartment,
which is better? (safe)
   I think it's better to live in an apartment,
   because it's safer.

pay thɛ́ksîi kàp dəən pay,
năy ca dii kwàa kan. (rew)
   chán wâa pay thɛ́ksîi dii kwàa,
   phrɔ́ʔ wâa rew kwàa.

Going by taxi and walking,
which is better? (fast)
   I think it's better to go by taxi,
   because it's faster.

pay thɛ́ksîi kàp dəən pay,
năy ca dii kwàa kan. (plɔ̀ɔtphay)
   chán wâa dəən pay dii kwàa
   phrɔ́ʔ wâa plɔ̀ɔtphay kwàa.

Going by taxi and walking,
which is better? (safe)
   I think it's better to walk,
   because it's safer.

phûut phasăa thay kàp phûut phasăa
ʔaŋkrìt, năy ca dii kwàa kan. (ŋâay)
   chán wâa phûut phasăa ʔaŋkrìt dii kwàa
   phrɔ́ʔ wâa ŋâay kwàa.

Speaking Thai and speaking English,
which is better? (easy)
   I think it's better to speak English,
   because it's easier.

Answers are not given to the following items, and students might differ in their choice. But whatever their choice, they must consider the meaning. This is the point.

khàp rót yon kàp khàp rót mɔɔtəəsay,
năy ca dii kwàa kan.
(thùuk, plɔ̀ɔtphay, sabaay, ŋâay)

Driving a car and driving a motorcycle,
which is better?
(cheap, safe, comfortable, easy)

kin ʔaahăan thay kàp kin ʔaahăan faràŋ,
năy ca dii kwàa kan.
(ʔarɔ̀y, thùuk, tham ŋâay)

Eating Thai food and eating Farang food,
which is better?
(taste good, cheap, easy to make)

yùu mɯaŋ thay kàp yùu mɯaŋ nɔ̂ɔk,
năy ca dii kwàa kan.
(thùuk, sabaay, yen, rɔ́ɔn)

Living in Thailand and living abroad,
which is better?
(cheap, comfortable, cool, hot)

tham ŋaan klaaŋwan kàp tham ŋaan
klaaŋkhɯɯn, năy ca dii kwàa kan.
(yen, ŋâay, sabaay)

Working during the day and working at night,
which is better?
(cool, easy, comfortable)

ข.

เขาเคยไปเมืองนอก   (อยู่ที่ซอยนั้น)

เขาเคยอยู่ที่ซอยนั้น   (ตื่นตีห้า)

เขาเคยตื่นตีห้า   (ไม่)

เขาไม่เคยตื่นตีห้า   (ไปเมืองนอก)

เขาไม่เคยไปเมืองนอก   (อยู่ที่ซอยนั้น)

เขาไม่เคยอยู่ที่ซอยนั้น

ค.

ไก่สองตัวนี่ คุณจะเอาตัวเดียวใช่ไหม   หนังสือสามเล่มนี่คุณจะเอาสองเล่มใช่ไหม
      ไม่ใช่ จะเอาทั้งสองตัว   ไม่ใช่ จะเอาทั้งสามเล่ม

ไก่ตัวนี้คุณจะเอาครึ่งตัวใช่ไหม   คุณทำงานครึ่งวันใช่ไหม
      ไม่ใช่ จะเอาทั้งตัว   ไม่ใช่ ทำทั้งวัน

เงินนี่คุณจะเอาร้อยบาทใช่ไหม   คุณเรียนภาษาไทยวันจันทร์ พุธ ศุกร์ ใช่ไหม
      ไม่ใช่ จะเอาทั้งหมด   ไม่ใช่ เรียนทุกวัน

เด็กห้องนี้คุณชอบคนเดียวใช่ไหม
      ไม่ใช่ ชอบทุกคน

๔๖.๘   การสนทนาโต้ตอบ

ห้องน้ำ	ครัว	สวน
ห้องนอน	ตู้เย็น	สนาม
ห้องกินข้าว	โรงรถ	ต้นไม้
ห้องรับแขก		

b. Substitution drill.

kháw khǝǝy pay mʉaŋ nɔ̂ɔk.
(yùu thîi sɔɔy nán)

He has been abroad.
(live on that Soi)

kháw khǝǝy yùu thîi sɔɔy nán.
(tʉ̀ʉn tii hâa)

He used to live on that Soi.
(get up at 5 o'clock)

kháw khǝǝy tʉ̀ʉn tii hâa.
(mây)

He usually gets up at 5 o'clock.
(not)

kháw mây khǝǝy tʉ̀ʉn tii hâa.
(pay mʉaŋ nɔ̂ɔk)

He has never gotten up at 5 o'clock.
(go abroad)

kháw mây khǝǝy pay mʉaŋ nɔ̂ɔk.
(yùu thîi sɔɔy nán)

He has never been abroad.
(live on that Soi)

kháw mây khǝǝy yùu thîi sɔɔy nán.

He has never lived on that Soi.

c. Response drill.

kày sɔ̌ɔŋ tua níi, khun ca ʔaw tua diaw,
chây máy.

Of these two chickens, you want only one.
Right?

   mây chây. ca ʔaw tháŋ sɔ̌ɔŋ tua.

   No. I want both of them.

kày tua níi, khun ca ʔaw khrʉ̂ŋ tua,
chây máy.

Of this chicken, you want half.
Right?

   mây chây. ca ʔaw tháŋ tua.

   No. I want all of it.

ŋǝn níi, khun ca ʔaw rɔ́ɔy bàat, chây máy.

Of this money, you want 100 baht. Right?

   mây chây. ca ʔaw tháŋmòt.

   No. I want all of it.

dèk hɔ̂ŋ níi, khun chɔ̂ɔp khon diaw,
chây máy.

Of the children in this room, you like
only one. Right?

   mây chây. chɔ̂ɔp thúk khon.

   No. I like all of them.

naŋsʉ̌ʉ sǎam lêm níi, khun ca ʔaw
sɔ̌ɔŋ lêm, chây máy.

Of these three books, you want two.
Right?

   mây chây. ca ʔaw tháŋ sǎam lêm.

   No. I want all three of them.

khun tham ŋaan khrʉ̂ŋ wan, chây máy.

You work half a day. Right?

   mây chây. tham tháŋ wan.

   No. I work all day.

khun rian phasǎa thay wan can,
phút, sùk, chây máy.

You study Thai on Mondays, Wednesdays,
and Fridays. Right?

   mây chây. rian thúk wan.

   No. I study it every day.

46.8 Conversation.   46.8

The teacher should ask each student about his home. The following words will be needed.

hɔ̂ŋ náam	Bathroom.	khrua	Kitchen.	sǔan	Garden.
hɔ̂ŋ nɔɔn	Bedroom.	tûu yen	Refrigerator.	sanǎam	Yard.
hɔ̂ŋ kin khâaw	Dining room.	rooŋ rót	Garage.	tôn máay	Trees.
hɔ̂ŋ ráp khὲὲk	Living room. (Room for receiving guests.)				

๔๖.๙ วลีท้ายประโยค

นะ

ผู้หญิงคนนั้นสวยนะ   พูดยังงั้นไม่ดีนะ
      ครับ สวยจริง ๆ   ครับ ไม่ดี

ผู้ชายคนนั้นอ้วนนะ   เก้าอี้ตัวนี้สบายนะ
      ไม่เห็นอ้วนเลย   ครับ สบายดี

วันนี้ร้อนนะ   หนังสือนี่ไม่ดีนะ
      ไม่หรอก กำลังดี   ทำไมว่ายังงั้นล่ะ

๔๖.๑๐ การเขียน

บทที่สี่   บทสนทนา   เลข   การเขียน

ná.

Speaker makes a comment or calls hearer's attention to something.

The teacher should make comments on pictures, the weather, and things or people in sight and the students should either agree or disagree.   Later, the students should make comments with the teacher and other students agreeing or disagreeing.   Examples are given below.

phûu yǐŋ khon nán sǔay ná.	Isn't that girl pretty? (Said with a falling intonation.)
khráp. sǔay ciŋciŋ.	Yes. She sure is.
phûu chaay khon nán ʔûan ná.	Isn't that man fat?
mây hěn ʔûan ləəy.	I don't think he's fat at all.
wan níi rɔ́ɔn ná.	Isn't it hot today?
mây lɔ̀k. kamlaŋ dii.	No it isn't. It's just right.
phûut yaŋŋán mây dii ná.	That was a terrible thing to say. Don't you agree?
khráp. mây dii.	Hmm.
kâwʔîi tua níi sabaay ná.	Isn't this chair comfortable?
khráp. sabaay dii.	Hmm.
naŋsɯ̌ɯ níi mây dii ná.	I don't think this book is any good. Don't you agree?
thammay wâa yaŋŋán lâ.	No. Why do you say that?

(The commonest way of agreeing with a **ná** comment is to quickly raise and lower the eyebrows (yák khíw), and the student should acquire this habit as part of the language. A conscious use of this gesture, however, is not recommended — it should be used naturally or not at all.   When you see Thais talking to each other, keep your eyes on their eyebrows and your ears on their **ná**'s and you will soon have it.

46.10 Writing.   46.10

Practice reading and writing lesson 4 of Book 1 in Thai. Notice, also, the following headings.

bòt thîi sìi	Lesson 4.
4.3 bòt sǒnthanaa	4.3 Dialog. (Literally, 'conversation text'.)
4.8 lêek	4.8 Numbers.
4.10 kaan khǐan	4.10 Writing.

บทที่ ๔๗

๔๗.๑ คำศัพท์

โดย

ทั่ว

ทั่วไป

โดยทั่วๆ ไป

บ้านอยู่

เช่าบ้านอยู่

การ........

การเช่าบ้านอยู่

อพาร์ตเมนต์

อยู่อพาร์ตเมนต์

การอยู่อพาร์ตเมนต์

ถึงจะ

มีมากขึ้น

ต้องมีคนใช้มากขึ้น

สำหรับ

แต่สำหรับฝรั่งแล้ว

ยัง

ยังถูกกว่า

นี่ยังถูกกว่านั้น

มี...ยังถูกกว่าไม่มี

บ้านทุกบ้าน

บ้านทุกหลัง

น้อย

อย่างน้อย

อย่างมาก

คนใช้อย่างน้อยสองคน

เฝ้าบ้าน

คนหนึ่งต้องเฝ้าบ้าน

เพิ่ม

เพิ่มขึ้น

เพิ่มขึ้นอีก

ต้องมี

อาจจะต้องมี

จ่าย

กับข้าว

จ่ายกับข้าว

ลำบาก

จ่ายกับข้าวก็ลำบาก

ซื้อของ

หาซื้อของ

เดินหาซื้อของ

ไปเดินหาซื้อของ

จ้างคนใช้

LESSON 47

47.1 Vocabulary and expansions.

dooy	By means of, with, by.
thûa	To be throughout, all over the place.
thûa pay	Throughout, everywhere.
dooy thûathûa pay	Generally.
bâan yùu	A house to live in.
châw bâan yùu	To rent a house to live in.
kaan ...	The action of ...
kaan châw bâan yùu	The renting of a house to live in.
ʔapháatmén	An apartment.
yùu ʔapháatmén	To live in an apartment.
kaan yùu ʔapháatmén	Living in an apartment.
thŭŋ ca	Even though.
mii mâak khûn	To have an increase.
tôŋ mii khon cháay mâak khûn	Must have more servants.
sámràp	For doing something, for someone, as for.
tɛ̀ɛ sámràp faràŋ lɛ́ɛw	But when it comes to Farangs, now.
yaŋ	Still more, even.
yaŋ thùuk kwàa	Is still cheaper than.
nîi yaŋ thùuk kwàa nân	This is even cheaper than that.
mii ... yaŋ thùuk kwàa mây mii	Having ... is even cheaper than not having.
bâan thúk bâan	Every home (the living unit).
bâan thúk lăŋ	Every house (the building).
nɔ́ɔy	To be small in number or amount. (Opposite of **mâak**.)
yàaŋ nɔ́ɔy	At least.
yàaŋ mâak	At most.
khon cháay yàaŋ nɔ́ɔy sɔ̆ɔŋ khon	At least two servants.
fâw bâan	To watch or guard the house.
khon nɯŋ tôŋ fâw bâan	One person must watch the house.
phə̂ə m	To increase.
phə̂əm khûn	To increase upwardly.
phə̂əm khûn ʔìik	To increase upwardly more so.
tôŋ mii	Must have.
ʔàat ca tôŋ mii	Might have to have.
càay	To pay out, spend.
kàp khâaw	The side dishes eaten *with the rice*.
càay kàpkhâaw	To buy groceries.
lambàak	Inconvenient, difficult.
càay kàpkhâaw kɔ̂ lambàak	When buying groceries, it is difficult.
sɯ́ɯ khɔ̆ɔŋ	To buy things.
hǎa sɯ́ɯ khɔ̆ɔŋ	To look for and buy things.
dəən hǎa sɯ́ɯ khɔ̆ɔŋ	To walk, look for, and buy things.
pay dəən hǎa sɯ́ɯ khɔ̆ɔŋ	To go, walk, look for, and buy things.
câaŋ khon cháay	To hire a servant.
(More.)	

กล้อง   กล่อง   กลอง   อ้าว

๔๗.๒ แบบฝึกหัดการสลับเสียงสูงต่ำ

หมูกับแมวอะไรจะอ้วนกว่ากัน
      หมูอ้วนกว่าแมว

หมูกับแมวอะไรจะผอมกว่ากัน
      แมวผอมกว่าหมู

บุหรี่กับไม้ขีดอะไรจะยาว (สั้น) กว่ากัน
คนไทยกับฝรั่งใครจะสูง (เตี้ย) กว่ากัน
เมืองไทยกับอังกฤษที่ไหนจะร้อน (หนาว) กว่ากัน
อาหารฝรั่งกับอาหารไทยอะไรจะเผ็ด (จืด) กว่ากัน
เมืองไทยกับอเมริกาที่ไหนจะใหญ่ (เล็ก) กว่ากัน
ไข่ไก่กับไข่เป็ดอะไรจะแพง (ถูก) กว่ากัน

๔๗.๓ โครงสร้างของประโยค
นั้น
โดยทั่ว ๆ ไปในกรุงเทพ ฯ นั้น

นี่ถูกกว่านั้น
การเช่าบ้านอยู่ถูกกว่าการอยู่อพาร์ตเมนต์

ถึงจะ........ก็จริง
แต่สำหรับ......แล้ว.........

ถึงจะต้องมีคนใช้มากขึ้นก็จริงแต่สำหรับฝรั่งแล้ว
การมีคนใช้ยังถูกกว่าไม่มี

klôŋ	A tobacco pipe, camera, binoculars, telescope, microscope.
	(These are distinguished when necessary by different modifiers.)
klòŋ	A small box.
klɔɔŋ	A drum.
ʔâaw	An exclamation of surprise.

47.2 Tone manipulation.   47.2

Response drill.

mǔu ka mɛɛw, ʔaray ca ʔûan kwàa kan.	Which is fatter, a pig or a cat?
mǔu ʔûan kwàa mɛɛw.	A pig is fatter than a cat.
mǔu ka mɛɛw, ʔaray ca phɔ̌ɔm kwàa kan.	Which is thinner, a pig or a cat?
mɛɛw phɔ̌ɔm kwàa mǔu.	A cat is thinner than a pig.

Do the following in the same way as the above.

burìi ka máykhìit, ʔaray ca yaaw (sân) kwàa kan.
khon thay ka faràŋ, khray ca sǔuŋ (tîa) kwàa kan.
mɯaŋ thay ka ʔaŋkrìt, thîi nǎy ca rɔ́ɔn (nǎaw) kwàa kan.
ʔaahǎan faràŋ ka ʔaahǎan thay, ʔaray ca phèt (cɯ̀ɯt) kwàa kan.
mɯaŋ thay ka ʔameerikaa, thîi nǎy ca yày (lék) kwàa kan.
khày kày ka khày pèt, ʔaray ca phɛɛŋ (thùuk) kwàa kan.

47.3 Sentence structure.   47.3

nán	This can modify a whole phrase or sentence, setting it apart as a unit from what follows. 'As for ...'
dooy thûathûa pay nay kruŋthêep nán,	Generally in Bangkok, as far as the preceding is concerned,
nîi thùuk kwàa nân.	This is cheaper than that.
kaan châw bâan yùu thùuk kwàa kaan yùu ʔapháatmén.	Renting a house to live in is cheaper than living in an apartment.
thɯ̌ŋ ca ... kɔ̂ ciŋ	Even though ... is true
tɛ̀ɛ sámràp ... lɛ́ɛw, ...	but in the case of ... , it is ... .
thɯ̌ŋ ca tôŋ mii khon cháay mâak khɯ̂n kɔ̂ ciŋ, tɛ̀ɛ sámràp faràŋ lɛ́ɛw, kaan mii khon cháay yaŋ thùuk kwàa mây mii.	Even though it is true that you need more servants, but for Farangs, it's actually cheaper to have them than not.

(More.)

บ้านทุกบ้านควรมีคนใช้อย่างน้อยสองคน
เพราะคนหนึ่งต้องเฝ้าบ้านเวลาอีกคนหนึ่งไปตลาด

นอกจากนี้คนที่มีบ้านหลังใหญ่ อาจจะต้องมีคนใช้ และคนสวนเพิ่มขึ้นอีก

ฝรั่งไปจ่ายกับข้าวก็ลำบาก เพราะพูดภาษาไทยไม่ได้

คนขายบอกขายเท่าไหร่ ก็ต่อราคาไม่เป็น

แล้วเขาก็ไม่รู้ว่าจะซื้ออะไรได้ที่ไหน

เขาจะเอาเวลาที่ต้องเดินหาซื้อของ
มาทำงาน จะได้เงินมากกว่าที่จะใช้จ้างคนใช้อีกมาก

๔๓.๔ แบบฝึกหัดการฟังเสียงสูงต่ำ

ลิ้นจี่	ลูกเงาะ
มะม่วง	ขนุน
แตงไทย	ทุเรียน
ส้มโอ	ชมพู่

๔๓.๕ บทบรรยาย

โดยทั่ว ๆ ไปในกรุงเทพ ฯ นั้น การเช่าบ้านอยู่ถูกกว่าการอยู่อพาร์ตเมนต์ ถึงจะต้องมีคนใช้มากขึ้นก็จริงแต่สำหรับฝรั่งแล้ว การมีคนใช้ยังถูกกว่าไม่มี* บ้าน ทุกบ้านควรมีคนใช้อย่างน้อยสองคนเพราะคนหนึ่งต้องเฝ้าบ้าน เวลาอีกคนหนึ่งไป ตลาด นอกจากนี้ คนที่มีบ้านหลังใหญ่อาจจะต้องมีคนใช้และคนสวนเพิ่มขึ้นอีก

---

*ฝรั่งไปจ่ายกับข้าวก็ลำบากเพราะพูดไทยไม่ได้ คนขายบอกขายเท่าไหร่ก็ต่อราคาไม่เป็น แล้วเขาก็ไม่รู้ว่าจะซื้ออะไรได้ที่ไหน ต้องเสียเวลาเดินหา เขาจะเอาเวลาที่ต้องไปเดินหาซื้อของ มาทำงาน จะได้เงินมากกว่าที่จะใช้จ้างคนใช้อีกมาก

bâan thúk bâan	Every household
khuan mii khon cháay	should have servants
yàaŋ nɔ́ɔy sɔ̌ɔŋ khon,	at least two,
phrɔ́ʔ khon nɯŋ tôŋ fâw bâan	because one must watch the house
weelaa ʔìik khon nɯŋ pay talàat.	while the other goes to the market.
nɔ̂ɔkcàak níi, khon thîi mii bâan lǎŋ yày	Besides this, people with big houses
ʔàat ca tôŋ mii khon cháay lɛ́ʔ khon sǔan	might have to have servants and a gardener
phɔ̂ɔm khɯ̂n ʔìik.	added on even more.
faràŋ pay càay kàpkhâaw	Farangs going to buy groceries
kɔ̂ lambàak	is difficult,
phrɔ́ʔ phûut phasǎa thay mây dây.	because they can't speak Thai.
khon khǎay bɔ̀ɔk khǎay thâwrày	When the seller says how much he will sell for,
kɔ̂ tɔ̀ɔ rakhaa mây pen.	they don't know how to bargain.
lɛ́ɛw kháw kɔ̂ mây rúu wâa	And then they don't know
ca sɯ́ɯ ʔaray dây thîi nǎy.	where they can buy what.
kháw ca ʔaw weelaa	If they would take this time
thîi tôŋ dəən hǎa sɯ́ɯ khɔ̌ɔŋ	that they must use to walk look buy things
maa tham ŋaan,	and bring it to use working,
ca dây ŋən mâak kwàa	they would get more money than
thîi ca cháy câaŋ khon cháay	that which they spend hiring a servant
ʔìik mâak.	by a lot.

47.4 Tone identification.

Fruits.

lincii	Litchi, lichee nuts.	luuk ŋɔ́ʔ	Rambutan.
mamuaŋ	Mango.	khanun	Jackfruit.
tɛɛŋthay	Muskmelon.	thurian	Durian.
som ʔoo	Pomelo.	chomphuu	Rose-apple.

47.5 Narrative.

dooy thûathûa pay nay kruŋthêep nán, kaan châw bâan yùu thùuk kwàa kaan yùu ʔapháatmén. thǔŋ ca tôŋ mii khon cháay mâak khɯ̂n kɔ̂ ciŋ, tɛ̀ɛ sámràp faràŋ lɛ́ɛw, kaan mii khon cháay yaŋ thùuk kwàa mây mii.* bâan thúk bâan khuan mii khon cháay yàaŋ nɔ́ɔy sɔ̌ɔŋ khon, phrɔ́ʔ khon nɯŋ tôŋ fâw bâan weelaa ʔìik khon nɯŋ pay talàat. nɔ̂ɔkcàak níi, khon thîi mii bâan lǎŋ yày ʔàat ca tôŋ mii khon cháay lɛ́ʔ khon sǔan phɔ̂ɔm khɯ̂n ʔìik.

---

*faràŋ pay càay kàpkhâaw kɔ̂ lambàak, phrɔ́ʔ phûut thay mây dây. khon khǎay bɔ̀ɔk khǎay thâwrày, kɔ̂ tɔ̀ɔ rakhaa mây pen. lɛ́ɛw kháw kɔ̂ mây rúu wâa ca sɯ́ɯ ʔaray dây thîi nǎy. tôŋ sǐa weelaa dəən hǎa. kháw ca ʔaw weelaa thîi tôŋ pay dəən hǎa sɯ́ɯ khɔ̌ɔŋ maa tham ŋaan, ca dây ŋən mâak kwàa thîi ca cháy câaŋ khon cháay ʔìik mâak.

๔๗.๖ ความแตกต่างระหว่างเสียงสูงต่ำ

พ่อมีกล้อง   แม่มีกล่อง   ลูกมีกลอง

ใครมีกล้อง   พ่อมีกล่องใช่ไหม
    พ่อ พ่อมีกล้อง   ไม่ใช่
ใครมีกล่อง   พ่อมีอะไร
    แม่ แม่มีกล่อง   กล้อง
ใครมีกลอง   แล้วใครมีกล่อง
    ลูก ลูกมีกลอง   แม่

พ่อมีอะไร   แม่มีกลองใช่ไหม
    กล้อง พ่อมีกล้อง   ไม่ใช่
แม่มีอะไร   แม่มีอะไร
    กล่อง แม่มีกล่อง   กล่อง
ลูกมีอะไร   แล้วใครมีกลอง
    กลอง ลูกมีกลอง   ลูก

พ่อมีกล้องใช่ไหม   ลูกมีกล้องใช่ไหม
    ใช่ พ่อมีกล้อง   ไม่ใช่
แม่มีกล่องใช่ไหม   ลูกมีอะไร
    ใช่ แม่มีกล่อง   กลอง
ลูกมีกลองใช่ไหม   แล้วใครมีกล้อง
    ใช่ ลูกมีกลอง   พ่อ

phɔ̂ɔ mii klɔ̂ŋ.	The father has a pipe.
mɛ̂ɛ mii klɔ̀ŋ.	The mother has a box.
lûuk mii klɔɔŋ.	The children have drums.

khray mii klɔ̂ŋ.
   phɔ̂ɔ. phɔ̂ɔ mii klɔ̂ŋ.
khray mii klɔ̀ŋ.
   mɛ̂ɛ. mɛ̂ɛ mii klɔ̀ŋ.
khray mii klɔɔŋ.
   lûuk. lûuk mii klɔɔŋ.

phɔ̂ɔ mii ʔaray.
   klɔ̂ŋ. phɔ̂ɔ mii klɔ̂ŋ.
mɛ̂ɛ mii ʔaray.
   klɔ̀ŋ. mɛ̂ɛ mii klɔ̀ŋ.
lûuk mii ʔaray.
   klɔɔŋ. lûuk mii klɔɔŋ.

phɔ̂ɔ mii klɔ̂ŋ, chây máy.
   chây. phɔ̂ɔ mii klɔ̂ŋ.
mɛ̂ɛ mii klɔ̀ŋ chây máy.
   chây. mɛ̂ɛ mii klɔ̀ŋ.
lûuk mii klɔɔŋ, chây máy.
   chây. lûuk mii klɔɔŋ.

phɔ̂ɔ mii klɔ̂ŋ, chây máy.
   mây chây.
phɔ̂ɔ mii ʔaray.
   klɔ̂ŋ.
lɛ́ɛw khray mii klɔ̀ŋ.
   mɛ̂ɛ.

mɛ̂ɛ mii klɔɔŋ, chây máy.
   mây chây.
mɛ̂ɛ mii ʔaray.
   klɔ̀ŋ.
lɛ́ɛw khray mii klɔɔŋ.
   lûuk.

lûuk mii klɔ̂ŋ, chây máy.
   mây chây.
lûuk mii ʔaray.
   klɔɔŋ.
lɛ́ɛw khray mii klɔ̂ŋ.
   phɔ̂ɔ.

๔๓.๗ คำถามบทบรรยาย

ในกรุงเทพ ฯ การเช่าบ้านอยู่ถูกกว่าการ
    อยู่อพาร์ตเมนต์ใช่ไหม   ใช่
การอยู่อพาร์ตเมนต์ต้องมีคนใช้มากขึ้น
    ใช่ไหม   ไม่ใช่
สำหรับฝรั่งแล้วไม่ต้องมีคนใช้ใช่ไหม   ไม่ใช่
ที่บ้านต้องมีคนเฝ้าเสมอใช่ไหม   ใช่
อยู่อพาร์ตเมนต์ต้องมีคนสวนใช่ไหม   ไม่ใช่
อยู่บ้านปลอดภัยกว่าอยู่อพาร์ตเมนต์
    ใช่ไหม   ไม่ใช่

อยู่อพาร์ตเมนต์ถูกกว่าอยู่บ้านใช่ไหม   ไม่ใช่ อยู่บ้านถูกกว่า
อยู่อพาร์ตเมนต์ต้องมีคนใช้มากกว่า
    อยู่บ้านใช่ไหม   ไม่ใช่ อยู่บ้านต้องมีมากกว่า
อยู่บ้านมีคนใช้คนเดียวพอใช่ไหม   ไม่ใช่ ต้องมีอย่างน้อยสองคน
อยู่อพาร์ตเมนต์ต้องมีคนใช้หลายคน
    ใช่ไหม   ไม่ใช่ มีคนเดียวก็พอ

อยู่บ้านควรจะมีคนใช้กี่คน   ควรจะมีอย่างน้อยสองคน
ทำไม   เพราะว่าคนหนึ่งต้องเฝ้าบ้าน เวลาอีก
                                                  คนหนึ่งไปตลาด
ทำไมฝรั่งมีคนใช้ถูกกว่าไม่มี   เพราะว่าเขาไม่ต้องไปกินข้าวที่ร้านอาหาร
อ้าว ฝรั่งทำกับข้าวเองไม่ได้หรือ   ทำเองก็ยังแพงกว่าจ้างแม่ครัวทำ
ทำไมยังงั้นล่ะ   คนไทยซื้อของได้ถูกกว่าฝรั่ง
ทำไม   ฝรั่งที่พูดไทยไม่ได้ ต้องซื้อของที่ร้าน
                                                  ใหญ่ ๆ
แล้วถ้าพูดได้ล่ะ   พูดได้ก็ไม่รู้จักต่อราคา
แล้วถ้ารู้จักล่ะ   ก็ไม่มีเวลาพอที่จะไปเดินหาซื้อ
แล้วถ้ามีล่ะ   ถ้ายังงั้นก็ทำเองได้

ŋay kruŋthêep kaan châw bâan yùu thùuk kwàa
kaan yùu ʔapháatmén, chây máy.   chây.

kaan yùu ʔapháatmén tôŋ mii khon cháay
mâak khûn, chây máy.   mây chây.

sámràp faràŋ lɛ́ɛw, mây tôŋ mii khon cháay,
chây máy.   mây chây.

thîi bâan tôŋ mii khon fâw samɔ̌ə, chây máy.   chây.

yùu ʔapháatmén, tôŋ mii khon sǔan, chây máy.   mây chây.

yùu bâan plɔ̀ɔtphay kwàa yùu ʔapháatmén, chây máy. mây chây.

yùu ʔapháatmén thùuk kwàa yùu bâan, chây máy.   mây chây.   yùu bâan thùuk kwàa.

yùu ʔapháatmén tôŋ mii khon cháay   mây chây.
mâak kwàa yùu bâan, chây máy.   yùu bâan tôŋ mii mâak kwàa.

yùu bâan, mii khon cháay khon diaw phɔɔ,   mây chây.
chây máy.   tôŋ mii yàaŋ nɔ́ɔy sɔ̌ɔŋ khon.

yùu ʔapháatmén, tôŋ mii khon cháay lǎay khon,   mây chây.
chây máy.   mii khon diaw kɔ̂ phɔɔ.

yùu bâan, khuan ca mii khon cháay kìi khon.   khuan ca mii yàaŋ nɔ́ɔy sɔ̌ɔŋ khon

thammay.   phrɔ́ʔ wâa khon nɯŋ tôŋ fâw bâan
                                                   weelaa ʔìik khon nɯŋ pay talàat.

thammay faràŋ mii khon cháay thùuk kwàa   phrɔ́ʔ wâa kháw mây tôŋ pay
mây mii.   kin khâaw thîi ráan ʔaahǎan.

ʔâaw. faràŋ tham kàpkhâaw ʔeeŋ mây dây lɔ̌ə.   tham ʔeeŋ, kɔ̂ yaŋ phɛɛŋ kwàa
                                                   câaŋ mɛ̂ɛ khrua tham.

thammay yaŋŋán lâ.   khon thay sɯ́ɯ khɔ̌ɔŋ dây
                                                   thùuk kwàa faràŋ.

thammay.   faràŋ thîi phûut thay mây dây
                                                   tôŋ sɯ́ɯ khɔ̌ɔŋ thîi ráan yàyyày.

lɛ́ɛw thâa phûut dây lâ.   phûut dây, kɔ̂ mây rúucàk
                                                   tɔ̀ɔ rakhaa.

lɛ́ɛw thâa rúucàk lâ.   kɔ̂ mây mii weelaa phɔɔ thîi
                                                   ca pay dəən hǎa sɯ́ɯ.

lɛ́ɛw thâa mii lâ.   thâa yaŋŋán, kɔ̂ tham ʔeeŋ dây.

๔๗.๘ **การสนทนาโต้ตอบ**

คนที่นุ่งกระโปรงกำลังทำอะไร   คนที่กำลังอ่านหนังสือพิมพ์นั่งที่ไหน

๔๗.๙ **วลีท้ายประโยค**

ซ่   ซิ

อ้าปากซิ   อ้าปากซ่

หนังสือเล่มนี้มีกี่หน้า เปิดดูซิ

หนังสือเล่มนี้มีกี่หน้า

          เปิดดูซ่

บทที่สี่สิบแปดอยู่หน้าอะไร เปิดดูซิ

เปิดดูบทที่สี่สิบแปดซ่ นั่นบทที่สี่สิบเจ็ด

A.   ผมอยากจะรู้ว่าบ้านคุณ C อยู่ที่ไหน ถามเขาซิ
B.   บ้านคุณอยู่ที่ไหน
C.   อยู่ที่ซอยร่วมฤดี
B.   บ้านคุณ C อยู่ที่ซอยร่วมฤดี
A.   ขอบคุณมาก

A.   ผมอยากจะรู้ว่าบ้านคุณ C อยู่ที่ไหน
B.   ถามเขาซ่
A.   บ้านคุณอยู่ที่ไหน
C.   อยู่ที่ซอยร่วมฤดี

๔๗.๑๐ **การเขียน**

74

47.8 Conversation.

Review the conversation sections on pages 23 and 45. This time the student should ask the questions. Suggestions for questions are given below.

Page 23. What are they each doing? What are they each wearing? Who is tall and fat, etc.? Who is doing this, and who is wearing that?

Page 45 Where are they each sitting? What are they each doing? Who is doing this, and who is sitting there?

If the straight questions can be asked quickly with good pronunciation, start using **khon thîi** constructions like the examples below.

khon thîi nûŋ kraprooŋ kamlaŋ tham ʔaray.
khon thîi kamlaŋ ʔàan naŋsüü phim nâŋ thîi nǎy.

47.9 Particles.

sî and sí.

A **sî** situation has two parts: A requests and B performs. A **sí** situation has three parts: A requests, B performs, and A reacts in some way to B's performance. Notice this distinction in the following examples.

Doctor (examining a child's throat):	ʔâa pàak sí.
Mother (after child fails to do so):	ʔâa pàak sî.
The teacher wants to know how many pages there are in the book, and asks a student:	naŋsüü lêm níi mii kìi nâa.
	pɔ̀ɔt duu sí.
A student wants to know how many pages there are and asks the teacher:	naŋsüü lêm níi mii kìi nâa.
And the teacher responds:	pɔ̀ɔt duu sî.

A **sî** request will change to a **sî** correction if the hearer does the wrong thing.

bòt thîi sìi sìp pὲεt yùu nâa ʔaray.   pɔ̀ɔt duu sí.
pɔ̀ɔt duu bòt thîi sìi sìp pὲεt sî.   nân bòt thîi sìi sìp cèt.

Act out the parts of the following dialogs.

A. phǒm yàak ca rúu wâa bâan khun C yùu thîi nǎy.   thǎam kháw sí.
B. bâan khun yùu thîi nǎy.
C. yùu thîi sɔ̌ɔy rûam rɯɯdii.
B. bâan khun C yùu thîi sɔ̌ɔy rûam rɯɯdii.
A. khɔ̀ɔpkhun mâak.

A. phǒm yàak ca rúu wâa bâan khun C yùu thîi nǎy.
B. thǎam kháw sî
A. bâan khun yùu thîi nǎy.
C. yùu thîi sɔ̌ɔy rûam rɯɯdii.

When the speaker says **sî** he is thinking about the hearer's action. When he says **sí**, he is thinking about his own needs or intentions.

47.10 Writing.

Practice reading and writing lesson 5 of Book 1 in Thai.

บทที่ ๔๘

๔๘.๑ คำศัพท์

กระป๋อง	ตาม
	ตามมา
บ้านว่าง	ตามมาทีหลัง
บ้านว่างให้เช่า	
ชั้น	ครอบ
ชั้นเดียว	ครอบครัว
ชั้นเดียวหรือสองชั้น	ครอบครัวเขาไม่ใหญ่
	ห้องนอนสามห้อง
ตึก	สามห้องนอน
ไม้	
ตึกหรือไม้	ติด
	ต่อ
ผมเช่าเอง	ติดต่อ
ผมไม่ได้เช่าเอง	ไปติดต่อกับเขาเอง
ผมไม่ได้เช่าเองหรอก	
	เคาท์เตอร์
เขาช่วยหาบ้านเช่า	
เขาให้ช่วยหาบ้านเช่า	บะหมี่
เขาให้ช่วยหาบ้านเช่าให้	
	เส้นหมี่
โสด	
เป็นโสด	ปลาหมึก
ชายโสด	
เขาเป็นโสดหรือแต่งงานแล้ว	ไข่เจียว
ภรรยา	ต่าง ๆ
ภรรยากับลูก ๆ ของเขา	

LESSON 48

48.1 Vocabulary and expansions.

krapɔ̌ŋ	A can, a tin.
bâan wâaŋ	A vacant house.
bâan wâaŋ hây châw	A vacant house for rent.
chán	A layer, storey, class, grade.
chán diaw	A single storey.
chán diaw rɯ́ sɔ̌ɔŋ chán	One or two storeys?
tɯ̀k	A building made of masonry.
máay	Wood.
tɯ̀k rɯ́ máay	Is the house of brick or wood?
phǒm châw ʔeeŋ.	I rent it myself.
phǒm **mây dây** châw ʔeeŋ.	It is not the case that...
phǒm mây dây châw ʔeeŋ **lɔk.**	... as you seem to think.
kháw chûay hǎa bâan châw.	He helped find a house for rent.
kháw **hây** chûay hǎa bâan châw.	He had me...
kháw hây chûay hǎa bâan châw **hây.**	... for him.
sòot	Unmarried.
pen sòot	To be single.
chaay sòot	A bachelor.
kháw pen sòot rɯ́ tɛ̀ŋŋaan lɛ́ɛw.	Is he single or married?
phanrayaa	Wife.
phanrayaa ka lûuklûuk khɔ̌ŋ kháw	His wife and children.
taam	To follow.
taam maa	To come after him.
taam maa thii lǎŋ	To come along later.
khrɔ̂ɔp	
khrɔ̂ɔpkhrua	Family.
khrɔ̂ɔpkhrua kháw mây yày.	His family isn't large.
hɔ̂ŋ nɔɔn sǎam hɔ̂ŋ	Three bedrooms (the number).
sǎam hɔ̂ŋ nɔɔn	Three-bedroomed (the characteristic).
tìt	To connect to.
tɔ̀ɔ	To join on to, continue on.
tìttɔ̀ɔ	To contact, get in touch with.
pay tìttɔ̀ɔ kàp kháw ʔeeŋ.	Get in touch with him yourself.
kháwtɤ̂ə	The counter or bar.
bamìi	Egg noodles.
sên mìi	Very fine rice noodles.
plamɯ̀k	Squid.
khày ciaw	Omelette.
tàaŋtàaŋ	Various.

77

๔๙.๒ แบบฝึกหัดการสลับเสียงสูงต่ำ

กางมุ้งที่ถนน และขายขวดที่ห้องนอน
　　กางมุ้งที่ห้องนอน
　　และขายขวดที่ถนน

ตัดหญ้าที่ห้อง และรีดเสื้อที่สนาม
　　ตัดหญ้าที่สนาม
　　และรีดเสื้อที่ห้อง

ตากหมอนที่ครัว และทอดหมูที่หน้าต่าง
　　ตากหมอนที่หน้าต่าง
　　และทอดหมูที่ครัว

ล้างจานที่บ้านและถูพื้นที่ครัว
　　ล้างจานที่ครัว
　　และถูพื้นที่บ้าน

๔๙.๓ โครงสร้างของประโยค

เพิ่งทำ
ทำเมื่อกี้นี้
กำลังทำอยู่
กำลังจะทำเดี๋ยวนี้
เดี๋ยวจะทำ

อีกที
หลายที
ทีนี้
ทีหลัง

ข้างหลัง
วันหลัง
ทีหลัง

เสื้อขนาดใหญ่
ขวดขนาดกลาง
กระป๋องขนาดเล็ก
บ้านขนาดสามห้องนอน

๔๙.๔ แบบฝึกหัดการฟังเสียงสูงต่ำ

มะเขือเทศ
ผักกาดหอม
ถั่วลันเตา

กะหล่ำปลี
ถั่วลิสง
แตงกวา

มันฝรั่ง
หัวหอม
เห็ด

78

48.2 Tone manipulation.

Transformation drill.

kaaŋ múŋ thîi thanŏn
léʔ khǎay khùat thîi hɔ̂ŋ nɔɔn.
  kaaŋ múŋ thîi hɔ̂ŋ nɔɔn
  léʔ khǎay khùat thîi thanŏn.

Put up the mosquito net in the road
and sell the bottles in the bedroom.
  Put up the mosquito net in the bedroom
  and sell the bottles in the road.

tàak mɔ̌ɔn thîi khrua
léʔ thɔ̂ɔt mǔu thîi nâatàaŋ.
  tàak mɔ̌ɔn thîi nâatàaŋ
  léʔ thɔ̂ɔt mǔu thîi khrua.

Air the pillow in the kitchen
and fry the pork at the window.
  Air the pillow at the window
  and fry the pork in the kitchen.

tàt yâa thîi hɔ̂ŋ
léʔ rîit sûa thîi sanǎam.
  tàt yâa thîi sanǎam
  léʔ rîit sûa thîi hɔ̂ŋ.

Cut the grass in the room
and iron the shirt in the yard.
  Cut the grass in the yard
  and iron the shirt in the room.

láaŋ caan thîi bâan
léʔ thǔu phǘʉn thîi khrua.
  láaŋ caan thîi khrua
  léʔ thǔu phǘʉn thîi bâan.

Wash the dishes in the house
and scrub the floor in the kitchen.
  Wash the dishes in the kitchen
  and scrub the floor in the house.

48.3 Patterns.

phôŋ tham.
tham mûa kîi níi.
kamlaŋ tham yùu.
kamlaŋ ca tham dǐawníi.
dǐaw ca tham.

I just did it.
I did it a few minutes ago.
I'm doing it.
I'm just going to do it now.
I'll do it in a few minutes.

ʔìik thîi.
lǎay thîi.
thîi níi.
thîi lǎŋ.

Another time, again.
Several times.
This time.
A later time, afterwards.

khâŋ lǎŋ.
wan lǎŋ.
thîi lǎŋ.

In back of, behind.
A later day, sometime.
Later.

sûa khanàat yày.
khùat khanàat klaaŋ.
krapɔ̌ŋ khanàat lék.
bâan khanàat sǎam hɔ̂ŋ nɔɔn.

A large-sized shirt.
A medium-sized bottle.
A small-sized can.
A three-bedroom house.

48.4 Tone identification.

Vegetables.

makhʉa theet	Tomatoes.	kalam plii	Cabbage.	man faraŋ	Potatoes.
phakkaat hɔɔm	Lettuce.	thua lisoŋ	Peanuts.	hua hɔɔm	Onions.
thua lantaw	Green peas.	tɛɛŋ kwaa	Cucumbers.	het	Mushrooms.

๔๙.๕ บทสนทนา

ก. คุณมีบ้านว่างให้เช่าใช่ไหมฮะ

  ข. ใช่ฮ่ะ คุณต้องการบ้านชั้นเดียว หรือสองชั้น
     แล้วก็ตึกหรือไม้

ก. ผมไม่ได้เช่าเองหรอกฮะ
   เพื่อนผมเพิ่งมาจากอเมริกา เขาให้ช่วยหาบ้านเช่าให้

  ข. ขอโทษ เขายังเป็นโสดหรือแต่งงานแล้วฮะ

ก. แต่งงานแล้วฮะ มีลูกสาวคนหนึ่ง ลูกชายคนหนึ่ง
   แต่ภรรยากับลูก ๆ ของเขายังอยู่อเมริกา   เขาจะตามมาทีหลัง

  ข. ครอบครัวเขาไม่ใหญ่ บ้านขนาดสามห้องนอนก็พอ

ก. ผมก็ว่ายังงั้นเหมือนกัน นี่เบอร์โทรศัพท์ของเขา
   แล้วคุณไปติดต่อกับเขาเองนะฮะ

๔๙.๖ ความแตกต่างระหว่างเสียงสูงต่ำ

ต้อยนั่งที่โต๊ะต๋อย และต๋อยนั่งที่โต๊ะต้อย

ต้อยนั่งที่ไหน   ใครนั่งที่โต๊ะต๋อย
   ที่โต๊ะต๋อย ต้อยนั่งที่โต๊ะต๋อย   ต้อย ต้อยนั่งที่โต๊ะต๋อย

ต๋อยนั่งที่ไหน   ใครนั่งที่โต๊ะต้อย
   ที่โต๊ะต้อย ต๋อยนั่งที่โต๊ะต้อย   ต๋อย ต๋อยนั่งที่โต๊ะต้อย

ต้อยนั่งที่โต๊ะต๋อยใช่ไหม   ต้อยนั่งที่โต๊ะต้อยใช่ไหม
   ใช่ ต้อยนั่งที่โต๊ะต๋อย   ไม่ใช่ ต้อยนั่งที่โต๊ะต๋อย

ต๋อยนั่งที่โต๊ะต้อยใช่ไหม   ต๋อยนั่งที่โต๊ะต้อยใช่ไหม
   ใช่ ต๋อยนั่งที่โต๊ะต้อย   ไม่ใช่ ต๋อยนั่งที่โต๊ะต้อย

48.5 Dialog.

A. khun mii bâan wâaŋ hây châw,
   chây máy há?.

  B. chây hâ.
     khun tôŋkaan bâan chán diaw
     rɨ́ sɔ̌ɔŋ chán.
     lɛ́ɛw kɔ̂ tɨ̀k rɨ́ máay.

A. phǒm mây dây châw ?eeŋ lɔk há?.
   phɨ̂an phǒm phɔ̂ŋ maa càak ?ameerikaa.
   kháw hây chûay hǎa bâan châw hây.
  B. khɔ̌ɔ thôot,*
     kháw yaŋ pen sòot rɨ́ tɛ̀ŋŋaan lɛ́ɛw há.

A. tɛ̀ŋŋaan lɛ́ɛw há?.
   mii lûuk sǎaw khon nɨŋ
   lûuk chaay khon nɨŋ.
   tɛ̀ɛ phanrayaa kàp lûuklûuk
   khɔ̌ŋ kháw yaŋ yùu ?ameerikaa.
   kháw ca taam maa thii lǎŋ.

  B. khrɔ̂ɔpkhrua kháw mây yày.
     bâan khanàat sǎam hɔ̂ŋ nɔɔn kɔ̂ phɔɔ.

A. phǒm kɔ̂ wâa yaŋŋán mɨ́ankan.
   nîi bɔɔ thoorasàp khɔ̌ŋ kháw.
   lɛ́ɛw khun pay tìttɔ̀ɔ kàp kháw
   ?eeŋ náhá?.

(I understand) you have houses to let.
Is that right?

That's right.
Do you want a house of one storey
or two?
Brick or wood?

Oh I'm not renting it for myself.
A friend of mine just came from America.
He wants me to help him find a house to rent.
Excuse me.
Is he single or married?

He's married.
He has a daughter
and a son.
But his wife and children
are still in America.
They'll join him later.

His family isn't large.
A three-bedroom house will be big enough.

I think so too.
Here's his phone number.
You can get in touch with him
yourself. O.K.?

48.6 Tone distinctions.

tɔ̌y nâŋ thîi tó? tɔ̌y,
lé? tɔ̌y nâŋ thîi tó? tɔ̌y.

tɔ̌y nâŋ thîi nǎy.
   thîi tó? tɔ̌y. tɔ̌y nâŋ thîi tó? tɔ̌y.
tɔ̌y nâŋ thîi nǎy.
   thîi tó? tɔ̌y. tɔ̌y nâŋ thîi tó? tɔ̌y.
tɔ̌y nâŋ thîi tó? tɔ̌y, chây máy.
   chây. tɔ̌y nâŋ thîi tó? tɔ̌y.
tɔ̌y nâŋ thîi tó? tɔ̌y, chây máy.
   chây. tɔ̌y nâŋ thîi tó? tɔ̌y.

Toy Fall is sitting at Toy Rise's desk,
and Toy Rise is sitting at Toy Fall's.

khray nâŋ thîi tó? tɔ̌y.
   tɔ̌y. tɔ̌y nâŋ thîi tó? tɔ̌y.
khray nâŋ thîi tó? tɔ̌y.
   tɔ̌y. tɔ̌y nâŋ thîi tó? tɔ̌y.
tɔ̌y nâŋ thîi tó? tɔ̌y, chây máy.
   mây chây. tɔ̌y nâŋ thîi tó? tɔ̌y.
tɔ̌y nâŋ thîi tó? tɔ̌y, chây máy.
   mây chây. tɔ̌y nâŋ thîi tó? tɔ̌y.

---

* Questions of a personal nature are usually preceded by **khɔ̌ɔ thôot**. When so introduced, many questions not normally asked in English are not impolite: 'How old are you?', 'Are you married?', 'How much do you pay for rent?', 'How much money do you make?'.

๔๘.๗ แบบฝึกหัดไวยากรณ์

ก.

เขาให้ช่วยหาแม่ครัวให้ (รีดเสื้อ)

เขาให้ช่วยรีดเสื้อให้ (ถูพื้น)

เขาให้ช่วยถูพื้นให้ (กางมุ้ง)

เขาให้ช่วยกางมุ้งให้ (ส่งที่เขี่ยบุหรี่)

เขาให้ช่วยส่งที่เขี่ยบุหรี่ให้ (หาบ้านเช่า)

เขาให้ช่วยหาบ้านเช่าให้

ข.

อยู่บ้านดีกว่าอยู่อพาร์ตเมนต์ (ถูก)

    ฉันก็ว่ายังงั้นเหมือนกัน เพราะว่าถูกกว่า

ไปรถมอเตอร์ไซด์ดีกว่าไปรถยนต์ (ถูก)

    ฉันก็ว่ายังงั้นเหมือนกัน เพราะว่าถูกกว่า

เดินไปดีกว่าไปแท๊กซี่ (ปลอดภัย)

    ฉันก็ว่ายังงั้นเหมือนกัน เพราะว่าปลอดภัยกว่า

นั่งที่โต๊ะดีกว่านั่งที่เคาท์เตอร์ (สบาย)

    ฉันก็ว่ายังงั้นเหมือนกัน เพราะว่าสบายกว่า

กินอาหารไทยดีกว่ากินอาหารฝรั่ง (อร่อย)

    ฉันก็ว่ายังงั้นเหมือนกัน เพราะว่าอร่อยกว่า

อยู่เมืองไทยดีกว่าอยู่เมืองนอก (สบาย)

    ฉันก็ว่ายังงั้นเหมือนกัน เพราะว่าสบายกว่า

48.7 Grammar drills.

a. Substitution drill.

kháw hây chûay hăa mêε khrua hây.

(rìit sûa)

kháw hây chûay rìit sûa hây.

(thŭu phúun)

kháw hây chûay thŭu phúun hây.

(kaaŋ múŋ)

kháw hây chûay kaaŋ múŋ hây.

(sòŋ thîi khìa burìi)

kháw hây chûay sòŋ thîi khìa burìi hây.

(hăa bâan châw)

kháw hây chûay hăa bâan châw hây.

He asked me to help find a cook for him.
(iron a shirt)

He asked me to help iron a shirt for him.
(scrub the floor)

He asked me to help scrub the floor for him.
(put up the mosquito net)

He asked me to help put up the mosquito net
for him. (pass him the ash tray)

He asked me to pass him the ash tray.
(find a house to rent)

He asked me to help find a house to rent
for him.

b. Response drill.

yùu bâan dii kwàa

yùu ?apháatmén. (thùuk)

 chán kɔ̂ wâa yaŋŋán mɯankan,

 phrɔ́? wâa thùuk kwàa.

pay rót mɔɔtəəsay dii kwàa

pay rót yon. (thùuk)

 chán kɔ̂ wâa yaŋŋan mɯankan,

 phrɔ́? wâa thùuk kwàa.

dəən pay dii kwàa

pay théksii. (plɔ̀ɔtphay)

 chán kɔ̂ wâa yaŋŋán mɯankan,

 phrɔ́? wâa plɔ̀ɔtphay kwàa.

nâŋ thîi tó? dii kwàa

nâŋ thîi kháwtə̂ə. (sabaay)

 chán kɔ̂ wâa yaŋŋán mɯankan,

 phrɔ́? wâa sabaay kwàa.

kin ?aahăan thay dii kwàa

kin ?aahăan faràŋ. (?arɔ̀y)

 chán kɔ̂ wâa yaŋŋán mɯankan,

 phrɔ́? wâa ?arɔ̀y kwàa.

yùu mɯaŋ thay dii kwàa

yùu mɯaŋ nɔ̂ɔk. (sabaay)

 chán kɔ̂ wâa yaŋŋán mɯankan,

 phrɔ́? wâa sabaay kwàa.

It's better to live in a house
than in an apartment.
 I think so too,
 because it's cheaper.

It's better to go by motorcycle
than by car.
 I think so too,
 because it's cheaper.

It's better to walk than
to go by taxi.
 I think so too,
 because it's safer.

It's better to sit at a table
than at the counter.
 I think so too,
 because it's more comfortable.

It's better to eat Thai food
than Farang food.
 I think so too,
 because it tastes better.

It's better to live in Thailand
than abroad.
 I think so too,
 because it's more comfortable.

ค.

แม่สูงกว่าลูกใช่ไหม
      ใช่ แล้วพ่อยังสูงกว่าแม่อีก

แม่ใหญ่กว่าลูกใช่ไหม
      ใช่ แล้วพ่อยังใหญ่กว่าแม่อีก

แม่เล็กกว่าพ่อใช่ไหม
      ใช่ แล้วลูกยังเล็กกว่าแม่อีก

แม่เตี้ยกว่าพ่อใช่ไหม
      ใช่ แล้วลูกยังเตี้ยกว่าแม่อีก

แม่อ้วนกว่าลูกใช่ไหม
      ใช่ แล้วพ่อยังอ้วนกว่าแม่อีก

สามล้อแพงกว่ารถเมล์ใช่ไหม
      ใช่ แล้วแท๊กซี่ยังแพงกว่าสามล้ออีก

๔๘.๘ การสนทนาโต้ตอบ

อาหารไทย

ก๋วยเตี๋ยว	ปลา
บะหมี่	
เส้นหมี่	ไก่
	กุ้ง
ข้าวต้ม	
ข้าวผัด	เนื้อ
	หมู
แกง	
แกงเผ็ด	ปู
แกงเขียวหวาน	
ผัด	
ผัดเผ็ด	เป็ด
ต้มยำ	ปลาหมึก
น้ำพริกปลาทู	
กุ้งทอด (เนื้อ หมู ปลา)	

อาหารฝรั่ง

ไข่ (ต้ม ดาว ลวก เจียว)
หมู (แฮม เบคอน)

ขนมปัง (ปิ้ง)
เนย
แซนวิช (ไก่ เนื้อ ไข่ เนยแข็ง)
ซุบ (ไก่ เนื้อ ผัก)
สลัด (ผัก มันฝรั่ง กุ้ง ไก่ เนื้อ ปู)

เนื้อทอด (ไก่ หมู ปลา)

เนื้ออบ (ไก่ หมู)

มันฝรั่ง
ผักต่าง ๆ
ผลไม้ต่าง ๆ

c. Response drill.

mɛ̂ɛ sǔuŋ kwàa lûuk, chây máy.
  chây.
lɛ́ɛw phɔ̂ɔ yaŋ sǔuŋ kwàa mɛ̂ɛ ʔìik.

The mother is taller than the child, right?
  Right.
And the father is even taller than the mother.

mɛ̂ɛ yày kwàa lûuk, chây máy.
  chây.
lɛ́ɛw phɔ̂ɔ yaŋ yày kwàa mɛ̂ɛ ʔìik.

The mother is bigger than the child, right?
  Right.
And the father is even bigger than the mother.

mɛ̂ɛ lék kwàa phɔ̂ɔ, chây máy.
  chây.
lɛ́ɛw lûuk yaŋ lék kwàa mɛ̂ɛ ʔìik.

The mother is smaller than the father, right?
  Right.
And the child is even smaller than the mother.

mɛ̂ɛ tîa kwàa phɔ̂ɔ, chây máy.
  chây.
lɛ́ɛw lûuk yaŋ tîa kwàa mɛ̂ɛ ʔìik.

The mother is shorter than the father, right?
  Right.
And the child is even shorter than the mother.

mɛ̂ɛ ʔûan kwàa lûuk, chây máy.
  chây.
lɛ́ɛw phɔ̂ɔ yaŋ ʔûan kwàa mɛ̂ɛ ʔìik.

The mother is fatter than the child, right?
  Right.
And the father is even fatter than the mother.

sǎamlɔ́ɔ phɛɛŋ kwàa rót mee, chây máy.
  chây. lɛ́ɛw thɛ́ksîi
yaŋ phɛɛŋ kwàa sǎamlɔ́ɔ ʔìik.

Samlors are more expensive than busses, right?
  Right. And taxis
are even more expensive than samlors.

48.8 Conversation.   **48.8**

The teacher should ask each student about the food he eats and the time he eats it here as compared to home. Some types of food are given below for reference.

ʔaahǎan thay		ʔaahǎan faràŋ
kúay tǐaw	plaa	khày (tôm, daaw, lûak, ciaw)
bamìi		mǔu (hɛm, beekhôn)
sên mii	kày	
		khanǒmpaŋ (pîŋ)
khâaw tôm	kûŋ	nəəy
khâaw phàt		sɛɛnwít (kày, núa, khày, nəəykhɛ̌ŋ)
	núa	
kɛɛŋ		súp (kày, núa, phàk)
kɛɛŋ phèt	mǔu	
kɛɛŋ khǐaw wǎan		salàt (phàk, man faràŋ, kûŋ, kày, núa, puu)
	puu	
phàt		núa thɔ̂ɔt (kày, mǔu, plaa)
phàt phèt	pèt	
		núa ʔòp (kày, mǔu)
tôm yam	plamùk	
		man faràŋ
námphrík plathuu		phàk tàaŋtàaŋ
kûŋ thɔ̂ɔt (núa, mǔu, plaa)		phǒnlamáay tàaŋtàaŋ

85

๔๘.๙ วลีท้ายประโยค

ล่ะ   นะ

จะกินอะไร   จะกินข้าวเมื่อไหร่
    จะกินอะไรดีล่ะ   จะกินเมื่อไหร่ดีล่ะ
ก็อยากจะกินอะไรล่ะ   ก็อยากจะกินเมื่อไหร่ล่ะ
    อยากจะกินแก้ว   อยากจะกินมะรืนนี้
อยากจะกินอะไรนะ   อยากจะกินเมื่อไหร่นะ

จะไปไหน   รถยนต์นี้จะขายเท่าไหร่
    จะไปไหนดีล่ะ   จะขายเท่าไหร่ดีล่ะ
ก็อยากจะไปไหนล่ะ   ก็อยากจะขายเท่าไหร่ล่ะ
    อยากจะไปตู้ยามตำรวจ   อยากจะขายร้อยบาท
อยากจะไปไหนนะ   อยากจะขายเท่าไหร่นะ

๔๘.๑๐ การเขียน

ฝึกหัด   เสียง   ต่ำ
แบบฝึกหัด   ออกเสียง   เสียงสูงต่ำ

lâ with questions.

Speaker shows a slight impatience; for some reason (reluctance of the hearer to answer, for example) he feels he has to press for an answer.

ná with questions.

Speaker asks for a repetition of the answer, either because he didn't hear it clearly or because he couldn't believe what he heard (surprise). In the following dialogs the **ná** shows surprise. To practice the more common use of **ná** (What was that again? I didn't hear you.), the teacher can give either an unclear answer (to which the student responds, for example, 'ca pay nǎy ná; mây dâyyin.'), or one that is too fast or has words that the student doesn't know (to which the student can respond 'ca pay nǎy ná. phûut cháchảa nɔ̀y, dây máy.').

ca kin ʔaray.	What do you want to eat?
ca kin ʔaray dii lâ.	What do you *think* I should eat?
kɔ̂ yàak ca kin ʔaray lâ.	Well what do you *want* to eat?
yàak ca kin kɛ̂ɛw.	I want to eat glass.
yàak ca kin ʔaray ná.	You want to eat *what*?
ca pay nǎy.	Where are you going to go?
ca pay nǎy dii lâ.	Where do you *think* I should go?
kɔ̂ yàak ca pay nǎy lâ.	Well where do you *want* to go?
yàak ca pay tûu yaam tamrùat.	I want to go to the police box.
yàak ca pay nǎy ná.	You want to go *where*?
ca kin khâaw mûarày.	When are you going to eat?
ca kin mûarày dii lâ.	When do you *think* I should eat?
kɔ̂ yàak ca kin mûarày lâ.	Well when do you *want* to eat?
yàak ca kin maruun níi.	I want to eat day after tomorrow.
yàak ca kin mûarày ná.	You want to eat *when*?
rót yon níi ca khǎay thâwrày.	How much are you going to sell this car for?
ca khǎay thâwrày dii lâ.	How much do you *think* I should sell it for?
kɔ̂ yàak ca khǎay thâwrày lâ.	Well how much do you *want* to sell it for?
yàak ca khǎay rɔ́ɔy bàat.	I want to sell it for 100 baht.
yàak ca khǎay thâwrày ná.	You want to sell it for *how* much?

48.10 Writing.   48.10

Practice reading and writing lessons 6 and 7 of book 1. Notice also heading 6.4.

fùk hàt	To practice.
bɛ̀ɛp fùk hàt	A drill or exercise in a textbook.
sǐaŋ	Sound.
ʔɔ̀ɔk sǐaŋ	To pronounce (to 'out' sound).
tàm	Low (in pitch, elevation, or status).
sǐaŋ sǔuŋ tàm	Tones.

บทที่ ๔๙

๔๙.๑ คำศัพท์

แรก	นายหน้า
ที่แรก	
	นายหน้าบ้านเช่า
บาง	
บางคน	เล่า
ที่สุด	แนะนำ
ในที่สุด	
	เตา
สะดวก	
	เต่า
ตกลง	
ตกลงใจ	ส้อม
ภายใน	สว่าง

๔๙.๒ แบบฝึกหัดการสลับเสียงสูงต่ำ

ทำไมกางมุ้งให้ตุ่มล่ะ	ทำไมล้างจานให้ศรีล่ะ
ก็ตุ่มให้กางให้นี่	ก็ศรีให้ล้างให้นี่
ทำไมตากหมอนให้ต้อยล่ะ	ทำไมถูพื้นให้แดงล่ะ
ก็ต้อยให้ตากให้นี่	ก็แดงให้ถูให้นี่
ทำไมทอดไก่ให้น้อยล่ะ	ทำไมรีดเสื้อให้ต้อยล่ะ
ก็น้อยให้ทอดให้นี่	ก็ต้อยให้รีดให้นี่

88

LESSON 49

49.1 Vocabulary and expansions.

rɛ̂ɛk	To be first.
thii rɛ̂ɛk	At first.
baaŋ	Some.
baaŋ khon	Some people.
thîisùt	The most.
nay thîisùt	Finally, in the end.
sadùak	Convenient (opposite of **lambàak**).
tòkloŋ	To decide.
tòkloŋ cay	To decide, make up one's mind.
phaaynay	Within.
naay nâa	An agent.
naay nâa bâan châw	A house agent.
lâw	To tell, relate.
nέʔnam	To suggest, advise, introduce.
taw	A stove.
tàw	A turtle.
sôm	A fork.
sawàaŋ	To be light, bright.

49.2 Tone manipulation.
Response drill.

thammay kaaŋ múŋ hây tùm lâ.
  kô tùm hây kaaŋ hây nî.
Why did you put up the mosquito net for Toom?
  Because she asked me to. That's why.

thammay tàak mɔ̌ɔn hây tôy lâ.
  kô tôy hây tàak hây nî.
Why did you air the pillows for Toy?
  Because she asked me to. That's why.

thammay thɔ̂ɔt kày hây nɔ́ɔy lâ.
  kô nɔ́ɔy hây thɔ̂ɔt hây nî.
Why did you fry the chicken for Noy?
  Because she asked me to. That's why.

thammay láaŋ caan hây sǐi lâ.
  kô sǐi hây láaŋ hây nî.
Why did you wash the dishes for Sri?
  Because she asked me to. That's why.

thammay thǔu phɄ́Ʉn hây dɛɛŋ lâ.
  kô dɛɛŋ hây thǔu hây nî.
Why did you scrub the floor for Daeng?
  Because she asked me to. That's why.

thammay rîit sɄ̂a hây tôy lâ.
  kô tôy hây rîit hây nî.
Why did you iron the blouse for Toy?
  Because she asked me to. That's why.

๔๕.๓ โครงสร้างของประโยค

ที่แรก	ภายใน
ตอนแรก	ภายนอก
คนแรก	
	ที่แรก
บางคน	จอนไม่รู้ว่า
บางวัน	อยู่บ้านหรืออยู่แฟล็ต
บางที	ดี
หนังสือบางเล่ม	
หนังสือบ้าง	
	จอนไปหาเขา
ทำยาก	และเล่าเรื่องนี้
ทำง่าย	ให้เขาทราบ
ทำลำบาก	และแนะนำให้เขา
ทำสะดวก	ไปติดต่อกับเดวิดเอง

๔๕.๔ แบบฝึกหัดการฟังเสียงสูงต่ำ

หัวผักกาดเหลือง	กระเทียม	หน่อไม้
ผักโขม	ผักชี	ถั่วงอก
ฟักทอง	มันเทศ	กะหล่ำดอก

๔๕.๕ บทบรรยาย

ที่แรกคุณจอนไม่รู้ว่าจะอยู่บ้านหรืออยู่แฟล็ตดี บางคนก็บอกว่าอยู่แฟล็ตดีกว่า เพราะว่าปลอดภัยกว่า และจ้างคนใช้คนเดียวก็พอ บางคนก็บอกว่าอยู่บ้านดีกว่า เพราะว่าสะดวกกว่าแล้วก็ถูกกว่าด้วย แต่ในที่สุดคุณจอนก็ตกลงใจเช่าบ้านอยู่

เวลานี้คุณเดวิดเพื่อนของคุณจอนกำลังหาบ้านเช่า คุณเดวิดเพิ่งมาถึงเมืองไทยและภรรยากับลูก ๆ ของเขาจะตามมาภายในหนึ่งเดือน คุณเดวิดขอให้คุณจอนช่วยหาบ้านเช่าขนาดสามห้องนอนให้ คุณจอนไปพบนายหน้าบ้านเช่าและเล่าเรื่องนี้ให้เขาทราบ และแนะนำให้เขาติดต่อกับคุณเดวิดเอง

49.3 Patterns and sentence structure.

thii rêɛk.	The first time, before, at first.
tɔɔn rêɛk.	At first.
khon rêɛk.	The first person.
baaŋ khon.	Some people.
baaŋ wan.	Some days.
baaŋ thii.	Sometimes, probably.
naŋsɰ̌ɰ baaŋ lêm.	Some (certain ones of the) books.
naŋsɰ̌ɰ bâaŋ.	Some (any) books.
tham yâak.	Hard to do.
tham ŋâay.	Easy to do.
tham lambàak.	Inconvenient to do.
tham sadùak.	Convenient to do.
phaay nay.	Inside, within.
phaay nɔ̂ɔk.	Outside.

thii rêɛk	At first
cɔɔn mây rúu wâa	John didn't know
yùu bâan rɰ́ yùu flɛ̀t	whether living in a house or in a flat
dii.	would be good.
cɔɔn pay hǎa kháw	John went to see him
lɛ́ʔ lâw rɰ̂aŋ níi	and told this matter
hây kháw sâap	for him to know
lɛ́ʔ nɛ́ʔŋam hây kháw	and advised him
pay tìttɔ̀ɔ kàp deewít ʔeeŋ.	to get in touch with David by himself.

49.4 Tone identification.

Vegetables.

hua phakkaat lɰaŋ	Carrots.	krathiam	Garlic.	nɔɔ maay	Bamboo shoots.
phak khoom	Spinach.	phak chii	Parsley.	thua ŋɔɔk	Bean sprouts.
fak thɔɔŋ	Pumpkin.	man theet	Yams.	kalam dɔɔk	Cauliflower.

49.5 Narrative.

thii rêɛk khun cɔɔn mây rúu wâa ca yùu bâan rɰ́ɰ yùu flɛ̀t dii. baaŋ khon kɔ̂ bɔ̀ɔk wâa yùu flɛ̀t dii kwàa phrɔ́ʔ wâa plɔ̀ɔtphay kwàa lɛ́ʔ câaŋ khon cháay khon diaw kɔ̂ phɔɔ. baaŋ khon kɔ̂ bɔ̀ɔk wâa yùu bâan dii kwàa phrɔ́ʔ wâa sadùak kwàa lɛ́ɛw kɔ̂ thùuk kwàa dûay. tɛ̀ɛ nay thîisùt khun cɔɔn kɔ̂ tòkloŋ cay châw bâan yùu.

weelaa níi khun deewít, phɰ̂an khɔ̌ŋ khun cɔɔn, kamlaŋ hǎa bâan châw. khun deewít phɰ̂ŋ maa thɯ̌ŋ mɰaŋ thay, lɛ́ʔ phanrayaa kàp lûuklûuk khɔ̌ŋ kháw ca taam maa phaaynay nɰ̀ŋ dɰan. khun deewít khɔ̌ɔ hây khun cɔɔn chûay hǎa bâan châw khanàat sǎam hɔ̂ŋ nɔɔn hây. khun cɔɔn pay phóp naay nâa bâan châw, lɛ́ʔ lâw rɰ̂aŋ níi hây kháw sâap. lɛ́ʔ nɛ́ʔŋam hây kháw tìttɔ̀ɔ kàp khun deewít ʔeeŋ.

๔๕.๖ ความแตกต่างระหว่างเสียงสูงต่ำ

เต่าอยู่ข้างบน   เตาอยู่ข้างล่าง

เต่าอยู่ที่ไหน	เต่าอยู่ข้างบนใช่ไหม
ข้างบน เต่าอยู่ข้างบน	ใช่ เต่าอยู่ข้างบน
เตาอยู่ที่ไหน	เตาอยู่ข้างล่างใช่ไหม
ข้างล่าง เตาอยู่ข้างล่าง	ใช่ เตาอยู่ข้างล่าง
อะไรอยู่ข้างบน	เต่าอยู่ข้างล่างใช่ไหม
เต่า เต่าอยู่ข้างบน	ไม่ใช่ เต่าอยู่ข้างบน
อะไรอยู่ข้างล่าง	เตาอยู่ข้างบนใช่ไหม
เตา เตาอยู่ข้างล่าง	ไม่ใช่ เตาอยู่ข้างล่าง

๔๕.๗ คำถามบทบรรยาย

คุณจอนตกลงใจเช่าแฟล็ตอยู่ใช่ไหม	ไม่ใช่
เขาตกลงใจเช่าบ้านอยู่ใช่ไหม	ใช่
คุณจอนไม่รู้จักคุณเดวิดใช่ไหม	ไม่ใช่
คุณเดวิดเป็นเพื่อนคุณจอนใช่ไหม	ใช่
คุณเดวิดอยู่บ้านเช่าใช่ไหม	ไม่ใช่
เขากำลังหาบ้านเช่าใช่ไหม	ใช่
คุณเดวิดมาอยู่เมืองไทยนานแล้วใช่ไหม	ไม่ใช่
เขายังอยู่ที่อเมริกาใช่ไหม	ไม่ใช่
เขาเพิ่งมาถึงเมืองไทยใช่ไหม	ใช่
ภรรยากับลูก ๆ ของเขามาถึงเมืองไทยแล้วใช่ไหม	ไม่ใช่
เขาจะตามมาทีหลังใช่ไหม	ใช่
เขาจะตามมาภายในหนึ่งอาทิตย์ใช่ไหม	ไม่ใช่
เขาจะตามมาภายในหนึ่งปีใช่ไหม	ไม่ใช่

49.6 Tone distinctions.

tàw yùu khâŋbon.

taw yùu khâŋlâaŋ.

tàw yùu thîi nǎy.

khâŋbon.   tàw yùu khâŋbon.

taw yùu thîi nǎy.

khâŋlâaŋ.   taw yùu khâŋlâaŋ.

ʔaray yùu khâŋbon.

tàw.   tàw yùu khâŋbon.

ʔaray yùu khâŋlâaŋ.

taw.   taw yùu khâŋlâaŋ.

tàw yùu khâŋbon, chây máy.

chây.   tàw yùu khâŋbon.

taw yùu khâŋlâaŋ, chây máy.

chây.   taw yùu khâŋlâaŋ.

tàw yùu khâŋlâaŋ, chây máy.

mây chây.   tàw yùu khâŋbon.

taw yùu khâŋbon, chây máy.

mây chây.   taw yùu khâŋlâaŋ.

The turtle is above.
The stove is below.

49.7 Questions on the narrative.

khun cɔɔn tòkloŋ cay châw flɛ̀t yùu, chây máy.	mây chây.
kháw tòkloŋ cay châw bâan yùu, chây máy.	chây.
khun cɔɔn mây rúucàk khun deewít, chây máy.	mây chây.
khun deewít pen phʉ̂an khun cɔɔn, chây máy.	chây.
khun deewít yùu bâan châw, chây máy.	mây chây.
kháw kamlaŋ hǎa bâan châw, chây máy.	chây.
khun deewít maa yùu mʉaŋ thay naan lɛ́ɛw, chây máy.	mây cháy.
kháw yaŋ yùu thîi ʔameerikaa, chây máy.	mây chây.
kháw phôŋ maa thʉ̌ŋ mʉaŋ thay, chây máy.	chây.
phanrayaa kàp lûuklûuk khɔ̌ŋ kháw maa thʉ̌ŋ mʉaŋ thay lɛ́ɛw, chây máy.	mây chây.
kháw ca taam maa thii lǎŋ, chây máy.	chây.
kháw ca taam maa phaaynay nʉ̀ŋ ʔathít, chây máy.	mây chây.
kháw ca taam maa phaaynay nʉ̀ŋ pii, chây máy.	mây chây.

(More.)

เขาจะตามมาภายในหนึ่งเดือนใช่ไหม	ใช่
คุณเดวิดขอให้คุณจอนช่วยหาบ้านเช่าให้ ใช่ไหม	ใช่
คุณเดวิดไปพบนายหน้าบ้านเช่าใช่ไหม	ไม่ใช่
คุณจอนไปพบนายหน้าบ้านเช่าใช่ไหม	ใช่
คุณเดวิดกำลังหาแฟล็ตเช่าใช่ไหม	ไม่ใช่ เขากำลังหาบ้านเช่า
คุณเดวิดมาอยู่เมืองไทยนานแล้วใช่ไหม	ไม่ใช่ เขาเพิ่งมา
ภรรยามาด้วยใช่ไหม	ไม่ใช่ เขาจะตามมาทีหลัง
ลูก ๆ ของคุณเดวิดอยู่เมืองไทยใช่ไหม	ไม่ใช่ เขาอยู่อเมริกา
คุณจอนแนะนำให้คุณเดวิดติดต่อกับ	ไม่ใช่ เขาแนะนำให้นายหน้า
นายหน้าบ้านเช่าใช่ไหม	บ้านเช่าติดต่อกับคุณเดวิด
ภรรยาของคุณเดวิดจะมาเมืองไทยภาย	
ในสองเดือนใช่ไหม	ไม่ใช่ เขาจะมาภายในหนึ่งเดือน
คุณจอนตกลงใจเช่าอะไรอยู่	เช่าบ้าน
ใครเป็นเพื่อนของเขา	คุณเดวิด
คุณเดวิดเป็นใคร	เป็นเพื่อนคุณจอน
คุณเดวิดกำลังทำอะไร	กำลังหาบ้านเช่า
เขามาถึงเมืองไทยเมื่อไหร่	เพิ่งมาถึง
เขาแต่งงานแล้วหรือยัง	แต่งงานแล้ว
เขามีลูกหรือเปล่า	มี
มีคนเดียวใช่ไหม	ไม่ใช่
มีกี่คน	สองคน
ภรรยาเขามาเมืองไทยแล้วหรือยัง	ยัง
ลูก ๆ มาแล้วหรือยัง	ยัง
คุณเดวิดขอให้คุณจอนทำอะไร	ขอให้ช่วยหาบ้านเช่าให้
เขาต้องการบ้านขนาดไหน	ขนาดสามห้องนอน
แล้วคุณจอนไปพบใคร	ไปพบนายหน้าบ้านเช่า
แล้วเขาพบหรือเปล่า	พบ
คุณจอนแนะนำใคร	แนะนำนายหน้าบ้านเช่า
แนะนำให้นายหน้าทำอะไร	ติดต่อกับคุณเดวิด

94

kháw ca taam maa phaaynay nɯ̀ŋ dɯan, chây máy.   chây.

khun deewít khɔ̌ɔ hây khun cɔɔn chûay
hǎa bâan châw hây, chây máy.   chây.

khun deewít pay phóp naay nâa bâan châw, chây máy.   mây chây.

khun cɔɔn pay phóp naay nâa bâan châw, chây máy.   chây.

khun deewít kamlaŋ hǎa flɛ̀t châw,
chây máy.   mây chây.
    kháw kamlaŋ hǎa bâan châw.

khun deewít maa yùu mɯaŋ thay naan lɛ́ɛw,
chây máy.   mây chây.
    kháw phɔ̂ŋ maa.

phanrayaa maa dûay,
chây máy.   mây chây.
    kháw ca taam maa thii lǎŋ.

lûuklûuk khɔ̌ɔŋ khun deewít yùu mɯaŋ thay,
chây máy.   mây chây.
    kháw yùu ʔameerikaa.

khun cɔɔn néʔnam hây khun deewít tìttɔ̀ɔ   mây chây. kháw néʔnam hây naay nâa
kàp naay nâa bâan châw, chây máy.   bâan châw tìttɔ̀ɔ kàp khun deewít.

phanrayaa khɔ̌ɔŋ khun deewít ca maa mɯaŋ thay   mây chây.
phaaynay sɔ̌ɔŋ dɯan, chây máy.   kháw ca maa phaaynay nɯ̀ŋ dɯan.

khun cɔɔn tòkloŋ cay châw ʔaray yùu.   châw bâan.

khray pen phɯan khɔ̌ɔŋ kháw.   khun deewít.

khun deewít pen khray.   pen phɯan khun cɔɔn.

khun deewít kamlaŋ tham ʔaray.   kamlaŋ hǎa bâan châw.

kháw maa thɯ̌ŋ mɯaŋ thay mɯarày.   phɔ̂ŋ maa thɯ̌ŋ.

kháw tɛ̀ŋŋaan lɛ́ɛw rɯ́ yaŋ.   tɛ̀ŋŋaan lɛ́ɛw.

kháw mii lûuk rɯ́ plàaw.   mii.

mii khon diaw, chây máy.   mây chây.

mii kìi khon.   sɔ̌ɔŋ khon.

phanrayaa kháw maa mɯaŋ thay lɛ́ɛw rɯ́ yaŋ.   yaŋ.

lûuklûuk maa lɛ́ɛw rɯ́ yaŋ.   yaŋ.

khun deewít khɔ̌ɔ hây khun cɔɔn tham ʔaray.   khɔ̌ɔ hây chûay hǎa bâan châw hây.

kháw tɔ̂ŋkaan bâan khanàat nǎy.   khanàat sǎam hɔ̂ŋ nɔɔn.

lɛ́ɛw khun cɔɔn pay phóp khray.   pay phóp naay nâa bâan châw.

lɛ́ɛw kháw phóp rɯ́ plàaw.   phóp.

khun cɔɔn néʔnam khray.   néʔnam naay nâa bâan châw.

néʔnam hây naay nâa tham ʔaray.   tìttɔ̀ɔ kàp khun deewít.

95

๔๕.๙   การสนทนาโต้ตอบ

จุดบุหรี่   ส้อม   ไม้

บุหรี่จุดอยู่   ช้อน   ตี๋

พัดลมเปิดอยู่   ส้อมอยู่ข้างขวามีด   ขึ้น

cùt burìi	To light a cigarette.
burìi cùt yùu.	The cigarette is lit.
phátlom pə̀ət yùu.	The fan is on.
sôm	Fork.
chɔ́ɔn	Spoon.
sôm yùu khâŋ khwǎa mîit.	The fork is to the right of the knife.
ˌmáay	Wood, stick.
tii	To hit with something, beat.
khûn	To get up on.

The students should listen while the teacher asks and answers questions suggested by the picture. Then the students should answer the teacher's questions. Finally, the students should ask questions.

๔๙.๙ วลีท้ายประโยค

ก็.....น่ะซิ

คุณแม่คุณเป็นผู้หญิงหรือผู้ชาย
  ก็ผู้หญิงน่ะซิ

ไปร้านตัดผมทำไม
  ก็ไปตัดผมน่ะซิ

ไปร้านขายผ้าทำไม
  ก็ไปซื้อผ้าน่ะซิ

กลางคืนมืดหรือสว่าง
  ก็มืดน่ะซิ

ไปร้านตัดรองเท้าทำไม
  ก็ไปตัดรองเท้าน่ะซิ

หนังสือนี่ทำด้วยกระดาษหรือไม้
  ก็กระดาษน่ะซิ

ไปโรงเรียนทำไม
  ก็ไปเรียนน่ะซิ

ไปร้านขายหนังสือทำไม
  ก็ไปซื้อหนังสือน่ะซิ

ขนมปังเป็นอาหารไทยหรืออาหารฝรั่ง
  ก็อาหารฝรั่งน่ะซิ

ไปร้านตัดเสื้อทำไม
  ก็ไปตัดเสื้อน่ะซิ

๔๙.๑๐ การเขียน

ฉัน   ข้างบน   อังกฤษ

98

kɔ̂ ... nâsi.

The speaker suggests that the answer he is giving should be obvious to everyone. The students should ask the questions and listen to the teacher's answers.   After they feel sure of the rhythm and tone of voice, they can answer questions from the teacher.

khun mɛ̂ɛ khun pen phûu yǐŋ rɤ́ phûu chaay.	Is your mother female or male?
kɔ̂ phûu yǐŋ nâsi.	Female, naturally.
klaaŋkhʉʉn mʉ̂ʉt rɤ́ sawàaŋ.	Is it dark or light at night?
kɔ̂ mʉ̂ʉt nâsi.	Dark, of course.
naŋsʉ̌ʉ nîi tham dûay kradàat rɤ́ máay.	Is this book made of paper or wood?
kɔ̂ kradàat nâsi.	Paper, of course.
khanǒmpaŋ pen ʔaahǎan thay	Is bread Thai food
rɤ́ ʔaahǎan faràŋ.	or Farang food?
kɔ̂ ʔaahǎan faràŋ nâsi.	Farang, as everyone knows.
pay ráan tàt phǒm thammay.	Why did you go to the barber shop?
kɔ̂ pay tàt phǒm nâsi.	To get a haircut, of course.
pay ráan khǎay phâa thammay.	Why did you go to the cloth shop?
kɔ̂ pay sʉ́ʉ phâa nâsi.	To buy some cloth, of course.
pay ráan tàt rɔŋtháaw thammay.	Why did you go to the shoemaker?
kɔ̂ pay tàt rɔŋtháaw nâsi.	To get some shoes made, of course.
pay rooŋrian thammay.	Why did you go to school?
kɔ̂ pay rian nâsi.	To study, of course.
pay ráan khǎay naŋsʉ̌ʉ thammay.	Why did you go to the bookstore?
kɔ̂ pay sʉ́ʉ naŋsʉ̌ʉ nâsi.	To buy some books, of course.
pay ráan tàt sʉ̂a thammay.	Why did you go to the shirt maker?
kɔ̂ pay tàt sʉ̂a nâsi.	To get a shirt made, of course.

Practice reading and writing lessons 8 and 9 of Book 1 in Thai. Notice the following irregularities.

chán   This is written as if it were **chǎn.**

khâŋ bon   This is written as if it were **khâaŋ bon.**

ʔaŋkrìt   The new symbol in this word stands for a combination of consonant.

           and vowel. It has three different readings: **rʉ, ri,** or **rəə.**

บทที่ ๕๐

๕๐. ก

๕๐. ข เรียงความ

การเดินทางในประเทศไทย

ในประเทศไทยถ้าจะเดินทางไปท่องเที่ยว หรือไปทำธุรกิจต่าง ๆ เราไปได้ถึง
สามทางด้วยกัน คือ ทางบก ทางน้ำ และทางอากาศ

ทางบก มีรถไฟ รถเมล์ และรถแท๊กซี่ ซึ่งจะพาเราไปได้ทั่วทุกจังหวัดใน
ประเทศไทยอย่างสะดวกสบาย และราคาก็ไม่แพงเกินไปนัก

ทางน้ำ มีเรือที่ใช้รับส่งคนโดยสารที่อยู่ตามจังหวัดใกล้ ๆ แม่น้ำ แต่คนส่วน
มากมักไม่ชอบไปทางเรือ เพราะว่าช้ามากทำให้เสียเวลา

ทางอากาศ มีเครื่องบินรับส่งคนโดยสารตามจังหวัดใหญ่ ๆ หลายจังหวัด
เช่น เชียงใหม่ ลำปาง อุบล อุดร และสงขลาเป็นต้น แต่คนที่ไม่มีธุระด่วนมักจะ
ไม่ไปทางอากาศ เพราะค่าโดยสารแพงมาก

เดินทาง	รับส่ง
ท่องเที่ยว	โดยสาร
	คนโดยสาร
ธุระ	ผู้โดยสาร
ธุรกิจ	ค่าโดยสาร
คือ	แม่น้ำ
บก	มัก (จะ)
จังหวัด	บิน
	เรือบิน
ไม่...นัก	เครื่องบิน
เรือ	ด่วน

100

LESSON 50

(Review)

50.a Review sections 2, 5, 6, 7, and 9 of lessons 46—49.

50.b Reading selection.   **50**

Classes that have time for the reading selection at this point but did not read the selection of 45.b should go back and read it first.   Even though the reading selections are separate from the rest of the book, they follow each other in order of difficulty and vocabulary presentation.

kaan dəən thaaŋ nay prathêet thay

nay prathêet thay, thâa ca dəən thaaŋ pay thôŋ thîaw rɯ́ pay tham thúrákìt tàaŋtàan, raw pay dây thɯ̌ŋ sǎam thaaŋ dûaykan. khɯɯ thaaŋ bòk, thaaŋ náam, lέʔ thaaŋ ʔaakàat.

thaaŋ bòk mii rót fay, rót mee, lέʔ rót théksîi, sɯ̂ŋ ca phaa raw pay dây thûa thúk caŋwàt ɲay prathêet thay yàaŋ sadùak sabaay, lέʔ rakhaa kɔ̂ mây phεεŋ kəən pay nák.

thaaŋ náam mii rɯa thîi cháy ráp sòŋ khon dooysǎan thîi yùu taam caŋwàt klâyklâay mɛ̂εnáam. tὲε khon sùan mâak mák mây chɔ̂ɔp pay thaaŋ rɯa, phrɔ́ʔ wâa chaa mâak, tham hây sǐa weelaa.

thaaŋ ʔaakàat mii khrɯ̂aŋ bin ráp sòŋ khon dooysǎan taam caŋwàt yàyyày lǎay caŋwàt chên chiaŋmày, lampaaŋ, ʔubon, ʔudɔɔn, lέʔ sǒŋkhlǎa pen tôn. tὲε khon thîi mây mii thúráʔ dùan mák ca mây pay thaaŋ ʔaakàat, phrɔ́ʔ khâa dooysǎan phεεŋ mâak.

dəən thaaŋ	To travel.
thôŋ thîaw	To tour, travel for pleasure.
thúráʔ	Business, affairs, errands.
thúrákìt	Business.
khɯɯ	To be as follows or defined, namely.
bòk	Land (as opposed to sea).
caŋwàt	Provinces of Thailand.
mây... nák	Not so..., not very.
rɯa	Ship, boat.
ráp sòŋ	To pick up and deliver, to take passengers.
dooysǎan	To take passage.
khon dooysǎan	Passengers.
phûu dooysǎan	Passengers.
khâa dooysǎan	Fare.
mɛ̂εnáam	River.
mák (ca)	Regularly, habitually, usually.
bin	To fly.
rɯa bin	Airplane (flying boat).
khrɯ̂aŋ bin	Airplane (flying machine).
dùan	To be urgent, express.

บทที่ ๕๑

๕๑.๑ คำศัพท์

บ้านเช่า

เรื่องบ้านเช่า

ติดต่อเรื่องบ้านเช่า

ยังไงบ้าง

ว่ายังไงบ้าง

ได้เรื่องว่ายังไงบ้าง

สมัย

ทัน

ทันสมัย

แบบ

แบบทันสมัย

น่า

น่าอยู่

บริเวณ

บริเวณบ้าน

กำลังทำ

กำลังดี

สนาม

หญ้า

สนามหญ้า

แขก

รับแขก

ห้องรับแขก

เรือน

เรือนคนใช้

เก็บ

ห้องเก็บของ

ต่างหาก

อยู่ต่างหาก

ลวด

มุ้งลวด

ค่าเช่า

ทาน

ขอทาน

อายุ

ขวบ

ปี

LESSON 51

51.1 Vocabulary and expansions.

bâan châw	A house for rent.
rûaŋ bâan châw	About a house to rent.
tìttɔ̀ɔ rûaŋ bâan châw	To contact someone about a house to rent.
yaŋŋay bâaŋ	How?
wâa yaŋŋay bâaŋ	What did he say?
dây rûaŋ wâa yaŋŋay bâaŋ.	What information did you get?
samǎy	An era.
than	To be on time.
than samǎy	Up to date.
bɛ̀ɛp	Type, style.
bɛ̀ɛp than samǎy	Modern style.
nâa	Good for ..., interesting to ... .
nâa yùu	Nice to live in.
bɔɔriween	Area, vicinity.
bɔɔriween bâan	The area around a house, yard.
kamlaŋ tham	Just doing it now.
kamlaŋ dii	Just good now, just right.
sanǎam	A yard, court, field.
yâa	Grass.
sanǎam yâa	Lawn.
khɛ̀ɛk	Guests.
ráp khɛ̀ɛk	To receive guests.
hɔ̂ŋ ráp khɛ̀ɛk	Living room.
rɯan	A house (used in certain combinations only).
rɯan khon cháay	A building for servants separate from the main house. Servants quarters.
kèp	To keep, store, collect.
hɔ̂ŋ kèp khɔ̌ɔŋ	A storeroom.
taŋhàak	To be separate.
yùu taŋhàak	To be situated separately.
lûat	Wire.
múŋ lûat	Screens (wire mosquito netting).
khâa châw	Rent.
thaan	Alms.
khɔ̌ɔ thaan	To beg.
ʔaayúʔ	Age.
khùap	A year of age (used for children only).
pii	A year, a year of age (for adults).

เหงื่อ อาเจียน
เหงื่อออก

ร้องไห้

สั่น
ตัวสั่น เจ็บ

หัวเราะ โกรธ

ขำ

๕๑.๒ แบบฝึกหัดการสลับเสียงสูงต่ำ

ลุงถามเพื่อน	ปู่ให้หมอ	น้าพบเพื่อน
เพื่อนถามลุง	หมอให้ปู่	เพื่อนพบน้า
ลุงเพื่อนถาม	ปู่หมอให้	น้าเพื่อนพบ
เพื่อนลุงถาม	หมอปู่ให้	เพื่อนน้าพบ
ถามลุงเพื่อน	ให้ปู่หมอ	พบน้าเพื่อน
ถามเพื่อนลุง	ให้หมอปู่	พบเพื่อนน้า

ŋ̀ua	Sweat.
ŋ̀ua ʔɔ̀ɔk	To sweat.
sàn	To tremble, vibrate.
tua sàn	To shiver.
hǔarɔ́ʔ	To laugh.
khǎm	To be funny.
ʔaacian	To vomit, throw up.
rɔ́ɔŋhâay	To cry, weep.
cèp	To hurt, be hurt.
kròot	To be mad at someone.

51.2 Tone manipulation. 51.2

Translation drill.

Practice saying the following sentences as fast as possible without losing tonal accuracy. Then, looking only at the English, translate from English to Thai.

luŋ thǎam phɨan.	My uncle asked his friend.
phɨan thǎam luŋ.	My friend asked my uncle.
luŋ phɨan thǎam.	My friend's uncle asked.
phɨan luŋ thǎam.	My uncle's friend asked.
thǎam luŋ phɨan.	Ask your friend's uncle.
thǎam phɨan luŋ.	Ask your uncle's friend.
pùu hây mɔ̌ɔ.	My grandfather gave it to the doctor.
mɔ̌ɔ hây pùu.	The doctor gave it to my grandfather.
pùu mɔ̌ɔ hây.	The doctor's grandfather gave it to me.
mɔ̌ɔ pùu hây.	My grandfather's doctor gave it to me.
hây pùu mɔ̌ɔ.	Give it to the doctor's grandfather.
hây mɔ̌ɔ pùu.	Give it to your grandfather's doctor.
náa phóp phɨan.	My nah saw a friend.
phɨan phóp náa.	My friend saw my nah.
náa phɨan phóp.	My friend's nah saw him.
phɨan náa phóp.	My nah's friend saw him.
phóp náa phɨan.	I saw my friend's nah.
phóp phɨan náa.	I saw my nah's friend.

๕๑.๓   โครงสร้างของประโยค

สมัยใหม่	ห้องน้ำ
สมัยก่อน	ห้องนอน
	ห้องกินข้าว
แบบไทย	ห้องอาหาร
แบบทันสมัย	ห้องรับแขก
แบบเก่า	ห้องเก็บของ
แบบฝรั่ง	ห้องคนใช้
	เรือนคนใช้
กำลังทำ	ครัว
กำลังดี	
กำลังพูด	
กำลังร้อน	เมื่อกี้นี้เอง
	เมื่อวานนี้เอง
น่าอยู่	เมื่อคืนนี้เอง
น่าดู	เมื่อเช้านี้เอง
น่าอ่าน	เมื่ออาทิตย์นี้เอง
น่าไป	เมื่อเย็นนี้เอง
น่ากิน	เมื่อสองสามวันนี้เอง

๕๑.๔   แบบฝึกหัดการฟังเสียงสูงต่ำ

เพดาน	ฝาผนัง
หลังคา	กำแพง
ระเบียง	กระจก
บันได	ประตูหน้าบ้าน

51.3 Patterns.

samăy mày.	Modern times.
samăy kɔ̀ɔn.	Old-fashioned times.
bɛ̀ɛp thay.	Thai style.
bɛ̀ɛp than samăy.	Modern style.
bɛ̀ɛp kàw.	Old style.
bɛ̀ɛp faràŋ.	Farang style.
kamlaŋ tham.	Just doing it now.
kamlaŋ dii.	It's just right.
kamlaŋ phûut.	He's talking right now.
kamlaŋ rɔ́ɔn.	It's hot now.
nâa yùu.	Good to live in.
nâa duu.	Good to look at, interesting.
nâa ʔàan.	Interesting to read.
nâa pay.	Interesting to go to.
nâa kin.	To look good to eat.
hɔ̂ŋ náam.	Bathroom.
hɔ̂ŋ nɔɔn.	Bedroom.
hɔ̂ŋ kin khâaw.	Dining room.
hɔ̂ŋ ʔaahăan.	Dining room (formal).
hɔ̂ŋ ráp khɛ̀ɛk.	Living room.
hɔ̂ŋ kèp khɔ̌ɔŋ.	Storeroom.
hɔ̂ŋ khon cháay.	Servant's room.
ruan khon cháay.	Servants quarters.
khrua.	Kitchen.
mûa kíi níi ʔeeŋ.	Just a moment ago.
mûa waan níi ʔeeŋ.	Just yesterday.
mûa khuun níi ʔeeŋ.	Just last night.
mûa cháaw níi ʔeeŋ.	Just this morning.
mûa ʔathít níi ʔeeŋ.	Just this week.
mûa yen níi ʔeeŋ.	Just this evening (said at night of the same day).
mûa sɔ̌ɔŋ săam wan níi ʔeeŋ.	Just two or three days ago.

51.4 Tone identification.

Parts of the house.

pheedaan	Ceiling.	faa phanaŋ	Wall (of a room or house).
laŋkhaa	Roof.	kamphɛɛŋ	Wall (enclosing a yard or city).
rabiaŋ	Veranda, porch.	kracok	Window pane, mirror.
banday	Stairway.	pratuu naa baan	Front gate.

ก. ผมไปติดต่อเรื่องบ้านเช่าให้คุณแล้ว

    ข. หรือครับ
       ได้เรื่องว่ายังไงบ้าง

ก. เป็นตึกชั้นครึ่งแบบทันสมัย
   น่าอยู่มาก ถ้าคุณเห็นต้องชอบแน่ๆ

    ข. บริเวณบ้านเป็นยังไงบ้าง

ก. กำลังดีเลยครับ
   หน้าบ้านเป็นสนามหญ้า

    ข. มีห้องทั้งหมดกี่ห้อง

ก. ชั้นบนมีห้องนอนสามห้อง ห้องน้ำ
   สองห้อง ชั้นล่างมีห้องรับแขก
   ห้องกินข้าว ครัว แล้วก็มีห้องน้ำ
   อีกห้องหนึ่ง

    ข. ไม่มีห้องคนใช้หรือฮะ

ก. มีครับ หลังบ้านมีเรือนคนใช้กับ
   ห้องเก็บของโรงรถอยู่ต่างหาก

    ข. บ้านมีมุ้งลวดหรือเปล่า

ก. มีครับ มีทุกห้อง

    ข. แล้วค่าเช่าล่ะฮะ เดือนละ
       เท่าไหร่

ก. สามพันห้า

๕๑.๖ ความแตกต่างระหว่างเสียงสูงต่ำ

หน่อยขอทาน   น้อยขอถ่าน

หน่อยทำอะไร
    ขอทาน หน่อยขอทาน

น้อยทำอะไร
    ขอถ่าน น้อยขอถ่าน

ใครขอทาน
    หน่อย หน่อยขอทาน

ใครขอถ่าน
    น้อย น้อยขอถ่าน

หน่อยขอทานใช่ไหม
    ใช่ หน่อยขอทาน

น้อยขอถ่านใช่ไหม
    ใช่ น้อยขอถ่าน

หน่อยขอถ่านใช่ไหม
    ไม่ใช่ หน่อยขอทาน

น้อยขอทานใช่ไหม
    ไม่ใช่ น้อยขอถ่าน

A. phǒm pay tìttɔ̀ɔ rɯ̂aŋ bâan châw
hây khun lɛ́ɛw.

B. lɔ̌ɔ khráp.
dây rɯ̂aŋ wâa yaŋŋay bâaŋ.

A. pen tɯ̀k chán khrɯ̂ŋ
bɛ̀ɛp than samǎy.
nâa yùu mâak.
thâa khun hěn, tɔ̂ŋ chɔ̂ɔp nɛ̂ɛnɛ̂ɛ.

B. bɔɔriween bâan pen yaŋŋay bâaŋ.

A. kamlaŋ dii lɔəy khráp.
nâa bâan pen sanǎam yâa.

B. mii hɔ̂ŋ tháŋmòt kìi hɔ̂ŋ.

A. chán bon mii hɔ̂ŋ nɔɔn sǎam hɔ̂ŋ,
hɔ̂ŋ náam sɔ̌ɔŋ hɔ̂ŋ.
chán lâaŋ mii hɔ̂ŋ ráp khɛ̀ɛk,
hɔ̂ŋ kin khâaw, khrua,
lɛ́ɛw kɔ̂ mii hɔ̂ŋ náam ʔìik hɔ̂ŋ nɯŋ.

B. mây mii hɔ̂ŋ khon cháay lɔ̌há?.

A. mii khráp.
lǎŋ bâan mii rɯan khon cháay
ka hɔ̂ŋ kèp khɔ̌ɔŋ.
rooŋ rót yùu taŋhàak.

B. bâan mii múŋ lûat rɯ́ plàaw.

A. mii khráp. mii thúk hɔ̂ŋ.

B. lɛ́ɛw khâa châw lahá?.
dɯan la thâwrày.

A. sǎam phan hâa.

I've already contacted somebody about a house
to rent for you.

Oh?
What did you find out?

It's a modern one and a half storey
brick house.
It's very cozy.
If you see it, you're sure to like it.

What's the compound like?

It's just right.
There's a lawn in front.

How many rooms are there altogether?

Upstairs there are three bedrooms
and two bathrooms.
Downstairs there's a living room,
a dining room, a kitchen,
and another bathroom.

Isn't there a servant's room?

Yes.
In back of the house there's a servants
quarters and a storeroom.
The garage is separate.

Does the house have screens?

Yes. All rooms have screens.

And how about the rent?
How much is it a month?

Three thousand five hundred.

nɔ̀y khɔ̌ɔ thaan.
nɔ́ɔy khɔ̌ɔ thàan.

Noy Low is begging (asking for alms).
Noy High is asking for charcoal.

nɔ̀y tham ʔaray.
khɔ̌ɔ thaan. nɔ̀y khɔ̌ɔ thaan.
nɔ́ɔy tham ʔaray.
khɔ̌ɔ thàan. nɔ́ɔy khɔ̌ɔ thàan.

khray khɔ̌ɔ thaan.
nɔ̀y. nɔ̀y khɔ̌ɔ thaan.
khray khɔ̌ɔ thàan.
nɔ́ɔy. nɔ́ɔy khɔ̌ɔ thàan.

nɔ̀y khɔ̌ɔ thaan, chây máy.
chây. nɔ̀y khɔ̌ɔ thaan.
nɔ́ɔy khɔ̌ɔ thàan, chây máy.
chây. nɔ́ɔy khɔ̌ɔ thàan.

nɔ̀y khɔ̌ɔ thàan, chây máy.
mây chây. nɔ̀y khɔ̌ɔ thaan.
nɔ́ɔy khɔ̌ɔ thaan, chây máy.
mây chây. nɔ́ɔy khɔ̌ɔ thàan.

๕๑.๗ แบบฝึกหัดไวยากรณ์

ก.

เขาเพิ่งมาเมื่อกี้นี้เอง (เช้า)

เขาเพิ่งมาเมื่อเช้านี้เอง (วาน)

เขาเพิ่งมาเมื่อวานนี้เอง (คืน)

เขาเพิ่งมาเมื่อคืนนี้เอง (เย็น)

เขาเพิ่งมาเมื่อเย็นนี้เอง (สองสามวัน)

เขาเพิ่งมาเมื่อสองสามวันนี้เอง (อาทิตย์)

เขาเพิ่งมาเมื่ออาทิตย์นี้เอง

ข.

ฉันไปติดต่อเรื่องบ้านเช่าให้คุณแล้ว (ซื้อรถ)

ฉันไปติดต่อเรื่องซื้อรถให้คุณแล้ว (คนใช้)

ฉันไปติดต่อเรื่องคนใช้ให้คุณแล้ว (ไปอเมริกา)

ฉันไปติดต่อเรื่องไปอเมริกาให้คุณแล้ว (เรียนภาษาอังกฤษ)

ฉันไปติดต่อเรื่องเรียนภาษาอังกฤษให้คุณแล้ว (ตัดรองเท้า)

ฉันไปติดต่อเรื่องตัดรองเท้าให้คุณแล้ว

ค.

ไม่มีโรงรถหรือฮะ

    มีฮะ โรงรถอยู่ต่างหาก

ไม่มีเรือนคนใช้หรือฮะ

    มีฮะ เรือนคนใช้อยู่ต่างหาก

ไม่มีครัวหรือฮะ

    มีฮะ กรัวอยู่ต่างหาก

ไม่มีห้องเก็บของหรือฮะ

    มีฮะ ห้องเก็บของอยู่ต่างหาก

ไม่มีห้องน้ำหรือฮะ

    มีฮะ ห้องน้ำอยู่ต่างหาก

ไม่มีห้องทำงานหรือฮะ

    มีฮะ ห้องทำงานอยู่ต่างหาก

a. Substitution drill.

kháw phôŋ maa mûa kíi níi ʔeeŋ. (cháaw)   He came just a few minutes ago. (morning)

kháw phôŋ maa mûa cháaw níi ʔeeŋ. (waan)   He came just this morning. (yesterday)

kháw phôŋ maa mûa waan níi ʔeeŋ. (khʉʉn)   He came just yesterday. (night)

kháw phôŋ maa mûa khʉʉn níi ʔeeŋ. (yen)   He came just last night. (evening)

kháw phôŋ maa mûa yen níi ʔeeŋ.   He came just this evening.
(sɔ̌ɔŋ sǎam wan)   (a few days)

kháw phôŋ maa mûa sɔ̌ɔŋ sǎam wan níi ʔeeŋ.   He came just a few days ago.
(ʔathít)   (week)

kháw phôŋ maa mûa ʔathít níi ʔeeŋ.   He came just this week.

b. Substitution drill.

chán pay tìttɔɔ rûaŋ bâan châw hây khun lɛ́ɛw. (sʉ́ʉ rót)   I've already made inquiries for you about houses for rent. (buying a car)

chán pay tìttɔɔ rûaŋ sʉ́ʉ rót hây khun lɛ́ɛw. (khon cháay)   I've already made inquiries for you about buying a car. (servants)

chán pay tìttɔɔ rûaŋ khon cháay hây khun lɛ́ɛw. (pay ʔameerikaa)   I've already contacted somebody for you about servants. (going to America)

chán pay tìttɔɔ rûaŋ pay ʔameerikaa hây khun lɛ́ɛw. (rian phasǎa ʔaŋkrìt)   I've already made contacts for you about going to America. (studying English)

chán pay tìttɔɔ rûaŋ rian phasǎa ʔaŋkrìt hây khun lɛ́ɛw. (tàt rɔŋtháaw)   I've already made inquiries for you about studying English. (getting shoes made)

chán pay tìttɔɔ rûaŋ tàt rɔŋtháaw hây khun lɛ́ɛw.   I've already contacted somebody for you about getting some shoes made.

c. Response drill.

mây mii rooŋ rót lɔ̌háʔ.   Isn't there a garage?
   mii háʔ. rooŋ rót yùu taŋhàak.   Yes. The garage is separate.

mây mii rʉan khon cháay lɔ̌háʔ.   Aren't there any servants quarters?
   mii háʔ. rʉan khon cháay yùu taŋhàak.   Yes. The servants quarters are separate.

mây mii khrua lɔ̌háʔ.   Isn't there a kitchen?
   mii háʔ. khrua yùu taŋhàak.   Yes. The kitchen is separate.

mây mii hɔ̂ŋ kèp khɔ̌ɔŋ lɔ̌háʔ.   Isn't there a storeroom?
   mii háʔ. hɔ̂ŋ kèp khɔ̌ɔŋ yùu taŋhàak.   Yes. The storeroom is separate.

mây mii hɔ̂ŋ náam lɔ̌háʔ.   Isn't there a bathroom?
   mii háʔ. hɔ̂ŋ náam yùu taŋhàak.   Yes. The bathroom is separate.

mây mii hɔ̂ŋ tham ŋaan lɔ̌háʔ.   Isn't there an office?
   mii háʔ. hɔ̂ŋ tham ŋaan yùu taŋhàak.   Yes. The office is separate.

๕๑.๘ การสนทนาโต้ตอบ

พ่อคุณอายุเท่าไหร่
    หกสิบปี

ลูกสาวคุณอายุเท่าไหร่
    สิบขวบ

๕๑.๙ วลีท้ายประโยค

ก็.........น่ะซิ

ทำไมถึงเหงื่อออก ร้อนหรือ
    ก็ร้อนน่ะซิ

ทำไมถึงอาเจียน ไม่สบายหรือ
    ก็ไม่สบายน่ะซิ

ทำไมถึงตัวสั่น หนาวหรือ
    ก็หนาวน่ะซิ

ทำไมถึงร้องไห้ เจ็บหรือ
    ก็เจ็บน่ะซิ

ทำไมถึงหัวเราะ ขำหรือ
    ก็ขำน่ะซิ

ทำไมถึงไม่พูดกับเขา โกรธเขาหรือ
    ก็โกรธน่ะซิ

๕๑.๑๐ การเขียน

51.8 Conversation.

The teacher should ask each student about his family at home.   How many brothers, sisters, children, aunts, uncles; their ages, what they do, etc.

phɔ̌ɔ khun ʔaayúʔ thâwrày.	How old is your father?
hòk sìp pii.	Sixty years old.
lûuk sǎaw khun ʔaayúʔ thâwrày.	How old is your daughter?
sìp khùap.	Ten years old.

51.9 Particles.

kɔ̂ ... nâsi (continued).

The student should repeat the following questions and answers after the teacher, mimicking rhythm, tone of voice, and even facial expressions as accurately as possible. Then, without books, he should answer questions from the teacher.   Finally, he should ask the questions himself.

thammay thǔŋ ...	How has it come about that ... ?
	Why has it arrived to the point that ... ?
thammay thǔŋ ŋùa ʔɔ̀ɔk.	How come you're sweating?
rɔ́ɔn lɔ̌ə.	Are you hot?
kɔ̂ rɔ́ɔn nâsi.	Of course I'm hot.
	(Why else would I be sweating?)
thammay thǔŋ tua sàn.	How come you're shivering?
nǎaw lɔ̌ə.	Are you cold?
kɔ̂ nǎaw nâsi.	Of course I'm cold.
	(Why else would I be shivering?)
thammay thǔŋ hǔarɔ́ʔ.	Why are you laughing?
khǎm lɔ̌ə.	Is it funny?
kɔ̂ khǎm nâsi.	Of course it's funny.
	(Why else would I be laughing?)
thammay thǔŋ ʔaacian.	How come you threw up?
mây sabaay lɔ̌ə.	Aren't you feeling well?
kɔ̂ mây sabaay nâsi.	Of course I'm not feeling well.
	(Why else would I throw up?)
thammay thǔŋ rɔ́ɔŋhâay.	Why are you crying?
cèp lɔ̌ə.	Does it hurt?
kɔ̂ cèp nâsi.	Of course it hurts.
	(Why else would I be crying.)
thammay thǔŋ mây phûut kàp kháw.	Why aren't you talking to him?
kròot kháw lɔ̌ə.	Are you mad at him?
kɔ̂ kròot nâsi.	Of course I'm mad at him.

51.10 Writing.

Practice reading and writing lesson 10 of Book 1 in Thai.

บทที่ ๕๒

๕๒.๑ คำศัพท์

จำเป็น	พอดี	ปากกา
จำเป็นต้อง		
ที่สำหรับจอดรถ	โทรทัศน์	ยา
	เครื่องโทรทัศน์	อาบน้ำ
บ้านเช่าหลังหนึ่ง		
หาบ้านเช่าได้		ยกข้าว
หาบ้านเช่าได้หลังหนึ่ง	ชาม	
	ตู้ถ้วยชาม	เก็บโต๊ะ

๕๒.๒ แบบฝึกหัดการสลับเสียงสูงต่ำ

ลุงสั่งกุ้ง (หมู)	ลุงทอดกุ้ง (น้อง)	ลุงสั่งเนื้อ (ซอ)	หลานทอดกุ้ง (สั่ง)
ลุงสั่งหมู (ซอ)	น้องทอดกุ้ง (กิน)	ลุงซอเนื้อ (น้อง)	หลานสั่งกุ้ง (พี่)
ลุงซอหมู (ปู่)	น้องกินกุ้ง (ไก่)	น้องซอเนื้อ (ปู่)	พี่สั่งกุ้ง (ปลา)
ปู่ซอหมู (ไก่)	น้องกินไก่ (หมู)	ปู่ซอเนื้อ (ขาย)	พี่สั่งปลา (หมู)
ปู่ซอไก่ (ขาย)	น้องกินหมู (ปู่)	ปู่ขายเนื้อ (กุ้ง)	พี่สั่งหมู (ซอ)
ปู่ขายไก่ (พี่)	ปู่กินหมู (เนื้อ)	ปู่ขายกุ้ง (ซอ)	พี่ซอหมู (น้อง)
พี่ขายไก่ (ปลา)	ปู่กินเนื้อ (ปลา)	ปู่ซอกุ้ง (ลุง)	น้องซอหมู (ไก่)
พี่ขายปลา (กิน)	ปู่กินปลา (ทอด)	ลุงซอกุ้ง (หลาน)	น้องซอไก่ (ขาย)
พี่กินปลา (น้อง)	ปู่ทอดปลา (ลุง)	หลานซอกุ้ง (ขาย)	น้องขายไก่ (หลาน)
น้องกินปลา (เนื้อ)	ลุงทอดปลา (ขาย)	หลานขายกุ้ง (เนื้อ)	หลานขายไก่ (ปลา)
น้องกินเนื้อ (ทอด)	ลุงขายปลา (น้อง)	หลานขายเนื้อ (สั่ง)	หลานขายปลา (กิน)
น้องทอดเนื้อ (หลาน)	น้องขายปลา (สั่ง)	หลานสั่งเนื้อ (หมู)	หลานกินปลา (ลุง)
หลานทอดเนื้อ (หมู)	น้องสั่งปลา (กุ้ง)	หลานสั่งหมู (ปลา)	ลุงกินปลา (เนื้อ)
หลานทอดหมู (ลุง)	น้องสั่งกุ้ง (เนื้อ)	หลานสั่งปลา (ทอด)	ลุงกินเนื้อ (ทอด)
ลุงทอดหมู (กุ้ง)	น้องสั่งเนื้อ (ลุง)	หลานทอดปลา (กุ้ง)	ลุงทอดเนื้อ (ปู่)

114

LESSON 52

52.1 Vocabulary and expansions.

campen	To be necessary.
campeŋ tôŋ	To be necessary or required.
thîi sámràp còɔt rót	A place to park the car.
bâan châw lǎŋ nɯŋ	A house for rent.
hǎa bâan châw dây	To find a house for rent.
hǎa bâan châw dây lǎŋ nɯŋ	To find a house for rent.
phɔɔdii	Just right.
thoorathát	Television.
khrɯaŋ thoorathát	Television set.
chaam	Bowl.
tûu thûay chaam	Dish cabinet.
pàakkaa	Pen.
yaa	Medicine, tobacco.
ʔàap náam	To bathe, take a bath.
yók khâaw	To bring on the food (lift the rice).
kèp tóʔ	To clear the table.

52.2 Tone manipulation.

Substitution drill.

luŋ sàŋ kûŋ. (mǔu)
luŋ sàŋ mǔu. (sɯɯ)
luŋ sɯɯ mǔu. (pùu)
pùu sɯɯ mǔu. (kày)
pùu sɯɯ kày. (khǎay)

pùu khǎay kày. (phîi)
phîi khǎay kày. (plaa)
phîi khǎay plaa. (kin)
phîi kin plaa. (nɔ́ɔŋ)
nɔ́ɔŋ kin plaa. (nɯ́a)

nɔ́ɔŋ kin nɯ́a. (thɔ̂ɔt)
nɔ́ɔŋ thɔ̂ɔt nɯ́a. (lǎan)
lǎan thɔ̂ɔt nɯ́a. (mǔu)
lǎan thɔ̂ɔt mǔu. (luŋ)
luŋ thɔ̂ɔt mǔu. (kûŋ)

luŋ thɔ̂ɔt kûŋ. (nɔ́ɔŋ)
nɔ́ɔŋ thɔ̂ɔt kûŋ. (kin)
nɔ́ɔŋ kin kûŋ. (kày)
nɔ́ɔŋ kin kày. (mǔu)
nɔ́ɔŋ kin mǔu. (pùu)

pùu kin mǔu. (nɯ́a)
pùu kin nɯ́a. (plaa)
pùu kin plaa. (thɔ̂ɔt)
pùu thɔ̂ɔt plaa. (luŋ)
luŋ thɔ̂ɔt plaa. (khǎay)

luŋ khǎay plaa. (nɔ́ɔŋ)
nɔ́ɔŋ khǎay plaa. (sàŋ)
nɔ́ɔŋ sàŋ plaa. (kûŋ)
nɔ́ɔŋ sàŋ kûŋ. (nɯ́a)
nɔ́ɔŋ sàŋ nɯ́a. (luŋ)

luŋ sàŋ nɯ́a. (sɯɯ)
luŋ sɯɯ nɯ́a. (nɔ́ɔŋ)
nɔ́ɔŋ sɯɯ nɯ́a. (pùu)
pùu sɯɯ nɯ́a. (khǎay)
pùu khǎay nɯ́a. (kûŋ)

pùu khǎay kûŋ. (sɯɯ)
pùu sɯɯ kûŋ. (luŋ)
luŋ sɯɯ kûŋ. (lǎan)
lǎan sɯɯ kûŋ. (khǎay)
lǎan khǎay kûŋ. (nɯ́a)

lǎan khǎay nɯ́a. (sàŋ)
lǎan sàŋ nɯ́a. (mǔu)
lǎan sàŋ mǔu. (plaa)
lǎan sàŋ plaa. (thɔ̂ɔt)
lǎan thɔ̂ɔt plaa. (kûŋ)

lǎan thɔ̂ɔt kûŋ. (sàŋ)
lǎan sàŋ kûŋ. (phîi)
phîi sàŋ kûŋ. (plaa)
phîi sàŋ plaa. (mǔu)
phîi sàŋ mǔu. (sɯɯ)

phîi sɯɯ mǔu. (nɔ́ɔŋ)
nɔ́ɔŋ sɯɯ mǔu. (kày)
nɔ́ɔŋ sɯɯ kày. (khǎay)
nɔ́ɔŋ khǎay kày. (lǎan)
lǎan khǎay kày. (plaa)

lǎan khǎay plaa. (kin)
lǎan kin plaa. (luŋ)
luŋ kin plaa. (nɯ́a)
luŋ kin nɯ́a. (thɔ̂ɔt)
luŋ thɔ̂ɔt nɯ́a. (pùu)

๕๒.๓ โครงสร้างของประโยค

โรงแรม	เป็นบ้านชั้นเดียวก็ได้
โรงเรียน	สองชั้นก็ได้
โรงหนัง	
โรงรถ	
โรงงาน	เป็นบ้านชั้นเดียว
โรงพยาบาล	หรือสองชั้นก็ได้

บ้านขนาดสามห้องนอน	
บ้านที่มีมุ้งลวด	
บ้านที่มีครัว	เป็นตึกก็ได้
บ้านที่มีห้องคนใช้	เป็นไม้ก็ได้
	เป็นตึกหรือไม้ก็ได้

เขาบอกว่าเขาต้องการ	
บ้านขนาดสามห้องนอน	
ที่มีมุ้งลวด	
มีครัว	เป็นบ้านชั้นเดียวหรือสองชั้น
และมีห้องคนใช้ด้วย	แล้วก็เป็นตึกหรือไม้ก็ได้

๕๒.๔ แบบฝึกหัดการฟังเสียงสูงต่ำ

สมุด	ปากกาหมึกซึม
ยางลบ	ไม้บรรทัด
แผนที่	แปรงลบกระดาน
กระดานดำ	กระดานประกาศ

๕๒.๕ บทบรรยาย

คุณเดวิดขอให้คุณประเสริฐช่วยหาบ้านเช่าให้เขาเหมือนกัน เขาบอกว่าเขาต้องการบ้านขนาดสามห้องนอนที่มีมุ้งลวด มีครัวและมีห้องคนใช้ด้วย บ้านนั้นไม่จำเป็นต้องมีโรงรถ แต่ต้องมีที่สำหรับจอดรถในบริเวณบ้าน จะเป็นบ้านชั้นเดียวหรือสองชั้น แล้วก็เป็นตึกหรือไม้ก็ได้ ไม่จำเป็นต้องเป็นบ้านที่ทันสมัยเพราะเขาไม่ต้องการจะให้ค่าเช่าเกินเดือนละสองพันห้า คุณประเสริฐหาบ้านเช่าได้หลังหนึ่งแล้วแต่ค่าเช่าแพงเกินไป

116

52.3 Patterns and sentence structure.

rooŋ rɛɛm	A hotel (rɛɛm means 'to spend the night').
rooŋ rian	A school.
rooŋ năŋ	A theater.
rooŋ rót	A garage.
rooŋ ŋaan	A factory.
rooŋ phayabaan	A hospital (**phayabaan** means 'to tend or nurse').

bâan khanàat săam hôŋ nɔɔn	A three-bedroom house.
bâan thîi mii múŋ lûat	A house that has screens.
bâan thîi mii khrua	A house that has a kitchen.
bâan thîi mii hôŋ khon cháay	A house that has a servant's room.

kháw bɔ̀ɔk wâa kháw tôŋkaan	He said that he wanted
bâan khanàat săam hôŋ nɔɔn	a three-bedroom house
thîi mii múŋ lûat,	that had screens,
mii khrua,	a kitchen,
lέʔ mii hôŋ khon cháay dûay.	and a servant's room, too.

pen bâan chán diaw kɔ̂ dây,	A house of one storey is all right,
sɔ̌ɔŋ chán kɔ̂ dây.	and two storeys is all right, too.
pen bâan chán diaw	A house of one storey
rú sɔ̌ɔŋ chán kɔ̂ dây.	or two, both will do.

pen tὺk kɔ̂ dây,	It can be brick
pen máay kɔ̂ dây.	or it can be wood.
pen tὺk rú máay kɔ̂ dây.	It can be either brick or wood.

pen bâan chán diaw rú sɔ̌ɔŋ chán,	It can be one or two storeys,
lέɛw kɔ̂ pen tὺk rú máay kɔ̂ dây.	and it can be brick or wood.
	All possibilities are all right.

52.4 Tone identification.

Things in the classroom.

samut	A notebook.	paakkaa mὺk sὺm	A fountain pen.
yaaŋ lop	A rubber eraser.	may banthat	A ruler.
phɛɛn thîi	A map.	prɛɛŋ lop kradaan	A blackboard eraser.
kradaan dam	A blackboard.	kradaan prakaat	A bulletin board.

52.5 Narrative.

khun deewít khɔ̌ɔ hây khun prasɤ̀ɤt chûay hǎa bâan châw hây kháw mŭankan. kháw bɔ̀ɔk wâa kháw tôŋkaan bâan khanàat săam hôŋ nɔɔn thîi mii múŋ lûat, mii khrua, lέʔ mii hôŋ khon cháay dûay. bâan nán mây campen tôŋ mii rooŋ rót, tὲɛ tôŋ mii thîi sámràp cɔ̀ɔt rót nay bɔɔriween bâan. ca pen bâan chán diaw rú sɔ̌ɔŋ chán, lέɛw kɔ̂ pen tὺk rú máay kɔ̂ dây. mây campen tôŋ pen bâan thîi than samǎy, phrɔ́ʔ kháw mây tôŋkaan ca hây khâa châw kɔɔn dὺan la sɔ̌ɔŋ phan hâa. khun prasɤ̀ɤt hǎa bâan châw dây lăŋ nὺŋ lέɛw, tὲɛ khâa châw phɛɛŋ kɤɤn pay.

๕๒.๖ ความแตกต่างระหว่างเสียงสูงต่ำ

ม้าอยู่ไกลกว่าหมา   หมาอยู่ใกล้กว่าม้า

อะไรอยู่ไกลกว่ากัน   หมา อยู่ไกลกว่าม้าใช่ไหม

    ม้า ม้าอยู่ไกลกว่าหมา   ไม่ใช่ หมาอยู่ใกล้กว่าม้า

อะไรอยู่ใกล้กว่ากัน   ม้า อยู่ใกล้กว่าหมาใช่ไหม

    หมา หมาอยู่ใกล้กว่าม้า   ไม่ใช่ ม้าอยู่ไกลกว่าหมา

ม้าอยู่ไกลกว่าหมาใช่ไหม

    ใช่ ม้าอยู่ไกลกว่าหมา

หมาอยู่ใกล้กว่าม้าใช่ไหม

    ใช่ หมาอยู่ใกล้กว่าม้า

๕๒.๗ คำถามบทบรรยาย

คุณเดวิดรู้จักคุณประเสริฐใช่ไหม	ใช่
เขาเช่าบ้านของคุณประเสริฐใช่ไหม	ไม่ใช่
เขาให้คุณประเสริฐช่วยหาบ้านเช่าให้ใช่ไหม	ใช่
คุณเดวิดต้องการบ้านขนาดสองห้องนอนใช่ไหม	ไม่ใช่
เขาต้องการบ้านที่มีมุ้งลวดใช่ไหม	ใช่
บ้านนั้นต้องเป็นบ้านที่ทันสมัยใช่ไหม	ไม่ใช่
บ้านนั้นจำเป็นต้องมีโรงรถใช่ไหม	ไม่ใช่
แต่ต้องมีที่จอดรถใช่ไหม	ใช่
บ้านจะเป็นตึกหรือไม้ก็ได้ใช่ไหม	ใช่
ต้องเป็นบ้านสองชั้นใช่ไหม	ไม่ใช่
คุณประเสริฐยังหาบ้านเช่าไม่ได้เลยใช่ไหม	ไม่ใช่
เขาหาได้หลังหนึ่งแล้วใช่ไหม	ใช่
ค่าเช่าถูกมากใช่ไหม	ไม่ใช่
ค่าเช่าแพงไปใช่ไหม	ใช่
คุณเดวิดไม่ต้องการจะให้ค่าเช่า	
เกินกว่าเดือนละสองพันห้าใช่ไหม	ใช่

52.6 Tone distinctions.

máa yùu klay kwàa mǎa. The horse is farther than the dog.
mǎa yùu klây kwàa máa. The dog is nearer than the horse.

ʔaray yùu klay kwàa kan.
 máa. máa yùu klay kwàa mǎa.
ʔaray yùu klây kwàa kan.
 mǎa. mǎa yùu klây kwàa máa.

máa yùu klay kwàa mǎa, chây máy.
 chây. máa yùu klay kwàa mǎa.
mǎa yùu klây kwàa máa, chây máy.
 chây. mǎa yùu klây kwàa máa.

mǎa yùu klay kwàa máa, chây máy.
 mây chây. mǎa yùu klây kwàa máa.
máa yùu klây kwàa mǎa, chây máy.
 mây chây. máa yùu klay kwàa mǎa.

52.7 Questions on the narrative.

khun deewít rúucàk khun prasòot, chây máy.	chây.
kháw châw bâan khɔ̌ŋ khun prasòot, chây máy.	mây chây.
kháw hây khun prasòot chûay hǎa bâan châw hây, chây máy.	chây.
khun deewít tɔ̂ŋkaan bâan khanàat sɔ̌ɔŋ hɔ̂ŋ nɔɔn, chây máy.	mây chây.
kháw tɔ̂ŋkaan bâan thîi mii múŋ lûat, chây máy.	chây.
bâan nán tɔ̂ŋ pen bâan thîi than sǎmǎy, chây máy.	mây chây.
bâan nán campen tɔ̂ŋ mii rooŋ rót, chây máy.	mây chây.
tɛ̀ɛ tɔ̂ŋ mii thîi cɔ̀ɔt rót, chây máy.	chây.
bâan ca pen tʉ̀k rʉ́ máay kɔ̂ dây, chây máy.	chây.
tɔ̂ŋ pen bâan sɔ̌ɔŋ chán, chây máy.	mây chây.
khun prasòot yaŋ hǎa bâan châw mây dây ləəy, chây máy.	mây chây.
kháw hǎa dây lǎŋ nʉ̀ŋ lɛ́ɛw, chây máy.	chây.
khâa châw thùuk mâak, chây máy.	mây chây.
khâa châw phɛɛŋ pay, chây máy.	chây.
khun deewít mây tɔ̂ŋkaan ca hây khâa châw kəən kwàa dʉan la sɔ̌ɔŋ phan hâa, chây máy.	chây.

(More.)

คุณเดวิดขอให้ภรรยาของคุณประเสริฐ
　　ช่วยหาบ้านเช่าให้ใช่ไหม
บ้านไม่ต้องมีมุ้งลวดใช่ไหม
บ้านต้องมีโรงรถใช่ไหม
ต้องเป็นบ้านชั้นเดียวใช่ไหม
ต้องเป็นตึกใช่ไหม
ค่าเช่าของบ้านที่คุณประเสริฐหาได้แล้ว
　　ไม่แพงเกินไปใช่ไหม

ใครให้คุณประเสริฐหาบ้านเช่าให้
คุณเดวิดต้องการบ้านขนาดไหน
บ้านนั้นจำเป็นต้องเป็นบ้านที่ทันสมัยไหม
จำเป็นต้องมีโรงรถไหม
ต้องมีที่จอดรถในบริเวณบ้านไหม
คุณเดวิดต้องการบ้านกี่ชั้น
แล้วก็เป็นตึกหรือไม้
เขาต้องการให้ค่าเช่าไม่เกินเดือนละเท่าไหร่

คุณประเสริฐหาบ้านเช่าได้แล้วหรือยัง
คุณเดวิดตกลงเช่าไหม
ทำไมเขาไม่ตกลง

ไม่ใช่ เขาขอให้คุณประเสริฐ
　　ช่วยหาบ้านเช่าให้
ไม่ใช่ ต้องมี
ไม่ใช่ แต่ต้องมีที่จอดรถ
ไม่ใช่ เป็นบ้านสองชั้นก็ได้
ไม่ใช่ เป็นไม้ก็ได้

ไม่ใช่ แพงเกินไป

คุณเดวิด
สามห้องนอน
ไม่จำเป็น
ไม่จำเป็น
ต้องมี
ชั้นเดียวหรือสองชั้นก็ได้
ตึกหรือไม้ก็ได้
สองพันห้า

หาได้แล้ว
ไม่ตกลง
แพงไป

khun deewít khɔ̌ɔ hây phanrayaa
khɔ̌ŋ khun prasəət chûay hǎa
bâan châw hây, chây máy.

bâan mây tɔ̂ŋ mii múŋ lûat,
chây máy.

bâan tɔ̂ŋ mii rooŋ rót,
chây máy.

tɔ̂ŋ pen bâan chán diaw,
chây máy.

tɔ̂ŋ pen tʉ̀k,
chây máy.

khâa châw khɔ̌ŋ bâan
thîi khun prasəət hǎa dây lέεw
mây phεεŋ kəən pay,
chây máy.

khray hây khun prasəət hǎa bâan
châw hây.

khun deewít tɔ̂ŋkaan bâan khanàat nǎy.

bâan nán campen tɔ̂ŋ pen bâan
thîi than samǎy máy.

campen tɔ̂ŋ mii rooŋ rót máy.

tɔ̂ŋ mii thîi cɔ̀ɔt rót
nay bɔɔriween bâan máy.

khun deewít tɔ̂ŋkaan bâan kìi chán.

lέεw kɔ̂ pen tʉ̀k rʉ́ máay.

kháw tɔ̂ŋkaan hây khâa châw
mây kəən dʉan la thâwrày.

khun prasəət hǎa bâan châw dây lέεw
rʉ́ yaŋ.

khun deewít tòkloŋ châw máy.

thammay kháw mây tòkloŋ.

mây chây.

kháw khɔ̌ɔ hây khun prasəət
chûay hǎa bâan châw hây.

mây chây.
tɔ̂ŋ mii.

mây chây.
tὲε tɔ̂ŋ mii thîi cɔ̀ɔt rót.

mây chây.
pen bâan sɔ̌ɔŋ chán kɔ̂ dây.

mây chây.
pen máay kɔ̂ dây.

mây chây.
phεεŋ kəən pay.

khun deewít.

sǎam hɔ̂ŋ nɔɔn.

mây campen.

mây campen.

tɔ̂ŋ mii.

chán diaw rʉ́ sɔ̌ɔŋ chán kɔ̂ dây.

tʉ̀k rʉ́ máay kɔ̂ dây.

sɔ̌ɔŋ phan hâa.

hǎa dây lέεw.

mây tòkloŋ.

phεεŋ pay.

121

๕๒.๘ การสนทนาโต้ตอบ

บนตู้ถ้วยชาม
หนังสือ ดินสอ ปากกา

บนตู้เย็น
กล้องสูบยา ที่เขี่ยบุหรี่ ไม้ขีด

บนตู้หนังสือ
จาน แก้ว ช้อน

บนเครื่องโทรทัศน์
หวี แปรงสีฟัน แว่นตา

บนโต๊ะ
ไม้ตีกลอง กลอง พัดลม

bon tûu thûay chaam:
naŋsŭu, dinsɔ́ɔ, pàakkaa.

On the dish cabinet:
a book, a pencil, and a pen.

bon tûu yen:
klɔ̂ŋ sùup yaa, thîi khìa burìi,
máykhìit.

On the refrigerator:
a pipe, an ash tray,
and matches.

bon tûu naŋsŭu:
caan, kɛ̂ɛw, chɔ́ɔn.

On the bookcase:
a plate, a glass, and a spoon.

bon khrûaŋ thoorathát:
wǐi, prɛɛŋ sǐi fan, wɛ̂n taa.

On the television set:
a comb, a toothbrush, and eyeglasses.

bon tó?:
máy tii klɔɔŋ, klɔɔŋ, phátlom.

On the table:
drum sticks, a drum, and a fan.

This lesson is intended to acquaint the student with the vocabulary of the picture only. Questions should be limited to the following types: ?aray yùu bon tó?. chɔ́ɔn yùu thîi nǎy. The picture will be used again in 54.8 for wider questioning.

๕๒.๙ วลีท้ายประโยค

เถอะ

แอ๊ดอยากจะรู้ว่า เขากินข้าวได้หรือยัง
    ได้ (พูดกับแอ๊ด)
        กินข้าวเถอะแอ๊ด

ตุ่มอยากจะรู้ว่าเขายกข้าวได้หรือยัง
    ได้ (พูดกับตุ่ม)
        ยกข้าวเถอะตุ่ม

ศรีอยากจะรู้ว่าเขากลับบ้านได้หรือยัง
    ได้ (พูดกับศรี)
        กลับบ้านเถอะศรี

แดงอยากจะรู้ว่าเขาเก็บโต๊ะได้หรือยัง
    ได้ (พูดกับแดง)
        เก็บโต๊ะเถอะแดง

ต้อยอยากจะรู้ว่าเขาอาบน้ำได้หรือยัง
    ได้ (พูดกับต้อย)
        อาบน้ำเถอะต้อย

๕๒.๑๐ การเขียน

เปล่า   ศาลาแดง   ดำริ   เชิญ   นาฬิกา

thəʔ.

The speaker gives permission or releases hearer to do something that the hearer wants to do or should do for his own good.   The speaker may also want the hearer to do it and may even be urging him with **thəʔ**, but he has no reason whatsoever to feel that he is imposing on the hearer in urging the action.   The feeling is indicated by the following English phrases.

> It's all right to ... now.
> There's no reason why you shouldn't ... now.
> Go ahead and ... .
> Come on and ... .

The following examples show permission or release, not urging.

ʔέεt yàak ca rúu wâa
kháw kin khâaw dây rɨ́ yaŋ.
  dây.
    (phûut kàp ʔέεt)
    kin khâaw thəʔ, ʔέεt.
	At wants to know whether she
	can eat yet.
	  Sure she can.
	    (Speaking to At)
	    Go ahead and eat, At.

sǐi yàak ca rúu wâa
kháw klàp bâan dây rɨ́ yaŋ.
  dây.
    (phûut kàp sǐi)
    klàp bâan thəʔ, sǐi.
	Sri wants to know whether she
	can go home yet.
	  Sure she can.
	    (Speaking to Sri)
	    You can go home now, Sri.

tɔ̂y yàak ca rúu wâa
kháw ʔàap náam dây rɨ́ yaŋ.
  dây.
    (phûut kàp tɔ̂y)
    ʔàap náam thəʔ, tɔ̂y.
	Toy wants to know whether she
	can take a bath now.
	  Sure she can.
	    (Speaking to Toy)
	    Go ahead and take a bath, Toy.

tùm yàak ca rúu wâa
kháw yók khâaw dây rɨ́ yaŋ.
  dây.
    (phûut kàp tùm)
    yók khâaw thəʔ, tùm.
	Toom wants to know whether she can
	bring on the food yet.
	  Sure she can.
	    (Speaking to Toom)
	    Serve the food now, Toom.

dεεŋ yàak ca rúu wâa
kháw kèp tóʔ dây rɨ́ yaŋ.
  dây.
    (phûut kàp dεεŋ)
    kèp tóʔ thəʔ, dεεŋ.
	Daeng wants to know whether she
	can clear the table now.
	  Sure she can.
	    (Speaking to Daeng)
	    You can clear the table now, Daeng.

52.10   Writing.   52.10

Practice reading and writing lesson 11 of Book 1 in Thai.   Notice the following irregularities.

plàaw	This is written short but pronounced long.
sǎaladεεŋ	The initial consonant is another high s (corresponding to Sanskrit ś). The second syllable is written long but pronounced short.
damriʔ	This is written as if it were **damríʔ**.
chəən	The irregular y initial consonant is pronounced n as a final consonant.
naalikaa	This is spelled with an irregular l consonant.

บทที่ ๕๓

๕๓.๑ คำศัพท์

เบา	แพทย์
	การแพทย์
ตรี	
(นาย) ร้อยตรี	
(นาย) พันตรี	วิทยา
	วิทยาศาสตร์
โท	วิทยาศาสตร์การแพทย์
(นาย) ร้อยโท	
(นาย) พันโท	กรุณา
เอก	ต่อ
(นาย) ร้อยเอก	
(นาย) พันเอก	ด๊อกเตอร์
ปริญญา	ครู่
	เมื่อสักครู่นี้เอง
ศาสตร์	
ภูมิ	นัด
ภูมิศาสตร์	ตามนัด
ประวัติ	มิสเตอร์
ประวัติศาสตร์	
	ตั้ง
ฮัลโหล	ตั้งนาน
หมอ	อีกนานถึงจะกิน

LESSON 53

53.1 Vocabulary and expansions.

baw	To be light in weight.
trii	Third rank.
(naay) rɔ́ɔy trii	Second lieutenant.
(naay) phan trii	Major.
thɔ̌ɔ	Second rank.
(naay) rɔ́ɔy thɔ̌ɔ	First lieutenant.
(naay) phan thɔ̌ɔ	Lieutenant colonel.
ʔèek	First rank.
(naay) rɔ́ɔy ʔèek	Captain.
(naay) phan ʔèek	Colonel.
prinyaa	An academic degree.
sàat	A suffix meaning 'field of knowledge'. -ology.
phuum, phuumíʔ	Earth, place (used mainly in compounds).
phuumísàat	Geography.
prawàt	Account, story, history.
prawàttisàat	The field or subject of History.
halɔ̌ɔ	The usual word for answering the phone. **sawàtdii khráp (khâ)** is also used by some people now and is gaining in popularity.
mɔ̌ɔ	Medical doctor.
phɛ̂ɛt	Medical doctor (formal).
kaan phɛ̂ɛt	The field of medicine, medical matters.
wítthayaa	Knowledge (used mainly in compounds).
wítthayasàat	Science.
wítthayasàat kaan phɛ̂ɛt	Medical sciences. The University of Medical Sciences.
karunaa	To be kind, merciful. 'Please' (used in written notices, formal telephone conversations, and when speaking to very high superiors).
tɔ̀ɔ	To connect. 'Connect me with ...', 'Give me extension ... .
dɔ́ktɔ̂ə	Doctor (the holder of a Ph.D.).
khrûu	A short period of time, a while.
mûa sák khrûu níi ʔeeŋ	Just a short while ago.
nát	To make an appointment, arrange a time.
taam nát	According to the appointment.
mítsatəə	Mr.
tâŋ	In front of a quantity this emphasizes its large size. As much as ... .
tâŋ naan	A *long* time.
ʔìik naan thǎŋ ca kin	It will be a long time before I eat. 'Another long time until (reaching) will eat.'

127

๕๓.๒ แบบผึกหัดการสลับเสียงสูงต่ำ

ถ้าเนื้อกิโลละ ๑๕ บาท หมูกิโลละ ๑๗
อะไรจะแพงกว่ากัน
    หมูแพงกว่าเนื้อ
อะไรจะถูกกว่ากัน
    เนื้อถูกกว่าหมู

ถ้าน้อยหนัก ๖๒ กิโล หน่อยหนัก ๖๑ กิโล
ใครจะหนักกว่ากัน
    น้อยหนักกว่าหน่อย
ใครจะเบากว่ากัน
    หน่อยเบากว่าน้อย

ถ้าลุงมีเงินพันบาท ป้ามีเงินสองพัน
ใครจะมีมากกว่ากัน
    ป้ามีมากกว่าลุง
ใครจะมีน้อยกว่ากัน
    ลุงมีน้อยกว่าป้า

ถ้าต๋อยสูง ๑๕๐ เซนต์ ต้อยสูง ๑๖๐ เซนต์
ใครจะสูงกว่ากัน
    ต้อยสูงกว่าต๋อย
ใครจะเตี้ยกว่ากัน
    ต๋อยเตี้ยกว่าต้อย

๕๓.๓ โครงสร้างของประโยค

(นาย) ร้อยตรี   ปริญญาตรี
(นาย) ร้อยโท   ปริญญาโท
(นาย) ร้อยเอก   ปริญญาเอก

(นาย) พันตรี   วิทยาศาสตร์
(นาย) พันโท   ภูมิศาสตร์
(นาย) พันเอก   ประวัติศาสตร์

๕๓.๔ แบบผึกหัดการฟังเสียงสูงต่ำ

น้ำมันเครื่อง   กุญแจถอดล้อ   แม่แรง
น้ำมันเบนซิน   ยางอะไหล่   ไฟท้าย

53.2 Tone manipulation.

Response drill.

thâa núa kiloo la sìp hâa bàat,
mǔu kiloo la sìp cèt,
ʔaray ca phɛɛŋ kwàa kan.
  mǔu phɛɛŋ kwàa núa.
ʔaray ca thùuk kwàa kan.
  núa thùuk kwàa mǔu.

If beef costs 15 baht a kilo,
and pork costs 17,
which is more expensive?
  Pork is more expensive than beef.
Which is cheaper?
  Beef is cheaper than pork.

thâa luŋ mii ŋən phan bàat,
pâa mii ŋən sɔ̌əŋ phan,
khray ca mii mâak kwàa kan.
  pâa mii mâak kwàa luŋ.
khray ca mii nɔ́əy kwàa kan.
  luŋ mii nɔ́əy kwàa pâa.

If Uncle has a thousand baht,
and Auntie has two thousand,
who has more?
  Auntie has more than Uncle.
Who has less?
  Uncle has less than Auntie.

thâa nɔ́əy nàk hòk sìp sɔ̌əŋ kiloo,
nɔ̀y nàk hòk sìp ʔèt kiloo,
khray ca nàk kwàa kan.
  nɔ́əy nàk kwàa nɔ̀y.
khray ca baw kwàa kan.
  nɔ̀y baw kwàa nɔ́əy.

If Noy High weighs 62 kilos,
and Noy Low weighs 61,
who is heavier?
  Noy High is heavier than Noy Low.
Who is lighter?
  Noy Low is lighter than Noy High.

thâa tɔ̌y sǔuŋ rɔ́əy hâa sìp sen,
tɔ̂y sǔuŋ rɔ́əy hòk sìp sen,
khray ca sǔuŋ kwàa kan.
  tɔ̂y sǔuŋ kwàa tɔ̌y.
khray ca tîa kwàa kan.
  tɔ̌y tîa kwàa tɔ̂y.

If Toy Rise is 150 centimeters tall,
and Toy Fall is 160,
who is taller?
  Toy Fall is taller than Toy Rise.
Who is shorter?
  Toy Rise is shorter than Toy Fall.

If the students can do these easily without books, the teacher should randomly change the figures.

53.3 Patterns.

(naay) rɔ́əy trii.	Second lieutenant.
(naay) rɔ́əy thoo.	First lieutenant.
(naay) rɔ́əy ʔèek.	Captain.
(naay) phan trii.	Major.
(naay) phan thoo.	Lieutenant colonel.
(naay) phan ʔèek.	Colonel.
prinyaa trii.	Bachelor's degree.
prinyaa thoo.	Master's degree.
prinyaa ʔèek.	Doctor's degree.
wítthayasàat.	Science.
phuumísàat.	Geography.
prawàttìsàat.	History.

53.4 Tone identification.

Things concerned with automobiles.

namman khrʉaŋ	Motor oil.	kuncɛɛ thɔɔt lɔɔ	A lug wrench.	mɛɛ rɛɛŋ	A jack.
namman bensin	Gasoline.	yaaŋ ʔalay	Spare tire.	fay thaay	Rear lights.

129

๕๓.๕ บทสนทนา

ก. ฮัลโหล

    ข. ฮัลโหล ที่ไหนครับ

ก. วิทยาศาสตร์การแพทย์ครับ

    ข. กรุณาต่อ ๒๑๕ หน่อยครับ

ค. ฮัลโหล

    ข. ขอพูดกับ ดร. วิชัยหน่อย
    ครับ

ค. ดร. วิชัยไม่อยู่ค่ะ
ออกไปข้างนอกเมื่อสักครู่นี้เอง

    ข. จะกลับเมื่อไหร่ทราบไหมครับ

ค. ไม่ทราบค่ะ

    ข. จะสั่งอะไรไว้หน่อยได้ไหมครับ

ค. เชิญค่ะ

    ข. ช่วยกรุณาบอกเขาด้วยนะครับ
ว่าพรุ่งนี้ หมอสมิตมีธุระ
ไปพบเขาตามนัดไม่ได้

ค. ค่ะ แล้วดิฉันจะบอกให้ค่ะ

    ข. เท่านั้นละครับ ขอบคุณมาก

๕๓.๖ ความแตกต่างระหว่างเสียงสูงต่ำ

แหวนอยู่บนเต่า   แว่นอยู่บนเตา

แหวนอยู่ที่ไหน
    บนเต่า แหวนอยู่บนเต่า
แว่นอยู่ที่ไหน
    บนเตา แว่นอยู่บนเตา

แหวนอยู่บนเต่าใช่ไหม
    ใช่ แหวนอยู่บนเต่า
แว่นอยู่บนเตาใช่ไหม
    ใช่ แว่นอยู่บนเตา

อะไรอยู่บนเต่า
    แหวน แหวนอยู่บนเต่า
อะไรอยู่บนเตา
    แว่น แว่นอยู่บนเตา

แหวนอยู่บนเตาใช่ไหม
    ไม่ใช่ แหวนอยู่บนเต่า
แว่นอยู่บนเต่าใช่ไหม
    ไม่ใช่ แว่นอยู่บนเตา

53.5 Dialog.

A. halǒo.

  B. halǒo. thîi nǎy khráp.

A. wítthayasàat kaan phê ɛt khráp.

  B. karunaa tɔ̀ɔ sɔ̌ɔŋ nừŋ hâa nɔ̀y khráp.

C. halǒo.

  B. khɔ̌ɔ phûut kàp dɔ́ktɘ̀ɘ wíchay nɔ̀y khráp.

C. dɔ́ktɘ̀ɘ wíchay mây yùu khâ.

  ʔɔ́ɔk pay khâŋ nɔ̂ɔk mûa sák khrûu níi ʔeeŋ.

  B. ca klàp mûarày, sâap máy khráp.

C. mây sâap khâ.

  B. ca sàŋ ʔaray wáy nɔ̀y, dây máy khráp.

C. chəən khâ.

  B. chûay karunaa bɔ̀ɔk kháw dûay ná

    khráp wâa phrûŋ níi mɔ̌ɔ samít mii

    thúráʔ. pay phóp kháw taam nát mây dây.

C. khâ. lɛ́ɛw dichán ca bɔ̀ɔk hây khâ.

  B. thâwnán la khráp. khɔ̀ɔpkhun mâak.

Hello.

Hello. Where is this?

The University of Medical Sciences.

Give me extension 215, please.

Hello.

May I speak to Dr. Wichai, please?

Dr. Wichai isn't here right now.

He went out just a little while ago.

Do you know when he'll be back?

No, I don't.

Can I leave a message?

Yes. Please do.

Please tell him that Dr. Smith will be busy tomorrow and won't be able to keep the appointment with him.

Yes. I'll tell him.

That's all. Thanks a lot.

53.6 Tone distinctions.

wɛ̌ɛn yùu bon tàw.   The ring is on the turtle.

wên yùu bon taw.   The eyeglasses are on the stove.

wɛ̌ɛn yùu thîi nǎy.

  bon tàw. wɛ̌ɛn yùu bon tàw.

wên yùu thîi nǎy.

  bon taw. wên yùu bon taw.

ʔaray yùu bon tàw.

  wɛ̌ɛn. wɛ̌ɛn yùu bon tàw.

ʔaray yùu bon taw.

  wên. wên yùu bon taw.

wɛ̌ɛn yùu bon tàw, chây máy.

  chây. wɛ̌ɛn yùu bon tàw.

wên yùu bon taw, chây máy.

  chây. wên yùu bon taw.

wɛ̌ɛn yùu bon taw, chây máy.

  mây chây. wɛ̌ɛn yùu bon tàw.

wên yùu bon tàw, chây máy.

  mây chây. wên yùu bon taw.

๕๓.๗   แบบฝึกหัดไวยากรณ์

ก.

ขอพูดกับร้อยเอกวิชัยครับ   (หมอ)
ขอพูดกับหมอวิชัยครับ.   (พันตรี)
ขอพูดกับพันตรีวิชัยครับ   (คุณ)
ขอพูดกับคุณวิชัยครับ   (ร้อยโท)
ขอพูดกับร้อยโทวิชัยครับ   (ด๊อกเตอร์)
ขอพูดกับ ดร. วิชัย ครับ

ข.

ขอพูดกับร้อยตรีประเสริฐหน่อยค่ะ   ขอพูดกับหมอทวีศักดิ์หน่อยค่ะ
    ร้อยตรีประเสริฐไม่อยู่ครับ   หมอทวีศักดิ์ไม่อยู่ครับ

ขอพูดกับ มร. สมิตหน่อยค่ะ   ขอพูดกับพันโทสมานหน่อยค่ะ
    มร. สมิตไม่อยู่ครับ   พันโทสมานไม่อยู่ครับ

ขอพูดกับพันเอกสวัสดิ์หน่อยค่ะ   ขอพูดกับ ดร. ยังหน่อยค่ะ
    พันเอกสวัสดิ์ไม่อยู่ครับ   ดร. ยังไม่อยู่ครับ

ค.

ผมร้อยตรีสมิตครับ   (มิสเตอร์)
ผม มร. สมิตครับ   (พันเอก)
ผมพันเอกสมิตครับ   (หมอ)
ผมหมอสมิตครับ   (พันโท)
ผมพันโทสมิตครับ   (ด๊อกเตอร์)
ผม ดร. สมิตครับ

53.7 Grammar drills.

a. Substitution drill.

khɔ̌ɔ phûut kàp rɔ́ɔy ʔèek wíchay khráp.	May I speak to Captain Wichai, please?
(mɔ̌ɔ)	(medical doctor)
khɔ̌ɔ phûut kàp mɔ̌ɔ wíchay khráp.	May I speak to Dr. Wichai, please?
(phan trii)	(Major)
khɔ̌ɔ phûut kàp phan trii wíchay khráp.	May I speak to Major Wichai, please?
(khun)	(Khun)
khɔ̌ɔ phûut kàp khun wíchay khráp.	May I speak to Khun Wichai, please?
(rɔ́ɔy thoo)	(1st lieutenant)
khɔ̌ɔ phûut kàp rɔ́ɔy thoo wíchay khráp.	May I speak to Lieutenant Wichai, please?
(dɔ́ktɚ̀)	(Ph.D.)
khɔ̌ɔ phûut kàp dɔ́ktɚ̀ wíchay khráp.	May I speak to Dr. Wichai, please?

b. Response dill.

khɔ̌ɔ phûut kàp rɔ́ɔy trii prasɚ̀ɚt nɔ̀y khâ.	May I speak to Lieutenant Prasert, please?
rɔ́ɔy trii prasɚ̀ɚt mây yùu khráp.	Lieutenant Prasert isn't here.
khɔ̌ɔ phûut kàp mítsatɚɚ samít nɔ̀y khâ.	May I speak to Mr. Smith, please?
mítsatɚɚ samít mây yùu khráp.	Mr. Smith isn't here.
khɔ̌ɔ phûut kàp phan ʔèek sawàt nɔ̀y khâ.	May I speak to Colonel Sawat, please?
phan ʔèek sawàt mây yùu khráp.	Colonel Sawat isn't here.
khɔ̌ɔ phûut kàp mɔ̌ɔ thawiisàk nɔ̀y khâ.	May I speak to Dr. Taweesak, please?
mɔ̌ɔ thawiisàk mây yùu khráp.	Dr. Taweesak isn't here.
khɔ̌ɔ phûut kàp phan thoo samǎan nɔ̀y khâ.	May I speak to Lt. Colonel Samarn, please?
phan thoo samǎan mây yùu khráp.	Lt. Colonel Samarn isn't here.
khɔ̌ɔ phûut kàp dɔ́ktɚ̀ yaŋ nɔ̀y khâ.	May I speak to Dr. Young. please?
dɔ́ktɚ̀ yaŋ mây yùu khráp.	Dr. Young isn't here.

c. Substitution drill.

phǒm rɔ́ɔy trii samít khráp.	This is 2nd Lieutenant Smith.
(mítsatɚɚ)	(Mr.)
phǒm mítsatɚɚ samít khráp.	This is Mr. Smith.
(phan ʔèek)	(Colonel)
phǒm phan ʔèek samít khráp.	This is Colonel Smith.
(mɔ̌ɔ)	(medical doctor)
phǒm mɔ̌ɔ samít khráp.	This is Dr. Smith.
(phan thoo)	(Lt. Colonel)
phǒm phan thoo samít khráp.	This is Lt. Colonel Smith.
(dɔ́ktɚ̀)	(Ph.D.)
phǒm dɔ́ktɚ̀ samít khráp.	This is Dr. Smith.

ง.

แดงล่ะฮะ   ตุ่มล่ะฮะ   ต้อยล่ะฮะ   น้อยล่ะฮะ   ศรีล่ะฮะ

แดงหรือฮะ   ตุ่มหรือฮะ   ต้อยหรือฮะ   น้อยหรือฮะ   ศรีหรือฮะ

จ.

แดงกินข้าวแล้วหรือยังฮะ   แล้วน้อยล่ะฮะ กินแล้วหรือยัง

     แดงหรือฮะ กินแล้ว   น้อยหรือฮะ ยัง

กินเมื่อไหร่ฮะ   จะกินเมื่อไหร่ฮะ

     กินตั้งนานแล้วฮะ   กำลังจะกินเดี๋ยวนี้ฮะ

แล้วตุ่มล่ะฮะ กินแล้วหรือยัง   แล้วศรีล่ะฮะ กินแล้วหรือยัง

     ตุ่มหรือฮะ กินแล้ว   ศรีหรือฮะ ยัง

กินเมื่อไหร่ฮะ   จะกินเมื่อไหร่ฮะ

     เพิ่งกินเมื่อกินเองฮะ   เดี๋ยวจะกินฮะ

แล้วต้อยล่ะฮะ กินแล้วหรือยัง   แล้วดำล่ะฮะ กินแล้วหรือยัง

     ต้อยหรือฮะ กำลังกินอยู่ฮะ   ดำหรือฮะ ยัง

                          จะกินเมื่อไหร่ฮะ

                          อีกนานถึงจะกินฮะ

แดง   ตุ่ม   ต้อย   น้อย   ศรี   ดำ

ตั้งนาน   เพิ่ง   กำลัง   กำลังจะ   เดี๋ยว   อีกนาน

๕๓.๘   การสนทนาโต้ตอบ

134

d. Contrast drill.

Notice the **há** after **lâ** is considerably higher than after **lŏ**.

dɛɛŋ lâhá	tùm lâhá	tôy lâhá	nɔ́ɔy lâhá	sĭi lâhá
dɛɛŋ lŏhá	tùm lŏhá	tôy lŏhá	nɔ́ɔy lŏhá	sĭi lŏhá

e. Response drill.

dɛɛŋ kin khâaw lɛ́ɛw rʉ́ yaŋ há.   Has Daeng eaten yet?
  dɛɛŋ lŏhá?. kin lɛ́ɛw.   Daeng? Yes.
kin mʉarày há.   When?
  kin tâŋ naan lɛ́ɛw há?.   Long ago.

lɛ́ɛw tùm lâhá.   And what about Toom?
kin lɛ́ɛw rʉ́ yaŋ.   Has she eaten yet?
  tùm lŏhá?. kin lɛ́ɛw.   Toom? Yes.
kin mʉarày há.   When?
  phɔ̂ŋ kin mʉa kíi níi ?eeŋ há?.   She ate just a minute ago.

lɛ́ɛw tôy lâhá.   And what about Toy?
kin lɛ́ɛw rʉ́ yaŋ.   Has she eaten yet?
  tôy lŏhá?.   Toy?
kamlaŋ kin yùu há?.   She's eating right now.

lɛ́ɛw nɔ́ɔy lâhá.   And what about Noy?
kin lɛ́ɛw rʉ́ yaŋ.   Has she eaten yet?
  nɔ́ɔy lŏhá?. yaŋ.   Noy? Not yet.
ca kin mʉarày há.   When is she going to eat?
  kamlaŋ ca kin dĭawníi há?.   She's just about to eat right now.

lɛ́ɛw sĭi lâhá.   And what about Sri?
kin lɛ́ɛw rʉ́ yaŋ.   Has she eaten yet?
  sĭi lŏhá?. yaŋ.   Sri? Not yet.
ca kin mʉarày há.   When is she going to eat?
  dĭaw ca kin há?.   In a few minutes.

lɛ́ɛw dam lâhá.   And what about Dum?
kin lɛ́ɛw rʉ́ yaŋ.   Has she eaten yet?
  dam lŏhá?. yaŋ.   Dum? Not yet.
ca kin mʉarày há.   When is she going to eat?
  ?ìik naan thʉ̌ŋ ca kin há?.   Not for a long time yet.

To do this drill without books, the teacher should write the following on the blackboard.

dɛɛŋ	tùm	tôy	nɔ́ɔy	sĭi	dam
tâŋ naan	phɔ̂ŋ	kamlaŋ	kamlaŋ ca	dĭaw	?ìik naan

53.8 Conversation.   53.8

The teacher should ask each student about his experiences in looking for a house or an apartment to rent.

135

๕๓.๙ วลีท้ายประโยค

เถอะ

ต้อยยังไม่กลับบ้านหรือ
          กลับไม่ได้ ยังทำงานไม่เสร็จ
กลับเถอะต้อย เย็นแล้ว

น้อยยังไม่เก็บโต๊ะหรือ
          ยัง นายยังไม่สั่งให้เก็บ
เก็บเถอะน้อย เขากินกันเสร็จแล้ว

ยังไม่กินข้าวหรือศรี
          ยัง ต้องคอยเพื่อนก่อน
กินเถอะศรี เขาไม่มาหรอก

๕๓.๑๐ การเขียน

เช้า   ทราบ   จันทร์   เกียรติ

thəʔ (continued).

When the speaker uses thəʔ to urge the hearer to do something, a reason is very often given. This reason lies in the situation or the well-being of the hearer — not in the needs or wishes of the speaker.

tôy yaŋ mây klàp bâan lə̌ə.	Aren 't you going home yet, Toy?
klàp mây dây.	I can't.
yaŋ tham ŋaan mây sèt.	I haven't finished my work yet.
klàp thəʔ, tôy.	Go on home, Toy.
yen lέεw.	It's evening already. (This implies that it is already past the time she usually goes home.)

nɔ́ɔy yaŋ mây kèp tóʔ lə̌ə.	You haven't cleared the table yet, Noy?
yaŋ.	No.
naay yaŋ mây sàŋ hây kèp.	The master hasn't said to yet.
kèp thəʔ, nɔ́ɔy.	Go ahead and clear it, Noy.
kháw kin kan sèt lέεw.	They've all finished eating.

yaŋ mây kin khâaw lə̌ə, sǐi.	Aren't you going to eat, Sri?
yaŋ.	Not yet.
tôŋ khɔɔy phûan kɔ̀ɔn.	I have to wait for my friends.
kin thəʔ, sǐi.	Go ahead and eat, Sri.
kháw mây maa lɔk.	They aren't coming.

53.10   **Writing.**

Practice reading and writing lessons 12 and 13 of Book 1 in Thai. Notice the following irregularities.

cháaw	This is written short but pronounced long.
sâap	Several words pronounced with an initial s are written with **thr**. They were most likely pronounced with this consonant cluster in an earlier stage of the language.
can	When there are two or more silenced consonants at the end of a syllable, the symbol **karan** is written over the last one only. Both **th** and **r** are silent in this word.
kìat	Neither the **r** nor the **i** are pronounced in this word.

บทที่ ๕๔

๕๔.๑ คำศัพท์

โทรเลข	เลื่อน	จดหมาย
ซึ่ง	เลื่อนนัด	เขียนจดหมาย
ดัง	เพื่อ	มัน
ดังนั้น	เลขานุการ	พยายาม

๕๔.๒ แบบฝึกหัดการสลับเสียงสูงต่ำ

ปู่ทอดเนื้อ	(กุ้ง)	ลุงขายกุ้ง	(กิน)	น้องทอดหมู	(ปู่)
ปู่ทอดกุ้ง	(สั่ง)	ลุงกินกุ้ง	(ปู่)	ปู่ทอดหมู	(ไก่)
ปู่สั่งกุ้ง	(เนื้อ)	ปู่กินกุ้ง	(ไก่)	ปู่ทอดไก่	(สั่ง)
ปู่สั่งเนื้อ	(พี่)	ปู่กินไก่	(พี่)	ปู่สั่งไก่	(ลุง)
พี่สั่งเนื้อ	(ซอ)	พี่กินไก่	(เนื้อ)	ลุงสั่งไก่	(ปลา)
พี่ซอเนื้อ	(กุ้ง)	พี่กินเนื้อ	(หลาน)	ลุงสั่งปลา	(ปู่)
พี่ซอกุ้ง	(น้อง)	หลานกินเนื้อ	(ซอ)	ปู่สั่งปลา	(ขาย)
น้องซอกุ้ง	(ขาย)	หลานซอเนื้อ	(หมู)	ปู่ขายปลา	(หมู)
น้องขายกุ้ง	(หมู)	หลานซอหมู	(ปลา)	ปู่ขายหมู	(สั่ง)
น้องขายหมู	(หลาน)	หลานซอปลา	(ปู่)	ปู่สั่งหมู	(น้อง)
หลานขายหมู	(กิน)	ปู่ซอปลา	(น้อง)	น้องสั่งหมู	(ไก่)
หลานกินหมู	(ไก่)	น้องซอปลา	(ทอด)	น้องสั่งไก่	(พี่)
หลานกินไก่	(ลุง)	น้องทอดปลา	(ไก่)	พี่สั่งไก่	(หลาน)
ลุงกินไก่	(ซอ)	น้องทอดไก่	(หลาน)	หลานสั่งไก่	(ซอ)
ลุงซอไก่	(ปลา)	หลานทอดไก่	(ลุง)	หลานซอไก่	(พี่)
ลุงซอปลา	(พี่)	ลุงทอดไก่	(ขาย)	พี่ซอไก่	(ทอด)
พี่ซอปลา	(ทอด)	ลุงขายไก่	(หมู)	พี่ทอดไก่	(กุ้ง)
พี่ทอดปลา	(เนื้อ)	ลุงขายหมู	(กิน)	พี่ทอดกุ้ง	(ขาย)
พี่ทอดเนื้อ	(ขาย)	ลุงกินหมู	(พี่)	พี่ขายกุ้ง	(กิน)
พี่ขายเนื้อ	(น้อง)	พี่กินหมู	(ขาย)	พี่กินกุ้ง	(หลาน)
น้องขายเนื้อ	(ลุง)	พี่ขายหมู	(ทอด)	หลานกินกุ้ง	
ลุงขายเนื้อ	(กุ้ง)	พี่ทอดหมู	(น้อง)		

LESSON 54

54.1 Vocabulary and expansions.

thooralêek	Telegram, to telegraph.
sûŋ	Relative pronoun (more literary thaŋ **thîi**).
daŋ	Like, as, according to.
daŋ nán	So, therefore.
lûan	To shift, slide, or move position, time, or grade.
lûan nát	To postpone an appointment.
phûa	In order to.
leekhǎanúkaan	A secretary.
còtmǎay	A letter.
khǐan còtmǎay	To write a letter.
man	Pronoun for things, animals, and disrespectfully for humans. It.
phayayaam	To try, make an attempt.

54.2 Tone manipulation.

Substitution drill.

This drill continues on from 52.2. Together they include all 125 combinations of five tones taken three at a time. It is not necessary to cover all 125 items, and the teacher may prefer to drill only parts of the full drill. But for those who enjoy doing this kind of drill, going through all 125 items at good speed offers good glottal exercise.

pùu thôot nʉ́a. (kûŋ)	luŋ khǎay kûŋ. (kin)	nɔ́ɔŋ thôot mǔu. (pùu)
pùu thôot kûŋ. (sàŋ)	luŋ kin kûŋ. (pùu)	pùu thôot mǔu. (kày)
pùu sàŋ kûŋ. (nʉ́a)	pùu kin kûŋ. (kày)	pùu thôot kày. (sàŋ)
pùu sàŋ nʉ́a. (phîi)	pùu kin kày. (phîi)	pùu sàŋ kày. (luŋ)
phîi sàŋ nʉ́a. (sʉ́ʉ)	phîi kin kày. (nʉ́a)	luŋ sàŋ kày. (plaa)
phîi sʉ́ʉ nʉ́a. (kûŋ)	phîi kin nʉ́a. (lǎan)	luŋ sàŋ plaa. (pùu)
phîi sʉ́ʉ kûŋ. (nɔ́ɔŋ)	lǎan kin nʉ́a. (sʉ́ʉ)	pùu sàŋ plaa. (khǎay)
nɔ́ɔŋ sʉ́ʉ kûŋ. (khǎay)	lǎan sʉ́ʉ nʉ́a. (mǔu)	pùu khǎay plaa. (mǔu)
nɔ́ɔŋ khǎay kûŋ. (mǔu)	lǎan sʉ́ʉ mǔu. (plaa)	pùu khǎay mǔu. (sàŋ)
nɔ́ɔŋ khǎay mǔu. (lǎan)	lǎan sʉ́ʉ plaa. (pùu)	pùu sàŋ mǔu. (nɔ́ɔŋ)
lǎan khǎay mǔu. (kin)	pùu sʉ́ʉ plaa. (nɔ́ɔŋ)	nɔ́ɔŋ sàŋ mǔu. (kày)
lǎan kin mǔu. (kày)	nɔ́ɔŋ sʉ́ʉ plaa. (thôot)	nɔ́ɔŋ sàŋ kày. (phîi)
lǎan kin kày. (luŋ)	nɔ́ɔŋ thôot plaa. (kày)	phîi sàŋ kày. (lǎan)
luŋ kin kày. (sʉ́ʉ)	nɔ́ɔŋ thôot kày. (lǎan)	lǎan sàŋ kày. (sʉ́ʉ)
luŋ sʉ́ʉ kày. (plaa)	lǎan thôot kày. (luŋ)	lǎan sʉ́ʉ kày. (phîi)
luŋ sʉ́ʉ plaa. (phîi)	luŋ thôot kày. (khǎay)	phîi sʉ́ʉ kày. (thôot)
phîi sʉ́ʉ plaa. (thôot)	luŋ khǎay kày. (mǔu)	phîi thôot kày. (kûŋ)
phîi thôot plaa. (nʉ́a)	luŋ khǎay mǔu. (kin)	phîi thôot kûŋ. (khǎay)
phîi thôot nʉ́a. (khǎay)	luŋ kin mǔu. (phîi)	phîi khǎay kûŋ. (kin)
phîi khǎay nʉ́a. (nɔ́ɔŋ)	phîi kin mǔu. (khǎay)	phîi kin kûŋ. (lǎan)
nɔ́ɔŋ khǎay nʉ́a. (luŋ)	phîi khǎay mǔu. (thôot)	lǎan kin kûŋ.
luŋ khǎay nʉ́a. (kûŋ)	phîi thôot mǔu. (nɔ́ɔŋ)	

139

๕๔.๓ โครงสร้างของประโยค

โทรศัพท์	เลื่อนนัด	เลื่อนที่
โทรทัศน์	เลื่อนเวลา	เลื่อนชั้น
โทรเลข	เลื่อนเก้าอี้	เลื่อนขึ้น
		เลื่อนลง

๕๔.๔ แบบฝึกหัดการฟังเสียงสูงต่ำ

พระนคร	ป้อมปราบศัตรูพ่าย
สัมพันธวงศ์	ลาดกระบัง
บางรัก	บางเขน
ยานนาวา	พระโขนง
ปทุมวัน	บางกะปิ
พญาไท	มินบุรี
ดุสิต	หนองจอก

๕๔.๕ บทบรรยาย

หมอสมิตได้รับโทรเลขจากภรรยาของเขาว่าจะมาถึงกรุงเทพ ฯ พรุ่งนี้ตอน
สี่โมงเช้า ซึ่งตรงกับเวลาที่หมอสมิตนัด ดร. วิชัยไว้ ดังนั้นหมอสมิตจึงต้องขอ
เลื่อนนัดกับ ดร. วิชัยเพื่อไปรับภรรยาเขา เขาโทร.ไปบอกที่ที่ทำงานของ ดร. วิชัย
แต่ ดร. วิชัยไม่อยู่ เลขานุการของเขาบอกว่า ดร.วิชัยออกไปข้างนอกไม่ทราบว่า
จะกลับเมื่อไหร่ หมอสมิตจึงขอให้เลขาช่วยบอก ดร. วิชัยว่าเขาไปพบ ดร. วิชัย
ตามนัดไม่ได้

54.3 Patterns.

thoorasàp.	Telephone.
thoorathát.	Television.
thooralêek.	Telegram.
lûan nát.	To postpone an appointment.
lûan weelaa.	To shift the time of something.
lûan kâwʔii.	To slide the chair over a little.
lûan thîi.	To be transferred to another position.
lûan chán.	To be promoted to a higher level or grade.
lûan khûn.	To be promoted.
lûan loŋ.	To be demoted.

54.4 Tone identification.
54.4

Districts in and around Bangkok.

phranakhɔɔn	Phra Nakhon.	pɔɔm praap satruu phaay	Pom Prap Sattru Phai.
samphanthawoŋ	Samphanthawong.	laat krabaŋ	Lat Krabang.
baaŋ rak	Bang Rak.	baaŋ kheen	Bang Khen.
yaannawaa	Yan Nawa	phrakhanooŋ	Phra Khanong.
pathumwan	Pathum Wan.	baaŋ kapiʔ	Bang Kapi.
phayaathay	Phaya Thai.	min burii	Min Buri.
dusit	Dusit.	nɔɔŋ cɔɔk	Nong Chok.

54.5 Narrative.
54.5

  mɔ̌ɔ samít dây ráp thooralêek càak phanrayaa khɔ̌ŋ kháw wâa ca maa thǔŋ kruŋthêep phrûŋ níi tɔɔn sìi mooŋ cháaw, sɯ̂ŋ troŋ kàp weelaa thîi mɔ̌ɔ samít nát dɔ́ktɚ wíchay wáy. daŋ nán mɔ̌ɔ samít cɯŋ tɔ̂ŋ khɔ̌ɔ lûan nát kàp dɔ́ktɚ wíchay phɯ̂a pay ráp phanrayaa kháw. kháw thoo pay bɔ̀ɔk thîi thîi tham ŋaan khɔ̌ŋ dɔ́ktɚ wíchay. tὲὲ dɔ́ktɚ wíchay mây yùu. leekhǎanúkaan khɔ̌ŋ kháw bɔ̀ɔk wâa dɔ́ktɚ wíchay ʔɔ̀ɔk pay khâŋ nɔ̂ɔk, mây sâap wâa ca klàp mɯ̂arày. mɔ̌ɔ samít cɯŋ khɔ̌ɔ hây leekhǎa chûay bɔ̀ɔk dɔ́ktɚ wíchay wâa kháw pay phóp dɔ́ktɚ wíchay taam nát mây dây.

141

๕๔.๖ ความแตกต่างระหว่างเสียงสูงต่ำ

กล้องอยู่ใกล้เสื้อ   กล่องอยู่ใกล้เสื้อ   กลองอยู่ใกล้เสื้อ
เสื้ออยู่ใกล้กล้อง   เสื้ออยู่ใกล้กล่อง   เสื้ออยู่ใกล้กลอง

กล้องอยู่ที่ไหน   กล้องอยู่ใกล้เสื้อใช่ไหม
     ใกล้เสื้อ   ใช่
กล่องอยู่ที่ไหน   กล่องอยู่ใกล้เสื้อใช่ไหม
     ใกล้เสื้อ   ใช่
กลองอยู่ที่ไหน   กลองอยู่ใกล้เสื้อใช่ไหม
     ใกล้เสื้อ   ใช่

เสื้ออยู่ที่ไหน   เสื้ออยู่ใกล้กล้องใช่ไหม
     ใกล้กล้อง   ใช่
เสื้ออยู่ที่ไหน   เสื้ออยู่ใกล้กล่องใช่ไหม
     ใกล้กล่อง   ใช่
เสื้ออยู่ที่ไหน   เสื้ออยู่ใกล้กลองใช่ไหม
     ใกล้กลอง   ใช่

อะไรอยู่ใกล้เสื้อ   กล้องอยู่ใกล้เสื้อใช่ไหม
     กล้อง   ไม่ใช่
อะไรอยู่ใกล้เสื้อ   กล่องอยู่ใกล้เสื้อใช่ไหม
     กล่อง   ไม่ใช่
อะไรอยู่ใกล้เสื้อ   กลองอยู่ใกล้เสื้อใช่ไหม
     กลอง   ไม่ใช่

อะไรอยู่ใกล้กล้อง   เสื้ออยู่ใกล้กล่องใช่ไหม
     เสื้อ   ไม่ใช่
อะไรอยู่ใกล้กล่อง   เสื้ออยู่ใกล้กลองใช่ไหม
     เสื้อ   ไม่ใช่
อะไรอยู่ใกล้กลอง   เสื้ออยู่ใกล้กล้องใช่ไหม
     เสื้อ   ไม่ใช่

54.6   Tone distinctions.

klɔ̂ŋ yùu klây sʉ̀a.
klɔ̀ŋ yùu klây sʉ̂a.
klɔɔŋ yùu klây sʉ̌a.

sʉ̀a yùu klây klɔ̂ŋ.
sʉ̂a yùu klây klɔ̀ŋ.
sʉ̌a yúu klây klɔɔŋ.

The pipe is near the mat.
The box is near the shirt.
The drum is near the tiger.

The mat is near the pipe.
The shirt is near the box.
The tiger is near the drum.

klɔ̂ŋ yùu thîi nǎy.
  klây sʉ̀a.

klɔ̀ŋ yùu thîi nǎy.
  klây sʉ̂a.

klɔɔŋ vùu thîi nǎy.
  klây sʉ̌a.

sʉ̀a yùu thîi nǎy.
  klây klɔ̂ŋ.

sʉ̂a yùu thîi nǎy.
  klây klɔ̀ŋ.

sʉ̌a yùu thîi nǎy.
  klây klɔɔŋ.

ʔaray yùu klây sʉ̀a.
  klɔ̂ŋ.

ʔaray yùu klây sʉ̂a.
  klɔ̀ŋ.

ʔaray yùu klây sʉ̌a.
  klɔɔŋ.

ʔaray yùu klây klɔ̂ŋ.
  sʉ̀a.

ʔaray yùu klây klɔ̀ŋ.
  sʉ̂a.

ʔaray yùu klây klɔɔŋ.
  sʉ̌a.

klɔ̂ŋ yùu klây sʉ̀a, chây may.
  chây.

klɔ̀ŋ yùu klây sʉ̂a, chây máy.
  chây.

klɔɔŋ yùu klây sʉ̌a, chây máy.
  chây.

sʉ̀a yùu klây klɔ̂ŋ, chây máy.
  chây.

sʉ̂a yùu klây klɔ̀ŋ, chây máy.
  chây.

sʉ̌a yùu klây klɔɔŋ, chây máy.
  chây.

klɔ̂ŋ yùu klây sʉ̀a, chây máy.
  mây chây.

klɔ̀ŋ yùu klây sʉ̌a, chây máy.
  mây chây.

klɔɔŋ yùu klây sʉ̀a, chây máy.
  mây chây.

sʉ̀a yùu klây klɔ̀ŋ, chây máy.
  mây chây.

sʉ̂a yùu klây klɔɔŋ, chây máy.
  mây chây.

sʉ̌a yùu klây klɔ̂ŋ, chây máy.
  mây chây.

๕๔.๗ คำถามบทบรรยาย

ภรรยาของหมอสมิตจะมาถึงกรุงเทพ ฯ พรุ่งนี้ใช่ไหม	ใช่
เขาโทรศัพท์มาบอกใช่ไหม	ไม่ใช่
เขาโทรเลขมาบอกใช่ไหม	ใช่
เขาบอกว่าจะมาถึงตอนสี่โมงเย็นใช่ไหม	ไม่ใช่
เขาบอกว่าจะมาถึงตอนสี่โมงเช้าใช่ไหม	ใช่
หมอสมิตมีเวลาว่างตอนสี่โมงเช้าใช่ไหม	ไม่ใช่
เขานัดกับ ดร. วิชัยใช่ไหม	ใช่
เขาจึงไม่ไปรับภรรยาเขาใช่ไหม	ไม่ใช่
เขาโทรศัพท์ไปเลื่อนนัดกับ ดร. วิชัยใช่ไหม	ใช่
ตอนที่เขาโทรไป ดร. วิชัยไม่อยู่ใช่ไหม	ใช่
เลขานุการของ ดร. วิชัยรับโทรศัพท์ใช่ไหม	ใช่
หมอสมิตบอกเลขาว่าเขามาหา ดร. วิชัยตามนัดไม่ได้ใช่ไหม	ใช่

ภรรยาของหมอสมิตจะมาถึงกรุงเทพ ฯ วันนี้ใช่ไหม	ไม่ใช่ เขาจะมาถึงพรุ่งนี้
เขาจะมาถึงตอนสี่โมงเย็นใช่ไหม	ไม่ใช่ เขาจะมาถึงตอนสี่โมงเช้า
เขาเขียนจดหมายมาบอกหมอสมิต ใช่ไหม	ไม่ใช่ เขาโทรเลขมาบอก
พรุ่งนี้หมอสมิตว่างใช่ไหม	ไม่ใช่ เขาไม่ว่าง
เขานัดกับหมอพิชัยใช่ไหม	ไม่ใช่ เขานัดกับ ดร. วิชัย
เขาให้คนโทรศัพท์ไปเลื่อนนัดกับ ดร. วิชัย ใช่ไหม	ไม่ใช่ เขาโทรไปเอง
ตอนที่เขาโทรไป ดร. วิชัยอยู่ใช่ไหม	ไม่ใช่ ดร. วิชัยออกไปข้างนอก
เขาพูดโทรศัพท์กับภรรยาของ ดร. วิชัย ใช่ไหม	ไม่ใช่ เขาพูดกับเลขานุการ
เขาบอกกับเลขาว่าเขาจะไปพบ ดร. วิชัยตามนัดใช่ไหม	ไม่ใช่ เขาบอกว่าเขาไปพบตามนัด**ไม่ได้**

144

phanrayaa khɔ̌ŋ mɔ̌ɔ samít ca maa thɯ̌ŋ kruŋthêep
phrûŋ níi, chây máy.   chây.

kháw thoorasàp maa bɔ̀ɔk, chây máy.   mây chây.

kháw thooralêek maa bɔ̀ɔk, chây máy.   chây.

kháw bɔ̀ɔk wâa ca maa thɯ̌ŋ tɔɔn sìi mooŋ yen,
chây máy.   mây chây.

kháw bɔ̀ɔk wâa ca maa thɯ̌ŋ tɔɔn sìi mooŋ cháaw,
chây máy.   chây.

mɔ̌ɔ samít mii weelaa wâaŋ tɔɔn sìi mooŋ cháaw,
chây máy.   mây chây.

kháw nát kàp dɔ́ktɚ̀ wíchay, chây máy.   chây.

kháw cɯŋ mây pay ráp phanrayaa kháw, chây máy.   mây chây.

kháw thoorasàp pay lɯ̂an nát kàp dɔ̀ktɚ̀ wíchay,
chây máy.   chây.

tɔɔn thîi kháw thoo pay dɔ́ktɚ̀ wíchay mây yùu,
chây máy.   chây.

leekhǎanúkaan khɔ̌ŋ dɔ́ktɚ̀ wíchay ráp thoorasàp,
chây máy.   chây.

mɔ̌ɔ samít bɔ̀ɔk leekhǎa wâa kháw maa hǎa
dɔ̀ktɚ̀ wíchay taam nát mây dây, chây máy.   chây.

phanrayaa khɔ̌ŋ mɔ̌ɔ samít ca maa thɯ̌ŋ kruŋthêep   mây chây.
wan níi. chây máy.   kháw ca maa thɯ̌ŋ phrûŋ níi.

kháw ca maa thɯ̌ŋ tɔɔn sìi mooŋ yen,   mây chây.
chây máy.   kháw ca maa thɯ̌ŋ tɔɔn sìi mooŋ cháaw.

kháw khǐan còtmǎay maa bɔ̀ɔk mɔ̌ɔ samít,   mây chây.
chây máy.   kháw thooralêek maa bɔ̀ɔk.

phrûŋ níi mɔ̌ɔ samít wâaŋ, chây máy.   mây chây.   kháw mây wâaŋ.

kháw nát kàp mɔ̌ɔ phíchay, chây máy.   mây chây. kháw nát kàp dɔ́ktɚ̀ wíchay.

kháw hây khon thoorasàp pay lɯ̂an nát   mây chây.
kàp dɔ́ktɚ̀ wíchay, chây máy.   kháw thoo pay ʔeeŋ.

tɔɔn thîi kháw thoo pay dɔ́ktɚ̀ wíchay yùu,   mây chây.
chây máy.   dɔ́ktɚ̀ wíchay ʔɔ̀ɔk pay khâŋ nɔ̂ɔk.

kháw phûut thoorasàp kàp phanrayaa   mây chây.   kháw phûut kàp
khɔ̌ŋ dɔ́ktɚ̀ wíchay, chây máy.   leekhǎanúkaan.

kháw bɔ̀ɔk kàp leekhǎa wâa kháw ca pay phóp   mây chây.   kháw bɔ̀ɔk wâa
dɔ́ktɚ̀ wíchay taam nát, chây máy.   kháw pay phóp taam nát mây dây.

(More.)   145

ภรรยาของหมอสมิตจะมาถึงกรุงเทพฯ
    เมื่อไหร่   พรุ่งนี้

เขาบอกสามีเขาหรือเปล่า   บอก

บอกว่ายังไง   บอกว่าจะมาถึงพรุ่งนี้ตอนสี่โมงเช้า

พรุ่งนี้หมอสมิตว่างไหม   ไม่ว่าง

ทำไมเขาไม่ว่าง   เพราะเขานัดกับ ดร. วิชัยไว้

แล้วเขาทำยังไง   เขาโทรศัพท์ไปที่ที่ทำงานของ ดร. วิชัย

เขาได้พูดกับ ดร. วิชัยไหม   ไม่ได้พูด

แล้วเขาพูดกับใคร   พูดกับเลขานุการ

เขาสั่งเลขาว่ายังไง   สั่งให้บอกกับ ดร.วิชัยว่าเขามาหาตามนัด
                                         ไม่ได้

๕๔.๙   การสนทนาโต้ตอบ

แม่ยืนที่ตู้ถ้วยชาม   ลูกสาวนั่งที่พื้น ข้างหน้าเครื่องโทรทัศน์

เขากำลังเก็บถ้วยชาม   เขากำลังดูโทรทัศน์

หมายืนที่ตู้เย็น   ลูกชายนั่งที่โต๊ะ

มันกำลังพยายามเปิดตู้เย็น   เขากำลังเปิดพัดลม

พ่อยืนที่ตู้หนังสือ

เขากำลังหาหนังสือ

phanrayaa khɔ̌ŋ mɔ̌ɔ samít ca maa thʉ̌ŋ kruŋthêep mʉarày.

phrûŋ níi.

kháw bɔ̀ɔk sǎamii kháw rʉ́ plàaw.

bɔ̀ɔk.

bɔ̀ɔk wâa yaŋŋay.

bɔ̀ɔk wâa ca maa thʉ̌ŋ phrûŋ níi tɔɔn sìi mooŋ cháaw.

phrûŋ níi mɔ̌ɔ samít wâaŋ máy.

mây wâaŋ.

thammay kháw mây wâaŋ.

phrɔ́ʔ kháw nát kàp dɔ́ɔktɚ̀ wíchay wáy.

lɛ́ɛw kháw tham yaŋŋay.

kháw thoorasàp pay thîi thîi tham ŋaan khɔ̌ŋ dɔ́ɔktɚ̀ wíchay.

kháw dây phûut kàp dɔ́ɔktɚ̀ wíchay máy.

mây dây phûut.

lɛ́ɛw kháw phûut kàp khray.

phûut kàp leekhǎanúkaan.

kháw sàŋ leekhǎa wâa yaŋŋay.

sàŋ hây bɔ̀ɔk kàp dɔ́ɔktɚ̀ wíchay wâa kháw maa hǎa taam nát mây dây.

54.8 Conversation.   54.8

Use the picture on page 123.

mɛ̂ɛ yʉʉn thîi tûu thûay chaam.	The mother is standing by the dish cabinet.
kháw kamlaŋ kèp thûay chaam.	She is putting away the dishes.
mǎa yʉʉn thîi tûu yen.	The dog is standing by the refrigerator.
man kamlaŋ phayayaam pɚ̀ɚt tûu yen.	It is trying to open the refrigerator.
phɔ̂ɔ yʉʉn thîi tûu naŋsʉʉ.	The father is standing by the bookcase.
kháw kamlaŋ hǎa naŋsʉʉ.	He is looking for a book.
lûuk sǎaw nâŋ thîi phʉʉn	The daughter is sitting on the floor
khâŋ nâa khrʉ̂aŋ thoorathát.	in front of the television set.
kháw kamlaŋ duu thoorathát.	She is watching television.
lûuk chaay nâŋ thîi tóʔ.	The son is sitting at the table.
kháw kamlaŋ pɚ̀ɚt phátlom.	He is turning on the fan.

The students should listen while the teacher asks and answers questions suggested by the picture. Then the students should answer the teacher's questions. Finally, the students should ask questions.

๕๔.๙ วลีท้ายประโยค

ซิ ล่ะ นี่ เถอะ

ก. ไหนลองยกมือซ้ายซิ

    ข. (ยกมือซ้าย)

ก. อ้าว ทำไมยกมือขวาล่ะ

    ข. ก็นี่มือซ้ายนี่

ก. อ้อ ขอโทษ ลืมไป ดีแล้ว เอาลงเถอะ

๕๔.๑๐ การเขียน

ศัพท์	สลับ
คำศัพท์	การสลับเสียงสูงต่ำ
โทรศัพท์	ไวยากรณ์
	แบบฝึกหัดไวยากรณ์
โครง	
สร้าง	ก็
โครงสร้าง	สร้าง
ประโยค	ประโยค
โครงสร้างของประโยค	ไวยากรณ์

พร   **ศร**   **นคร**   **ละคร**

54.9 Particles.

sí, lâ, nî, thǝʔ.

In the dialog below, **A** elicits an action from **B** with the particle **sí**. He accuses **B** of doing the wrong thing with **lâ**. **B** defends himself with **nî**. **A** releases **B** from what he is doing with **thǝʔ**. The crucial words in this English explanation that point to the meaning, use, or flavor of the Thai particles are shown below.

sí: elicits	lâ: accuses	nî: defends	thǝʔ: releases

A. nǎy lɔɔŋ yók mɯɯ sáay sí.   Let's see you raise your left hand.

  B. (yók mɯɯ sáay.)   (Raises left hand.)

A. ʔâaw.   Hey!

    thammay yók mɯɯ khwǎa lâ.   Why did you raise your *right* hand?

  B. kɔ̂ nîi mɯɯ sáay nî.   But this is my *left* hand.

A. ʔɔ̂ɔ. khɔ̌ɔ thôot.   Oh. I'm sorry.

    lɯɯm pay.   My mistake. (My attention strayed.)

    dii lɛ́ɛw. ʔaw loŋ thǝʔ.   All right. You can put it down now.

54.10 Writing.

Practice reading and writing lesson 14 of Book 1 in Thai. The headings for sections 1, 2, 5, and 7 are given below.

sàp	Word, term.
kham sàp	Vocabulary.
thoorasàp	Telephone (far words).
khrooŋ	Frame, skeleton.
sâaŋ	To build.
khrooŋ sâaŋ	Structure.
prayòok	Sentence.
khrooŋ sâaŋ khɔ̌ŋ prayòok.	Sentence structures, patterns.
salàp	To alternate.
kaan salàp sǐaŋ sǔuŋ tàm	The alternation of tones.
wayyakɔɔn	Grammar.
bɛ̀ɛp fɯ̀k hàt wayyakon	Grammar drills.

Notice the following irregularities.

kɔ̂	Written with the vowel shortener but no vowel.
sâaŋ	Spelled as if it were **srâaŋ**.
prayòok	Spelled as if it were **prayôok**.
wayyakɔɔn	When **rɔɔ** appears as a final consonant with no vowel symbol, it is pronounced **ɔɔn** instead of the expected **on**. Some more examples of this are given below.

พร   ศร   นคร   ละคร

phɔɔn   sɔ̌ɔn   nakhɔɔn   lakhɔɔn

Blessings.   Arrow.   City.   A play, drama.

บทที่ ๕๕

๕๕. ก

๕๕. ข เรียงความ

ร้านขายอาหารในประเทศไทย

ในประเทศไทยมีร้านขายอาหารและเครื่องดื่มทั่ว ๆ ไป ทั้งร้านเล็กและร้าน
ใหญ่ ร้านเล็กส่วนมากก็เป็นร้านกาแฟ ร้านก๋วยเตี๋ยว ร้านข้าวแกงและร้าน
ข้าวต้มเป็นต้น ร้านเหล่านี้ราคาไม่แพงนัก

ร้านกาแฟจะเปิดขายตั้งแต่เช้าไปจนถึงสองทุ่มสามทุ่ม ที่ร้านกาแฟนี้ไม่ได้
ขายกาแฟอย่างเดียว แต่จะมีน้ำอัดลมชนิดต่าง ๆ รวมทั้งบุหรี่และไม้ขีดด้วย

ร้านก๋วยเตี๋ยวจะเปิดขายเวลาประมาณสี่โมงเช้าจนถึงราว ๆ บ่ายสามโมง แต่
บางร้านอาจจะเปิดถึงกลางคืน ถ้าร้านนั้นตั้งอยู่ในที่ที่มีคนผ่านไปมามากๆ สำหรับ
ก๋วยเตี๋ยวที่ขายก็มีทั้งก๋วยเตี๋ยวหมู เนื้อ ไก่ เป็ด และปู

ร้านข้าวแกงจะเปิดและปิดร้านเช่นเดียวกับร้านก๋วยเตี๋ยว อาหารในร้าน
ส่วนมากจะมีแกงเผ็ดเนื้อ ไก่ ปลา และผัดต่าง ๆ

ร้านข้าวต้มจะเปิดขายทั้งตอนเช้าและตอนกลางคืน และบางร้านจะเปิด
ตลอดทั้งคืน มีข้าวต้ม หมู ไก่ ปลา กุ้งเป็นต้น

ส่วนร้านอาหารใหญ่ที่คนส่วนมากเรียกว่า ภัตตาคารนั้นจะมีทั้งไทย จีน
และฝรั่งให้เราเลือกไปรับประทานได้ตามความพอใจ แต่ราคาค่อนข้างจะแพง

ดื่ม	อัด	ตั้ง	ภัตตาคาร
เครื่องดื่ม	อัดลม		เลือก
	น้ำอัดลม	เช่นเดียวกับ	
ทั้ง.....และ			พอใจ
		ตลอด	ความพอใจ
	ชนิด		
เหล่า		ส่วน	ค่อน
เหล่านี้	รวม	ส่วน.....นั้น	ค่อนข้างแพง

150

LESSON 55

(Review)

55.a Review sections 2, 5, 6, 7, and 9 of lessons 51 – 54.

55.b Reading selection.

ráan khăay ʔaahăan nay prathêet thay

nay prathêet thay mii ráan khăay ʔaahăan lέʔ khrûaŋ dùɯm thûathûa pay tháŋ ráan lék lέʔ ráan yày. ráan lék sùan mâak kô pen ráan kafεε, ráan kúay tĭaw, ráan khâaw kεεŋ, lέʔ ráan khâaw tôm pen tôn. ráan làw níi rakhaa mây phεεŋ nák.

ráan kafεε ca pòət khăay tâŋtὲε cháaw pay con thŭŋ sɔ̌ɔŋ thûm săam thûm. thîi ráan kafεε níi mây dây khăay kafεε yàaŋ diaw, tὲε ca mii náam ʔàt lom chanít tàaŋtàaŋ ruam tháŋ burìi lέʔ máykhìit dûay.

ráan kúay tĭaw ca pòət khăay weelaa pramaan sìi mooŋ cháaw con thŭŋ rawraaw bàay săam mooŋ. tὲε baaŋ ráan ʔàat ca pòət thŭŋ klaaŋ khɯɯn thâa ráan nán tâŋ yùu nay thîi thîi mii khon phàan pay maa mâakmâak. sámràp kúay tĭaw thîi khăay kô mii tháŋ kúay tĭaw mǔu, núa, kày, pèt, lέʔ puu.

ráan khâaw kεεŋ ca pòət lέʔ pìt ráan chên diaw kàp ráan kúay tĭaw. ʔaahăan nay ráan sùan mâak ca mii kεεŋ phèt núa, kày, plaa, lέʔ phàt tàaŋtàaŋ.

ráan khâaw tôm ca pòət khăay tháŋ tɔɔn cháaw lέʔ tɔɔn klaaŋ khɯɯn, lέʔ baaŋ ráan ca pòət talɔ̀ɔt tháŋ khɯɯn. mii khâaw tôm mǔu, kày, plaa, kûŋ pen tôn.

sùan ráan ʔaahăan yày thîi khon sùan mâak rîak wâa pháttakhaan nán ca mii tháŋ thay, ciin, lέʔ faràŋ hây raw lûak pay rápprathaan dây taam khwaam phɔɔ cay, tὲε rakhaa khônkhâaŋ ca phεεŋ.

dùɯm	To drink.
khrûaŋ dùɯm	Drinks.
tháŋ ... lέʔ	Both ... and.
làw	Group.
làw níi	These.
ʔàt	To compress.
ʔàt lom	To compress air.
náam ʔàt lom	Carbonated drinks.
chanít	Kind, type, variety.
ruam	To combine, include.
tâŋ	To set up, to be situated.
chên diaw kàp	The same as, in like manner.
talɔ̀ɔt	Throughout.
sùan	Part.
sùan ... nán	As for ... .
pháttakhaan	A large restaurant.
lûak	To choose.
phɔɔ cay	To be satisfied.
khwaam phɔɔ cay	Satisfaction.
khôn	More than half.
khônkhâaŋ ca	More than half way in the direction of, rather, quite.

151

บทที่ ๕๖

๕๖.๑ คำศัพท์

ข้าม	ถอด
ตรงข้ามกับ	หลับ
ตรงกันข้าม	หลับตา
	นอนหลับ
ต่ออายุ	จำ
	จำได้
ต่างด้าว	ฟัง
คนต่างด้าว	ทัน
ใบต่างด้าว	ฟังทัน
ต่ออายุใบต่างด้าว	
	มอง
เซ็น	มองเห็น
เซ็นชื่อ	
	ได้ยิน
ย้าย	ฟังได้ยิน
	ชนะ
แจ้ง	
	แห่ง
ทะเบียน	
ลงทะเบียน	หัน
ใบทะเบียน	หันหน้า
ครั้ง	
บันทึก	

152

LESSON 56

56.1 Vocabulary and expansions.

khâam	To cross.
troŋ khâam kàp	Right across from, just opposite to.
troŋ kan khâam	Just opposite (in position), just the opposite (in meaning).
tɔ̀ɔ ʔaayúʔ	To renew (continue on the age of something).
tàaŋ dâaw	Foreign.
khon tàaŋ dâaw	Foreigner.
bay tàaŋ dâaw	Foreigner's registration card, papers, or book.
tɔ̀ɔ ʔaayúʔ bay tàaŋ dâaw	To renew one's foreigner's registration papers.
sen	To sign.
sen chʉ̂ʉ	To sign one's name.
yáay	To relocate. The meaning of the English word 'move' is very broad and is covered by many different words in Thai. **yáay** refers to a relocation of things that are relatively fixed. In addition to moving one's residence, it can refer to rearranging the furniture in a room or changing tables in a restaurant.
cɛ̂ɛŋ	To make known, inform, report.
thabian	A registration.
loŋ thabian	To register.
bay thabian	Registration papers.
khráŋ	A time, occasion.
banthʉ́k	To note, to record.
thɔ̀ɔt	To take off.
làp	To close the eyes.
làp taa	To close the eyes.
nɔɔn làp	To sleep. (To lie down with the eyes closed.)
cam	To remember, recognize.
cam dây	To be able to remember or recognize.
faŋ	To listen to.
than	To be on time, to keep up with.
faŋ than	To listen fast enough to catch what is being said.
mɔɔŋ	To look at, direct one's eyes. (**duu** refers to the attention of the eyes; **mɔɔŋ** to their direction.)
mɔɔŋ hěn	To look toward and see.
dâyyin	To hear.
faŋ dâyyin	To listen to and hear.
chanáʔ	To win.
hɛ̀ŋ	Place. Classifier for places.
hǎn	To turn in place (not in line of motion).
hǎn nâa	To turn the head.

153

๕๖.๒ แบบฝึกหัดการสลับเสียงสูงต่ำ

คนใช้ทำแกงที่ร้าน
และซื้อไข่ที่ครัวใช่ไหม
    ไม่ใช่ เขาทำแกงที่ครัว
    และซื้อไข่ที่ร้าน

คนใช้ตัดหญ้าที่ห้อง
และรีดเสื้อที่สนามใช่ไหม
    ไม่ใช่ เขาตัดหญ้าที่สนาม
    และรีดเสื้อที่ห้อง

คนใช้กางมุ้งที่ถนน
และขายขวดที่ห้องนอนใช่ไหม
    ไม่ใช่ เขากางมุ้งที่ห้องนอน
    และขายขวดที่ถนน

คนใช้ล้างจานที่บ้าน
และถูพื้นที่ครัวใช่ไหม
    ไม่ใช่ เขาล้างจานที่ครัว
    และถูพื้นที่บ้าน

คนใช้ตากหมอนที่ครัว
และทอดหมูที่หน้าต่างใช่ไหม
    ไม่ใช่ เขาตากหมอนที่หน้าต่าง
    และทอดหมูที่ครัว

๕๖.๓ โครงสร้างของประโยค

ครั้งแรก
ตอนแรก
คนแรก
ประตูแรก

ครั้งนี้
ครั้งนั้น
ทุกครั้ง

เขาไปทุกที่
เขาไม่ไปสักที

กินได้   กินไม่ได้

จำได้   จำไม่ได้

นอนหลับ   นอนไม่หลับ

คิดออก   คิดไม่ออก

ฟังทัน   ฟังไม่ทัน

มองเห็น   มองไม่เห็น

Response drill.

khon cháay tham kɛɛŋ thîi ráan | The servant made the curry at the shop
lɛ́ʔ súu khày thîi khrua, chây máy. | and bought the eggs in the kitchen. Right?
 mây chây. kháw tham kɛɛŋ thîi khrua | No. She made the curry in the kitchen
lɛ́ʔ súu khày thîi ráan. | and bought the eggs at the shop.

khon cháay kaaŋ múŋ thîi thanǒn | The servant put up the mosquito net in the road
lɛ́ʔ khǎay khùat thîi hɔ̂ŋ nɔɔn, chây máy. | and sold the bottles in the bedroom. Right?
 mây chây. kháw kaaŋ múŋ thîi hɔ̂ŋ nɔɔn | No. She put up the mosquito net in the bed-
lɛ́ʔ khǎay khùat thîi thanǒn. | room and sold the bottles in the street.

khon cháay tàak mɔ̌ɔn thîi khrua | The servant aired the pillows in the kitchen
lɛ́ʔ thɔ̂ɔt mǔu thîi nâatàaŋ, chây máy. | and fried the pork at the window. Right?
 mây chây. kháw tàak mɔ̌ɔn thîi nâatàaŋ | No. She aired the pillows at the window
lɛ́ʔ thɔ̂ɔt mǔu thîi khrua. | and fried the pork in the kitchen.

khon cháay tàt yâa thîi hɔ̂ŋ | The servant cut the grass in the room
lɛ́ʔ rîit sûa thîi sanǎam, chây máy. | and ironed the shirt in the yard. Right?
 mây chây. kháw tàt yâa thîi sanǎam | No. He cut the grass in the yard
lɛ́ʔ rîit sûa thîi hɔ̂ŋ. | and ironed the shirt in the room.

khon cháay láaŋ caan thîi bâan | The servant washed the dishes in the house
lɛ́ʔ thǔu phúun thîi khrua, chây máy. | and scrubbed the floor in the kitchen. Right?
 mây chây. kháw láaŋ caan thîi khrua | No. She washed the dishes in the kitchen
lɛ́ʔ thǔu phúun thîi bâan. | and scrubbed the floor in the house.

56.3   Patterns.   56.3

khráŋ rɛ̂ɛk.	The first time.
tɔɔn rɛ̂ɛk.	At first.
khon rɛ̂ɛk.	The first person.
pratuu rɛ̂ɛk.	The first door.
khráŋ níi.	This time.
khráŋ nán.	That time.
thúk khráŋ.	Every time.
kháw pay thúk thii.	He goes every time.
kháw mây pay sák thii.	He never goes. He doesn't go even once.
kin dâay.	Able to eat.
cam dâay.	Able to remember.
nɔɔn làp.	To sleep.
khít ʔɔ̀ɔk.	To figure out.
faŋ than.	To keep up with while listening.
mɔɔŋ hěn.	To look at and see.
kin mây dâay.	Unable to eat.
cam mây dâay·	Unable to remember or recognize.
nɔɔn mây làp.	Unable to sleep, to lie awake.
khít mây ʔɔ̀ɔk.	Unable to figure it out.
faŋ mây than.	Unable to listen fast enough.
mɔɔŋ mây hěn.	To look at but be unable to see.

155

๕๖.๔   แบบฝึกหัดการฟังเสียงสูงต่ำ

เกษตร   ศึกษาธิการ
การคลัง   คมนาคม
มหาดไทย   อุตสาหกรรม
กลาโหม   การต่างประเทศ
เศรษฐการ   สาธารณะสุข
ยุติธรรม   พัฒนาการแห่งชาติ

๕๖.๕   บทสนทนา

ก.   ขอโทษครับ สถานีตำรวจลุมพินีอยู่ที่ไหนครับ

   ข.   อยู่ที่ถนนวิทยุ ตรงข้ามกับสวนลุม ฯ

ก.   ขอโทษครับ ผมจะต่ออายุใบต่างด้าวได้ที่ไหนครับ

   ค.   ที่โน่นครับ ประตูแรกทางขวานั่น

ก.   ต่ออายุใบต่างด้าวที่นี่ใช่ไหมครับ

   ง.   ครับ ขอดูหน่อยซิครับ เซ็นชื่อที่นี่ครับ
       ๒๐๕ บาท ครับ

ก. อ้อ เดือนหน้าผมจะย้ายบ้าน ต้องมาแจ้งที่นี่ใช่ไหมครับ

   ง.   ครับ หลังจากย้ายแล้ว เอาใบทะเบียนบ้านใหม่
       กับใบต่างด้าวมาแจ้งที่นี่อีกครั้งหนึ่งครับ เราต้องบันทึกไว้

ก.   ขอบคุณครับ พรุ่งนี้ผมจะมาใหม่ มาสักกี่โมงดีครับ

   ง.   มาตอนนี้ก็ดีครับ

56.4 Tone identification.

The ministries (krasuaŋ) of the Thai government.

kaseet	Agriculture.	sùksaathikaan	Education.
kaan khlaŋ	Finance.	khamanaakhom	Communications.
mahaatthay	Interior.	ʔutsaahakam	Industry.
kalaahoom	Defense.	kaan taaŋ pratheet	Foreign Affairs.
seetthakaan	Economics.	saathaaranasuk	Public Health.
yuttitham	Justice.	phatthanaakaan hɛŋ chaat	National Development.

56.5 Dialog.

A. khɔ̌ɔ thôot khráp.
sathǎanii tamrùat lumphinii
yùu thîi nǎy khráp.

Excuse me.
Could you tell me where the Lumpini
Police Station is?

 B. yùu thîi thanǒn wítthayúʔ.
troŋ khâam kàp sǔan lum.

It's on Wireless Road.
Right across from Lumpini Park.

A. khɔ̌ɔ thôot khráp.
phǒm ca tɔ̀ɔ ʔaayúʔ bay tàaŋ dâaw
dây thîi nǎy khráp.

Excuse me.
Could you tell me where I go to renew
my Foreigner's Registration Book?

 C. thîi nôon khráp.
pratuu rɛ̂ɛk thaaŋ khwǎa nân.

Over there.
First door on the right.

A. tɔ̀ɔ ʔaayúʔ bay tàaŋ dâaw thîi nîi,
chây máy khráp.

Is this where I get my Foreigner's
Registration Book renewed?

 D. khráp.
khɔ̌ɔ duu nɔ̀y si khráp.
sen chʉʉ thîi nîi khráp.
sɔ̌ɔŋ rɔ́ɔy hâa bàat khráp.

Yes.
Let me see it.
Sign your name here.
205 baht, please.

A. ʔɔ́ɔ, dʉan nâa phǒm ca yáay bâan.
tɔ̂ŋ maa cɛ̂ɛŋ thîi nîi, chây máy khráp.

Oh, I'm going to move house next month.
I have to come report it here, don't I?

 D. khráp.
lǎŋcàak yáay lɛ́ɛw,
ʔaw bay thabian bâan mày
kàp bay tàaŋ dâaw maa cɛ̂ɛŋ thîi nîi
ʔìik khráŋ nʉ̀ŋ khráp.
raw tɔ̂ŋ banthʉ́k wáy.

Yes.
After you have moved,
bring your new house registration form
and your Foreigner's Registration Book here
once more.
We have to record the move.

A. khɔ̀ɔpkhun khráp.
phrûŋ níi phǒm ca maa mày.
maa sák kìi mooŋ dii khráp.

Thank you.
I'll come back tomorrow.
What would be the best time to come?

 D. maa tɔɔn níi kɔ̂ dii khráp.

About this same time would be good.

157

๕๖.๖ ความแตกต่างระหว่างเสียงสูงต่ำ

ที่แรกผู้ชายใส่แว่น และผู้หญิงใส่แหวน
ผู้ชายถอดแว่นให้ผู้หญิงใส่ และผู้หญิงถอดแหวนให้ผู้ชายใส่
ที่หลังผู้ชายใส่แหวนและผู้หญิงใส่แว่น

ที่แรกผู้ชายใส่อะไร
    แว่น ที่แรกผู้ชายใส่แว่น

ที่แรกผู้หญิงใส่อะไร
    แหวน ที่แรกผู้หญิงใส่แหวน

ที่แรกใครใส่แว่น
    ผู้ชาย ที่แรกผู้ชายใส่แว่น

ที่แรกใครใส่แหวน
    ผู้หญิง ที่แรกผู้หญิงใส่แหวน

ใครถอดแว่นให้ใครใส่
    ผู้ชาย ผู้ชายถอดแว่นให้ผู้หญิงใส่

ใครถอดแหวนให้ใครใส่
    ผู้หญิง ผู้หญิงถอดแหวนให้ผู้ชายใส่

ที่หลังผู้ชายใส่อะไร
    แหวน ที่หลังผู้ชายใส่แหวน

ที่หลังผู้หญิงใส่อะไร
    แว่น ที่หลังผู้หญิงใส่แว่น

ที่หลังใครใส่แว่น
    ผู้หญิง ที่หลังผู้หญิงใส่แว่น

ที่หลังใครใส่แหวน
    ผู้ชาย ที่หลังผู้ชายใส่แหวน

thii rɛ̂ɛk phûu chaay sày wên
lɛ́ʔ phûu yǐŋ sày wɛ̌ɛn.

phûu chaay thɔ̀ɔt wên
hây phûu yǐŋ sày,
lɛ́ʔ phûu yǐŋ thɔ̀ɔt wɛ̌ɛn
hây phûu chaay sày.

thii lǎŋ phûu chaay sày wɛ̌ɛn
lɛ́ʔ phûu yǐŋ sày wên.

At first the man was wearing the glasses
and the woman was wearing the ring.

The man took off the glasses
and let the woman put them on,
and the woman took off the ring
and let the man put it on.

Afterwards the man was wearing the ring
and the woman was wearing the glasses.

thii rɛ̂ɛk phûu chaay sày ʔaray.
 wên.
 thii rɛ̂ɛk phûu chaay sày wên.

thii rɛ̂ɛk phûu yǐŋ sày ʔaray.
 wɛ̌ɛn.
 thii rɛ̂ɛk phûu yǐŋ sày wɛ̌ɛn.

thii rɛ̂ɛk khray sày wên.
 phûu chaay.
 thii rɛ̂ɛk phûu chaay sày wên.

thii rɛ̂ɛk khray sày wɛ̌ɛn.
 phûu yǐŋ.
 thii rɛ̂ɛk phûu yǐŋ sày wɛ̌ɛn.

khray thɔ̀ɔt wên hây khray sày.
 phûu chaay.
 phûu chaay thɔ̀ɔt wên hây phûu yǐŋ sày.

khray thɔ̀ɔt wɛ̌ɛn hây khray sày.
 phûu yǐŋ.
 phûu yǐŋ thɔ̀ɔt wɛ̌ɛn hây phûu chaay sày.

thii lǎŋ phûu chaay sày ʔaray.
 wɛ̌ɛn.
 thii lǎŋ phûu chaay sày wɛ̌ɛn.

thii lǎŋ phûu yǐŋ sày ʔaray.
 wên.
 thii lǎŋ phûu yǐŋ sày wên.

thii lǎŋ khray sày wên.
 phûu yǐŋ.
 thii lǎŋ phûu yǐŋ sày wên.

thii lǎŋ khray sày wɛ̌ɛn.
 phûu chaay.
 thii lǎŋ phûu chaay sày wɛ̌ɛn

๔๖.๗ แบบฝึกหัดไวยากรณ์

ก.

กินได้ไหมฮะ

    ไม่ได้ฮะ กินไม่ได้

นอนหลับไหมฮะ

    ไม่หลับฮะ นอนไม่หลับ

คิดออกไหมฮะ

    ไม่ออกฮะ คิดไม่ออก

จำได้ไหมฮะ

    ไม่ได้ฮะ จำไม่ได้

ฟังทันไหมฮะ

    ไม่ทันฮะ ฟังไม่ทัน

มองเห็นไหมฮะ

    ไม่เห็นฮะ มองไม่เห็น

ฟังได้ยินไหมฮะ

    ไม่ได้ยินฮะ ฟังไม่ได้ยิน

ข.

เขาจำได้ทุกที แต่ฉันจำไม่ได้สักที

    (ทำเสร็จ)

เขาทำเสร็จทุกที แต่ฉันทำไม่เสร็จสักที

    (เข้าใจ)

เขาเข้าใจทุกที แต่ฉันไม่เข้าใจสักที

    (มาทัน)

เขามาทันทุกที แต่ฉันมาไม่ทันสักที

    (มองเห็น)

เขามองเห็นทุกที แต่ฉันมองไม่เห็นสักที

    (ชนะ)

เขาชนะทุกที แต่ฉันไม่ชนะสักที

    (คิดออก)

เขาคิดออกทุกที แต่ฉันคิดไม่ออกสักที

ค.

คุณทำงานตอนเช้าหรือตอนบ่าย

    ตอนเช้าก็ทำ ตอนบ่ายก็ทำ ทำทั้งวัน

คุณชอบอาหารไทยหรืออาหารฝรั่ง

    อาหารไทยก็ชอบ อาหารฝรั่งก็ชอบ ชอบทั้งสองอย่าง

คุณเคยไปบางแสนหรือพัทยา

    บางแสนก็เคย พัทยาก็เคย เคยไปทั้งสองแห่ง

a. Response drill.

kin dây máy há.	Can you eat it?
mây dây há?. kin mây dây.	No. I can't eat it.
nɔɔn làp máy há.	Did you sleep?
mây làp há?. nɔɔn mây làp.	No. I didn't sleep.
khít ?ɔ̀ɔk máy há.	Can you figure it out?
mây ?ɔ̀ɔk há?. khít mây ?ɔ̀ɔk.	No. I can't figure it out.
cam dây máy há.	Can you remember? (Do you recognize it?)
mây dây há?. cam mây dây.	No. I can't remember. (I don't recognize it.)
faŋ than máy há.	Can you keep up with what he's saying?
mây than há?. faŋ mây than.	No. I can't keep up.
mɔɔŋ hěn máy há.	Can you see it?
mây hěn há?. mɔɔŋ mây hěn.	No. I can't see it.
faŋ dâyyin máy há.	Can you hear it?
mây dâyyin há?. faŋ mây dâyyin.	No. I can't hear it.

b. Substitution drill.

kháw cam dây thúk thii, tὲὲ chán cam mây dây sák thii. (tham sèt)	He can remember every time, but I can never remember. (finish)
kháw tham sèt thúk thii, tὲὲ chán tham mây sèt sák thii. (khâwcay)	He finishes it every time, but I can never finish it. (understand)
kháw khâwcay thúk thii, tὲὲ chán mây khâwcay sák thii. (maa than)	He understands every time, but I never understand. (get here on time)
kháw maa than thúk thii, tὲὲ chán maa mây than sák thii. (mɔɔŋ hěn)	He gets here on time every time, but I never get here on time. (see)
kháw mɔɔŋ hěn thúk thii, tὲὲ chán mɔɔŋ mây hěn sák thii. (chaná?)	He sees it every time, but I never see it. (win)
kháw chaná? thúk thii, tὲὲ chán mây chaná? sák thii. (khít ?ɔ̀ɔk)	He wins every time, but I never win. (figure it out)
kháw khít ?ɔ̀ɔk thúk thii, tὲὲ chán khít mây ?ɔ̀ɔk sák thii.	He figures it out every time, but I never figure it out.

c. Response drill.

khun tham ŋaan tɔɔn cháaw rú tɔɔn bàay. tɔɔn cháaw kô tham, tɔɔn bàay kô tham. tham tháŋ wan.	Do you work in the morning or the afternoon? I work both in the morning and in the afternoon. I work all day.
khun chɔ̂ɔp ?aahǎan thay rú ?aahǎan faràŋ. ?aahǎan thay kô chɔ̂ɔp, ?aahǎan faràŋ kô chɔ̂ɔp. chɔ̂ɔp tháŋ sɔ̌ɔŋ yàaŋ.	Do you like Thai food or Farang food? I like Thai food and Farang food. I like both kinds.
khun khəəy pay baaŋsɛ̌ɛn rú phátthayaa. baaŋsɛ̌ɛn kô khəəy, phátthayaa kô khəəy. khəəy pay tháŋ sɔ̌ɔŋ hὲŋ.	Do you usually go to Bangsaen or Pataya? I go to Bangsaen and Pataya. I go to both places.

161

๕๖.๘ การสนทนาโต้ตอบ

๕๖.๙ วลีท้ายประโยค

ซิ   ล่ะ   นี่   เถอะ

ก. ไหนลองหันหน้าไปทางขวาซิ

    ข. (หันหน้าไปทางขวา)

ก. อ้าว ทำไมหันไปทางขวาล่ะ

    ข. ก็คุณบอกให้ผมหันไปทางขวานี่

ก. เหลอ งั้นขอโทษ หันกลับมาเถอะ
    เอ้า หันไปทางซ้ายซิ

    ข. (หันไปทางซ้าย)

ก. ดีแล้ว หันกลับมาเถอะ

ยกมือ   หลับตา

๕๖.๑๐ การเขียน

สนทนา   โต้   ตอบ   โต้ตอบ

162

56.8 Conversation.

The teacher should ask each student about the weather and clothing in his native country.

56.9 Particles.

sí, lâ, nî, thə̂ʔ (continued).

As in 54.9, **A** elicits performance with **sí** and accuses performer of being wrong with **lâ**. **B** defends himself with **nî**, and **A** releases performer with **thə̂ʔ**.

A. năy lɔɔŋ hăn nâa pay thaaŋ khwăa sí.	Let's see you turn your head to the right.
B. (hăn nâa pay thaaŋ khwăa.)	(Turns head to the right.)
A. ʔâaw. thammay hăn pay thaaŋ khwăa lâ.	Hey! Why did you turn to the right?
B. kô khun bɔ̀ɔk hây phŏm hăn pay thaaŋ khwăa nî.	Because you told me to turn to the right.
A. lɔ̌ə. ŋán khɔ̌ɔ thôot. hăn klàp maa thə̂ʔ. ʔâw. hăn pay thaaŋ sáay sí.	Oh? I'm sorry, then. Turn back. Okay. Turn to the left.
B. (hăn pay thaaŋ sáay.)	(Turns to the left.)
A. dii lɛ́ɛw. hăn klàp maa thə̂ʔ	Good. You can turn back now.

Use, also, **yók muu** and **làp taa** in place of **hăn nâa**.

56.10 Writing.

Practice reading and writing lessons 15 and 16 of Book 1 in Thai. The heading for 16.9 is given below.

sŏnthanaa	Conversation.
tôo	To counter, back and forth.
tɔ̀ɔp	To answer.
tôo tɔ̀ɔp	To interchange, talk or write back and forth.

บทที่ ๕๗

๕๗.๑ คำศัพท์

ความ	อำเภอ
	ที่ว่าการอำเภอ
เครื่อง	
	ลงชื่อ
คนตามถนน	
	สำเนา
นายสิบ	สำเนาทะเบียนบ้าน
	จะได้
เวร	กำ
นายสิบเวร	กำมือ
เสมียน	แบ
เสมียนต่างด้าว	แบมือ
ชี้	
	วาด
	รูป
ธรรมเนียม	วาดรูป
ค่าธรรมเนียม	
	เหลี่ยม
คืน	รูปสามเหลี่ยม
	รูปสี่เหลี่ยม
รุ่ง	
รุ่งขึ้น	ลบ

LESSON 57

57.1 Vocabulary and expansions.

khwaam	-ness, -ity, essence, stuff. This word serves to nominalize characteristics in the same way that **kaan** nominalizes actions.
khrûaŋ	Implements.
khon taam thanŏn	A person along the street.
naay sìp	Corporal, sergeant.
ween	In turn, by shifts.
naay sìp ween	The sergeant on duty.
samĭan	Clerk.
samĭan tàaŋ dâaw	The clerk who handles the registration of foreigners.
chíi	To point.
thamniam	Custom, tradition.
khâa thamniam	Fee.
khʉʉn	To return, give back.
rûŋ	Dawn.
rûŋ khʉ̂n	The next day.
ʔamphəə	District, county. Subdivisions of a province.
thîi wâa kaan ʔamphəə	The building where **ʔamphəə** administrative matters are handled. Usually referred to simply as **ʔamphəə**.
loŋ chʉ̂ʉ	To enter one's name.
sămnaw	A copy.
sămnaw thabian bâan	A copy of the house registration paper.
ca dây	So that, in order that, in order to.
kam	To close the hand, clench the fist.
kam mʉʉ	To close the hand, clench the fist.
bɛɛ	To spread out, unfold.
bɛɛ mʉʉ	To open the hand.
wâat	To draw.
rûup	A picture, form, shape.
wâat rûup	To draw a picture.
lìam	An angle, corner, edge.
rûup săam lìam	A triangle.
rûup sìi lìam	A quadrilateral.
lóp	To erase, subtract.

165

๕๓.๒ แบบฝึกหัดการสลับเสียงสูงต่ำ

	ใคร		อะไร	ที่ไหน
ก. ใครขาย				
ข. พี่ขาย	ลุง	กิน	ปลา	ครัว
อ. พี่ขาย	ปู่	สั่ง	ไก่	ตลาด
ข. พี่ขายอะไร	พ่อ	ทอด	กุ้ง	บ้าน
ค. พี่ขายเนื้อ	น้อง	ซ้อ	เนื้อ	ร้าน
อ. พี่ขายเนื้อ	หลาน	ขาย	หมู	ถนน

ค. พี่ขายเนื้อที่ไหน

   ง. พี่ขายเนื้อที่ตลาด

     อ. พี่ขายเนื้อที่ตลาด

ง. ใครสั่ง

๕๓.๓ โครงสร้างของประโยค

(นาย)สิบตรี	ความจริง
(นาย)สิบโท	ความร้อน
(นาย)สิบเอก	ความเห็น
	ความเร็ว
เอาขวดไปคืน	ความยาว
เอาหนังสือไปคืน	ความดี
	ความรู้
ได้เงินคืน	
รับใบต่างด้าวคืน	เครื่องโทรทัศน์
	เครื่องโทรศัพท์
การเรียน	เครื่องเย็น
การขายของ	เครื่องเรือน
การเช่าบ้าน	เครื่องครัว
การอยู่อพาร์ตเมนต์	เครื่องฉายหนัง
การขับรถ	เครื่องแกง

57.2 Tone manipulation.

Chain response drill.

The students should play the game suggested by the matrix at the right and the example at the left below.

	khray	ʔaray	thîi nǎy
A. khray khǎay.			
B. phîi khǎay.			
T. phîi khǎay.	luŋ	kin	plaa	khrua
B. phîi khǎay ʔaray.			
C. phîi khǎay núa.	pùu	sàŋ	kày	talàat
T. phîi khǎay núa.			
C. phîi khǎay núa thîi nǎy.	phîi	thɔ̂ɔt	kûŋ	bâan
D. phîi khǎay núa thîi talàat.			
T. phîi khǎay núa thîi talàat.	nɔ́ɔŋ	súu	núa	ráan
D. khray sàŋ.			
Etc.	lǎan	khǎay	mǔu	thanǒn

A total of 625 different tunes can be produced, but it is probably best to restrict these with the rule that no two like tones can appear together; otherwise the habits formed from similar drills in Book 1 will lead the student to use the same tones in a string. In Book 1 the purpose was to practice each tone separately. Here, it is to mix them up.

The teacher's confirmations after each answer (T) are to ensure that the tunes do not stray.

57.3 Patterns.

(naay) sìp trii.	Private first class.
(naay) sìp thoo.	Corporal.
(naay) sìp ʔèek.	Sergeant.
ʔaw khùat pay khɯɯn.	Return the bottles.
ʔaw naŋsɯɯ pay khɯɯn.	Return the book.
dây ŋən khɯɯn.	Get the money back.
ráp bay tàaŋ dâaw khɯɯn.	Get back one's foreigner's registration papers.
kaan rian.	Studying.
kaan khǎay khɔ̌ɔŋ.	Selling things.
kaan châw bâan.	Renting houses.
kaan yùu ʔapháatmén.	Living in an apartment.
kaan khàp rót.	Driving a car.
khwaam ciŋ.	Truth.
khwaam rɔ́ɔn.	Heat.
khwaam hěn.	Opinion.
khwaam rew.	Speed.
khwaam yaaw.	Length.
khwaam dii.	Goodness.
khwaam rúu.	Knowledge.
khrɯ̂aŋ thoorathát.	Television set.
khrɯ̂aŋ thoorasàp.	A telephone.
khrɯ̂aŋ yen.	Air conditioner.
khrɯ̂aŋ rɯan.	Furniture.
khrɯ̂aŋ khrua.	Kitchen utensils.
khrɯ̂aŋ chǎay nǎŋ.	A movie projector.
khrɯ̂aŋ kɛɛŋ.	The spices for making a curry.

167

๕๗.๔ แบบฝึกหัดการฟังเสียงสูงต่ำ

อาร์เจนตินา	ลาว
อาหรับ	มาเลเซีย
อเมริกา	เนเธอร์แลนด์
อังกฤษ	นิวซีแลนด์
อินเดีย	นอรเว
อินโดนีเซีย	ปากีสถาน
อิหร่าน	ปานามา
อิตาลี	พม่า
อิสราเอล	โปรตุเกส
ออสเตรเลีย	รัสเซีย (รุสเซีย)
ออสเตรีย	ซาอุดิอาเรเบีย
เบลเยียม	สเปน
บราซิล	สวีเดน
จีน	สวิสเซอร์แลนด์
เดนมาร์ก	ซีลอน
ฝรั่งเศส	สิงค์โปร์
ฟีลิปปีนส์	เตอรกี
ฟินแลนด์	เวียดนาม
เกาหลี	เยอรมัน
แคนาดา	ญี่ปุ่น

๕๗.๕ บทบรรยาย

หมอสมิตต้องต่ออายุใบต่างด้าว แต่เขาไม่ทราบว่าสถานีตำรวจลุมพินีอยู่ที่ไหน เขาเลยต้องถามคนตามถนน เมื่อทราบแล้วเขาก็ไปที่สถานีตำรวจ เขาไปที่โต๊ะนายสิบเวรและถามว่าเขาจะต่ออายุใบต่างด้าวได้ที่ไหน นายสิบเวรบอกว่าที่ห้องเสมียนต่างด้าว แล้วชี้ไปทางขวา เมื่อหมอสมิตเข้าไปในห้องนั้นและบอกว่าจะมาต่อใบต่างด้าว เสมียนได้ขอดูใบต่างด้าว แล้วให้หมอสมิตเซ็นชื่อ และบอกว่าต้องเสียค่าธรรมเนียมทั้งหมดสองร้อยห้าบาท และให้มารับใบต่างด้าวคืนได้ในวันรุ่งขึ้น

หมอสมิตกำลังคิดจะย้ายบ้าน เขาเลยถามเสมียนว่า จะต้องทำอย่างไรบ้าง เสมียนบอกว่าหลังจากที่เขาไปแจ้งที่อำเภอและลงชื่อในทะเบียนบ้านใหม่แล้ว เขาจะต้องเอาสำเนาทะเบียนบ้านกับใบต่างด้าวกลับมาแจ้งที่เสมียนต่างด้าวอีกครั้งหนึ่ง เขาจะได้บันทึกไว้

168

57.4 Tone identification.

Countries having embassies or consulates in Thailand.

About eighty percent of the syllables have mid tone. With this mid tone level in mind as a background sound, the student should try to catch all the syllables that deviate from it as the teacher reads through the list at fairly good speed.

ʔaaceentinaa	Argentina.	laaw	Laos.
ʔaarap	United Arab Republic.	maaleesia	Malaysia.
ʔameerikaa	U. S. A.	neethɔɔlɛɛn	The Netherlands.
ʔaŋkrit	England.	niwsiilɛɛn	New Zealand.
ʔindia	India.	nɔɔrawee	Norway.
ʔindooniisia	Indonesia.	paakiisathaan	Pakistan.
ʔiraan	Iran.	panamaa	Panama.
ʔitaalii	Italy.	phamaa	Burma.
ʔitsaraaʔeen	Israel.	pootukeet	Portugal.
ʔɔɔtsatreelia	Australia.	ratsia (rutsia)	U. S. S. R.
ʔɔɔtsatria	Austria.	saaʔudii ʔaareebia	Saudi Arabia.
beenyiam	Belgium.	sapeen	Spain.
braasin	Brazil.	sawiideen	Sweden.
ciin	China.	sawitsɔɔlɛɛn	Switzerland.
denmaak	Denmark.	siilɔɔn	Ceylon.
faraŋseet	France.	siŋkapoo	Singapore.
filippin	The Philippines.	tɔɔrakii	Turkey.
finlɛɛn	Finland.	wiatnaam	Vietnam.
kawlii	Korea.	yɔɔraman	Germany.
khɛɛnadaa	Canada.	yiipun	Japan.

57.5 Narrative.

mɔ̌ɔ samít tôŋ tɔ̀ɔ ʔaayúʔ bay tàaŋ dâaw tɛ̀ɛ kháw mây sâap wâa sathǎanii tamrùat lumphinii yùu thîi nǎy. kháw ləəy tôŋ thǎam khon taam thanǒn. mɨ̂a sâap lɛ́ɛw, kháw kô pay thîi sathǎanii tamrùat. kháw pay thîi tóʔ naay sìp ween lɛ́ʔ thǎam wâa kháw ca tɔ̀ɔ ʔaayúʔ bay tàaŋ dâaw dây thîi nǎy. naay sìp ween bɔ̀ɔk wâa thîi hɔ̂ŋ samǐan tàaŋ dâaw, lɛ́ɛw chíi pay thaaŋ khwǎa. mɨ̂a mɔ̌ɔ samít khâw pay nay hɔ̂ŋ nán lɛ́ʔ bɔ̀ɔk wâa ca maa tɔ̀ɔ bay tàaŋ dâaw, samǐan dây khɔ̌ɔ duu bay tàaŋ dâaw, lɛ́ɛw hây mɔ̌ɔ samít sen chɨ̂ɨ, lɛ́ʔ bɔ̀ɔk wâa tôŋ sǐa khâa thamniam tháŋmòt sɔ̌ɔŋ rɔ́ɔy hâa bàat, lɛ́ʔ hây maa ráp bay tàaŋ dâaw khɨɨn dây nay wan rûŋ khɨ̂n.

mɔ̌ɔ samít kamlaŋ khít ca yáay bâan, kháw ləəy thǎam samǐan wâa ca tôŋ tham yaŋŋay bâaŋ. samǐan bɔ̀ɔk wâa lǎŋcàak thîi kháw pay cɛɛŋ thîi ʔamphəə lɛ́ʔ loŋ chɨ̂ɨ nay thabian bâan mày lɛ́ɛw, kháw ca tôŋ ʔaw sǎmnaw thabian bâan kàp bay tàaŋ dâaw klàp maa cɛɛŋ thîi samǐan tàaŋ dâaw ʔìik khráŋ nɨɨŋ, kháw ca dây banthúk wáy.

๕๗.๖ ความแตกต่างระหว่างเสียงสูงต่ำ

คนขอถ่านอยู่ไกลกว่าคนขอทาน
คนขอทานอยู่ใกล้กว่าคนขอถ่าน

ใครอยู่ไกลกว่ากัน	ใครอยู่ใกล้กว่ากัน
คนขอถ่านอยู่ไกลกว่าคนขอทาน	คนขอทานอยู่ใกล้กว่าคนขอถ่าน
คนขอถ่านอยู่ไกลกว่าคนขอทานใช่ไหม	คนขอทาน อยู่ใกล้กว่าคนขอถ่านใช่ไหม
ใช่ คนขอถ่านอยู่ไกลกว่าคนขอทาน	ใช่ คนขอทานอยู่ใกล้กว่าคนขอถ่าน
คนขอทานอยู่ไกลกว่าคนขอถ่านใช่ไหม	คนขอถ่านอยู่ใกล้กว่าคนขอทานใช่ไหม
ไม่ใช่ คนขอทานอยู่ใกล้กว่าคน	ไม่ใช่ คนขอถ่านอยู่ไกลกว่าคน
ขอถ่าน	ขอทาน

๕๗.๗ คำถามบทบรรยาย

หมอสมิตต้องต่ออายุใบต่างด้าวใช่ไหม	ใช่
เขาต้องไปสถานทูตใช่ไหม	ไม่ใช่
เขาต้องไปที่สถานีตำรวจใช่ไหม	ใช่
เขารู้จักสถานีตำรวจลุมพินีใช่ไหม	ไม่ใช่
เขาต้องถามคนตามถนนใช่ไหม	ใช่
เมื่อเขาไปถึงสถานีตำรวจลุมพินี เขาไปที่โต๊ะนายร้อยเวรใช่ไหม	ไม่ใช่
เขาไปที่โต๊ะนายสิบเวรใช่ไหม	ใช่
เขาบอกว่าเขามาต่อทะเบียนบ้านใช่ไหม	ไม่ใช่
นายสิบเวรบอกให้เขาไปที่ห้องเสมียนต่างด้าวใช่ไหม	ใช่
เสมียนบอกเขาว่าต้องเสียค่าธรรมเนียม ๑๐๕ บาทใช่ไหม	ไม่ใช่
แล้วให้เขามารับคืนวันรุ่งขึ้นใช่ไหม	ใช่

170

57.6 Tone distinctions.

khon khɔ̌ɔ thàan yùu klay kwàa khon khɔ̌ɔ thaan.

The person asking for charcoal is farther away than the beggar.

khon khɔ̌ɔ thaan yùu klây kwàa khon khɔ̌ɔ thàan.

The beggar is nearer than the person asking for charcoal.

khray yùu klay kwàa kan.
  khon khɔ̌ɔ thàan yùu
  klay kwàa khon khɔ̌ɔ thaan.

khon khɔ̌ɔ thàan yùu klay kwàa khon khɔ̌ɔ thaan, chây mǎy.
  chây. khon khɔ̌ɔ thàan yùu
  klay kwàa khon khɔ̌ɔ thaan.

khon khɔ̌ɔ thaan yùu klay kwàa khon khɔɔ thàan, chây mǎy.
  mây chây. khon khɔ̌ɔ thaan yùu
  klây kwàa khon khɔ̌ɔ thàan.

khray yùu klây kwàa kan.
  khon khɔ̌ɔ thaan yùu
  klây kwàa khon khɔ̌ɔ thàan.

khon khɔ̌ɔ thaan yùu klây kwàa khon khɔ̌ɔ thàan, chây mǎy.
  chây. khon khɔ̌ɔ thaan yùu
  klây kwàa khon khɔ̌ɔ thàan.

khon khɔ̌ɔ thàan yùu klây kwàa khon khɔ̌ɔ thaan, chây mǎy.
  mây chây. khon khɔ̌ɔ thàan yùu
  klay kwàa khon khɔ̌ɔ thaan.

57.7 Questions on the narrative.

mɔ̌ɔ samít tɔ̂ŋ tɔ̀ɔ ʔaayúʔ bay tàaŋ dâaw, chây mǎy.   chây.
kháw tɔ̂ŋ pay sathǎanthûut, chây mǎy.   mây chây.
kháw tɔ̂ŋ pay thîi sathǎanii tamrùat, chây mǎy.   chây.
kháw ruucàk sathǎanii tamrùat lumphinii, chây mǎy.   mây chây.
kháw tɔ̂ŋ thǎam khon taam thanǒn, chây mǎy.   chây.

mûa kháw pay thǔŋ sathǎanii tamrùat lumphinii,
kháw pay thîi tɔ́ʔ naay rɔ́ɔy ween, chây mǎy.   mây chây.
kháw pay thîi tɔ́ʔ naay sìp ween, chây mǎy.   chây.
kháw bɔ̀ɔk wâa kháw maa tɔ̂ɔ thabian bâan, chây mǎy.   mây chây.
naay sìp ween bɔ̀ɔk hây kháw pay thîi hɔ̂ŋ samǐan tàaŋ dâaw, chây mǎy.   chây.
samǐan bɔ̀ɔk kháw wâa tɔ̂ŋ sǐa khâa thamniam 105 bàat, chây mǎy.   mây chây.
lɛ́ɛw hây kháw maa ráp khɯ̌ɯn nay wan rûŋ khɯ̂n, chây mǎy.   chây.
(More.)

171

หมอสมิตกำลังคิดจะย้ายบ้านใช่ไหม	ใช่
เขาถามเสมียนว่าจะต้องทำอย่างไรใช่ไหม	ใช่
เสมียนบอกให้เขาไปที่สถานทูตใช่ไหม	ไม่ใช่
เสมียนบอกให้เขาไปที่อำเภอก่อนใช่ไหม	ใช่
แล้วไปที่สถานีตำรวจทีหลังใช่ไหม	ใช่

หมอสมิตไปที่สวนลุมฯ ใช่ไหม	ไม่ใช่ เขาไปที่สถานีตำรวจลุมพินี
เขาไปต่อทะเบียนรถใช่ไหม	ไม่ใช่ เขาไปต่อใบต่างด้าว
เขาไปหานายร้อยเวรใช่ไหม	ไม่ใช่ เขาไปหานายสิบเวร
นายสิบเวรให้เขาไปหานายร้อยเวรใช่ไหม	ไม่ใช่ ให้ไปหาเสมียนต่างด้าว
ห้องของเสมียนต่างด้าวอยู่ทางซ้ายมือใช่ไหม	ไม่ใช่ อยู่ทางขวามือ

หมอสมิตต้องเสียค่าธรรมเนียม ๕๐๒ บาท ใช่ไหม	ไม่ใช่ ต้องเสีย ๒๐๕ บาท
เสมียนให้เขามารับใบต่างด้าวคืนอาทิตย์หน้า ใช่ไหม	ไม่ใช่ ให้มารับวันรุ่งขึ้น
หมอสมิตบอกเสมียนว่าเขาจะซื้อบ้านใช่ไหม	ไม่ใช่ เขาบอกว่าจะย้ายบ้าน
เสมียนบอกหมอสมิตว่าเขาต้องไปที่สถานี ตำรวจก่อนใช่ไหม	ไม่ใช่ เขาบอกว่าต้องไปที่อำเภอก่อน
แล้วต้องไปที่สถานทูตทีหลังใช่ไหม	ไม่ใช่ ต้องไปที่สถานีตำรวจทีหลัง

หมอสมิตจะไปไหน	สถานีตำรวจลุมพินี
ไปทำไม	ไปต่ออายุใบต่างด้าว
เขาไปถูกไหม	ไม่ถูก
แล้วเขาทำอย่างไร	เขาถามคนตามถนน
เมื่อเขาไปถึงสถานีตำรวจเขาพูดกับใคร	นายสิบเวร
นายสิบเวรให้เขาไปหาใคร	เสมียนต่างด้าว
เสมียนบอกเขาว่าต้องเสียค่าธรรมเนียม เท่าไหร่	๒๐๕ บาท
แล้วให้เขามารับใบต่างด้าวคืนเมื่อไหร่	วันรุ่งขึ้น
หมอสมิตถามอะไรเสมียนอีก	เรื่องย้ายบ้าน

mɔ̌ɔ samít kamlaŋ khít ca yáay bâan, chây máy   chây.

kháw thǎam samǐan wâa ca tɔ̂ŋ tham yaŋŋay, chây máy.   chây.

samǐan bɔ̀ɔk hây kháw pay thîi sathǎanthûut, chây máy.   mây chây.

samǐan bɔ̀ɔk hây kháw pay thîi ʔamphəə kɔ̀ɔn, chây máy.   chây.

lɛ́ɛw pay thîi sathǎanii tamrùat thii lǎŋ, chây máy.   chây.

mɔ̌ɔ samít pay thîi sǔan lum, chây máy.   mây chây. kháw pay thîi sathǎanii tamrùat lumphinii.

kháw pay tɔ̀ɔ thabian rót, chây máy.   mây chây. kháw pay tɔ̀ɔ bay tàaŋ dâaw.

kháw pay hǎa naay rɔ́ɔy ween, chây máy.   mây chây. kháw pay hǎa naay sìp ween.

naay sìp ween hây kháw pay hǎa naay rɔ́ɔy ween, chây máy.   mây chây. hây pay hǎa samǐan tàaŋ dâaw.

hɔ̂ŋ khɔ̌ŋ samǐan tàaŋ dâaw yùu thaaŋ sáay mɯɯ, chây máy.   mây chây. yùu thaaŋ khwǎa mɯɯ.

mɔ̌ɔ samít tɔ̂ŋ sǐa khâa thamniam 502 bàat, chây máy.   mây chây. tɔ̂ŋ sǐa 205 bàat.

samǐan hây kháw maa ráp bay tàaŋ dâaw khɯɯn ʔathít nâa, chây máy.   mây chây. hây maa ráp wan rûŋ khɯ̂n.

mɔ̌ɔ samít bɔ̀ɔk samǐan wâa kháw ca sɯ́ɯ bâan, chây máy.   mây chây. kháw bɔ̀ɔk wâa ca yáay bâan.

samǐan bɔ̀ɔk mɔ̌ɔ samít wâa kháw tɔ̂ŋ pay thîi sathǎanii tamrùat kɔ̀ɔn, chây máy.   mây chây. kháw bɔ̀ɔk wâa tɔ̂ŋ pay thîi ʔamphəə kɔ̀ɔn.

lɛ́ɛw tɔ̂ŋ pay thîi sathǎanthûut thii lǎŋ, chây máy.   mây chây. tɔ̂ŋ pay thîi sathǎanii tamrùat thii lǎŋ.

mɔ̌ɔ samít ca pay nǎy   sathǎanii tamrùat lumphinii.

pay thammay.   pay tɔ̀ɔ ʔaayúʔ bay tàaŋ dâaw.

kháw pay thùuk máy.   mây thùuk.

lɛ́ɛw kháw tham yaŋŋay.   kháw thǎam khon taam thanǒn.

mɯ̂a kháw pay thɯ̌ŋ sathǎanii tamrùat, kháw phûut kàp khray.   naay sìp ween.

naay sìp ween hây kháw pay hǎa khray.   samǐan tàaŋ dâaw.

samǐan bɔ̀ɔk kháw wâa tɔ̂ŋ sǐa khâa thamniam thâwrày.   205 bàat.

lɛ́ɛw hây kháw maa ráp bay tàaŋ dâaw khɯɯn mɯ̂arày.   wan rûŋ khɯ̂n.

mɔ̌ɔ samít thǎam ʔaray samǐan ʔìik.   rɯ̂aŋ yáay bâan.

173

๕๓.๘ การสนทนาโต้ตอบ

The students should listen while the teacher asks and answers questions suggested by the picture. Then the students should answer the teacher's questions. Finally, the students should ask questions.

๕๗.๙ วลีท้ายประโยค

ซิ   ล่ะ   นี่   เถอะ

ก. ไหนลองกำมือขวาซิ

   ข. (กำมือซ้าย)

ก. อ้าว ทำไมกำมือซ้ายล่ะ

   ข. อ๋อ ขอโทษ ลืมไป
        (แบมือซ้ายกำมือขวา)

ก. ดีแล้ว แบเถอะ

ก. ไหนลองวาดรูปสี่เหลี่ยมซิ

   ข. (วาดรูปสามเหลี่ยม)

ก. อ้าว ทำไมวาดรูปสามเหลี่ยมล่ะ

   ข. ก็ผมอยากวาดรูปสามเหลี่ยมนี่

ก. ก็ดิฉันบอกให้วาดรูปสี่เหลี่ยมนี่

   ข. ก็ผมอยากวาดรูปสามเหลี่ยมนี่

ก. ไม่เอา ลบ

ยกมือ   หลับตา   หันหน้า

๕๗.๑๐ การเขียน

สระ   เสียงสระ   พยัญชนะ   เสียงพยัญชนะ

แบบฝึกหัดการออกเสียงสระและพยัญชนะ

176

sí, lâ, nî, thəʔ (continued).

In 54.9 and 56.9, **B** did what he was told to; the mistake was **A**'s and **B** pointed this out with a bit of righteous indignation (**nî**)   In the next situation the mistake is **B**'s, and when **A** calls his attention to this (with **lâ**) **B** has no defense.

A. nǎy lɔɔŋ kam mɯɯ khwǎa sí.   Let's see you clench your right fist.

  B. (kam mɯɯ sáay.)   (Clenches left fist.)

A. ʔâaw. thammay kam mɯɯ sáay lâ.   Hey! Why did you clench your *left* fist?

  B. ʔɔ́ɔ. khɔ̌ɔ thôot. lɯɯm pay.   Oh. I'm sorry. My mistake.
     (bɛɛ mɯɯ sáay, kam mɯɯ khwǎa.)   (Opens left hand, clenches right hand.)

A. dii lɛ́ɛw. bɛɛ thəʔ.   Good. You can unclench now.

     Use also **yók mɯɯ, làp taa,** and **hǎn nâa.**

     Finally, **B** purposely does the wrong thing and an argument starts.   **B** insists (with **nî**) that he is free to do whatever he wants to, and **A** insists (also with **nî**) that **B** should do what he is told.   The final imperative is not modified by any particle (see **nɔ̀y, thii, dûay, sí, sî,** and **thəʔ**).   It is an order.

A. nǎy lɔɔŋ wâat rûup sìi liam sí.   Let's see you draw a square.

  B. (wâat rûup sǎam liam.)   (Draws a triangle.)

A. ʔâaw. thammay wâat rûup sǎam liam lâ. Hey! Why did you draw a triangle?

  B. kɔ̂ phǒm yàak wâat rûup sǎam liam nî. Because I *wanted* to draw a triangle.

A. kɔ̂ dichán bɔ̀ɔk hây wâat rûup   But I told you to draw a square.
     sìi liam nî.

  B. kɔ̂ phǒm yàak wâat rûup sǎam liam nî. But I wanted to draw a triangle.

A. mây ʔaw. lóp.   I won't accept it. Erase it!

57.10 Writing.   **57.10**

     Practice reading and writing lesson 17 of Book 1 in Thai. The heading for 17.6 is given below.

saràʔ   Vowels.
sǐaŋ saràʔ   Vowel sounds.

phayanchanáʔ   Consonants.
sǐaŋ phayanchanáʔ   Consonant sounds.

bɛ̀ɛp fùk hàt kaan ʔɔ̀ɔk sǐaŋ saràʔ lɛ́ʔ phayanchanáʔ.
A drill for practicing the sounds of vowels and consonants.

บทที่ ๕๘

๕๘.๑ คำศัพท์

ย่า	หม้อ
ยาย	หม้อน้ำ
ตา	อัด
	ฉีด
ตอบ	อัดฉีด
ชวน	เปลี่ยน
โทษ	รู้สึก
เกลียด	ยาง
	อ่อน
	ยางอ่อน
เลี้ยง	
	แบน
กลัว	ยางแบน
รัก	แม่แรง
เติม	ล้อ
เติมน้ำมัน	ถอด
เต็ม	ถอดล้อ
เติมน้ำมันให้เต็ม	กุญแจ
	กุญแจถอดล้อ
พิเศษ	
น้ำมันเครื่อง	ปอนด์
เบนซิน	อะไหล่
น้ำมันเบนซิน	ยางอะไหล่
กลั่น	เรียบร้อย
น้ำกลั่น	แม่ครัว

58.1 Vocabulary and expansions.

yâa	Father's mother.
yaay	Mother's mother.
taa	Mother's father.
tɔ̀ɔp	To answer.
chuan	To invite.
thôot	To blame, punishment.
klìat	To hate.
líaŋ	To treat, raise (as a child).
klua	To fear.
rák	To love.
tɤ̀ɤm	To add to, fill.
tɤ̀ɤm námman	To put in gasoline.
tem	To be full.
tɤ̀ɤm námman hây tem	To fill up with gasoline.
phísèet	Special.
námman khrûaŋ	Motor oil.
bensin	Benzine.
námman bensin.	Gasoline. The modifier **bensin** is added only when necessary to distinguish it from other kinds of **námman.**
klàn	To distill.
nám klàn	Distilled water.
mɔ̂ɔ	A pot.
mɔ̂ɔ náam	A car radiator.
ʔàt	To compress.
chìit	To inject, inoculate, spray.
ʔàt chìit	To lubricate a car.
plìan	To change.
rúusὺk	To feel.
yaaŋ	Rubber, a tire.
ʔɔ̀ɔn	To be weak, soft, young.
yaaŋ ʔɔ̀ɔn	A low (partially flat) tire.
bɛɛn	Flat.
yaaŋ bɛɛn	A flat tire.
mɛ̂ɛ rɛɛŋ	A car jack.
lɔ́ɔ	A wheel.
thɔ̀ɔt	To take something off.
thɔ̀ɔt lɔ́ɔ	To take off a wheel.
kuncɛɛ	A key, wrench.
kuncɛɛ thɔ̀ɔt lɔ́ɔ	A lug wrench.

(More.)

แดงถามศรี	แดงถามศรีใช้ไหม	ไม่ใช่ ศรีถามแดง	
น้องบอกพี่	หน่อยชอบป้า	ตาทักหน่อย	หน่อยทักป้า
ตาโกรธยาย	แม่ตอบพ่อ	น้าตอบตุ่ม	น้าส่งน้อย
พี่โกรธหน่อย	ศรีขอแดง	หลานรับอา	ตาตียาย
ลูกถามแม่	ตุ่มคอยป้า	แอ๊ดตีป้า	หลานเห็นย่า
น้อยขอแอ๊ด	ลุงถามแม่	น้อยให้ปู่	ต้อยขอน้า
พ่อชอบต้อย	อาช่วยป้า	แดงหาอา	ป้าเลี้ยงลุง
หลานโกรธตา	ตุ่มเกลียดหน่อย	ป้าตีหลาน	แดงเห็นปู่
ยายหมบพ่อ	ป้าชอบศรี	ปู่รับแดง	หน่อยรับพี่
พี่ถามอา	พ่อรักลูก	ลุงบอกศรี	แอ๊ดรักตา
น้อยเรียกหลาน	อาโทษหน่อย	หน่อยกลัวแม่	ตุ่มให้น้อง
ป้าชอบแดง	ตาชวนตุ่ม	น้อยรักป้า	ปู่เรียกย่า
ยายโกรธหน่อย	หน่อยเกลียดศรี	ลุงหาน้อง	ป้าสอนศรี
หลานคอยตุ่ม	ลูกหมบตุ่ม	ตุ่มส่งแดง	ตุ่มส่งพ่อ
น้าช่วยน้อย	ปู่ถามย่า	ยายรับยุง	หลานรับปู่
พ่อโทษศรี	แอ๊ดขอแม่	น้ากลัวหน่อย	หน่อยพบน้า
ป้าชวนหลาน	ต้อยชวนอา	ตุ่มเตือนปู่	แม่ส่งหลาน
พี่เรียกน้อง	ย่าชอบหน่อย	ป้าให้แอ๊ด	แดงตีน้า
ปู่ถามน้อย	ศรีเกลียดป้า	ศรีสอนปู่	น้องหาหน่อย
แอ๊ดคอยลุง	แอ๊ดรักน้า	แม่ตอบตา	ศรีตีพี่
หลานเกลียดป้า	หน่อยสอนแดง	หน่อยขอปู่	น้าเลี้ยงตุ่ม
น้อยช่วยลุง	ตุ่มโทษอา	ตาเลี้ยงศรี	ย่าสอนหน่อย
อาโกรธลูก	ลูกทักป้า	อาเตือนแม่	น้าตอบศรี
ป้าคอยน้อย	อาชานศรี	ศรีตอบน้า	ลุงเห็นหลาน
ลุงช่วยน้อง	ปู่เตือนน้อง	น้าเห็นหลาน	ตาส่งแดง
พ่อบอกแอ๊ด	น้อยเลี้ยงป้า	ป้าให้ลูก	ปู่ตอบน้า
ยายหมบน้อย	ศรีเกลียดตุ่ม	ปู่เตือนตา	ศรีหาแอ๊ด
อาโทษหลาน	ลุงบอกน้อย	ป้ารักหลาน	ตุ่มเรียกปู่
น้องเรียกพี่	ต้อยถามป้า	ย่ากลัวปู่	ย่าเตือนต้อย
หลานกลัวยาย	น้อยเห็นแดง	ศรีให้ยาย	หลานรักน้า
แอ๊ดโกรธตา	ป้าช่วยตุ่ม	แม่พบน้า	ปู่สอนป้า
ป้าชวนน้อย	น้องกลัวป้า	ปู่เลี้ยงหน่อย	ศรีทักต้อย
น้ากอยน้อง			

pɔɔn	A pound.
ʔalày	Spare.
yaaŋ ʔalày	Spare tire.
rîaprɔ́ɔy	To be in good condition, all set.
mɛ̂ɛ khrua	A female cook.

58.2 Tone manipulation.

58.2

Response drill.

As in 52.2 and 54.2, this drill covers all 125 combinations of 5 tones taken 3 at a time; but there is no need to cover all items. In fact, the whole drill can be skipped if teacher and students are bored with this kind of drilling. It is included here only for those classes who might need and want it. The purpose is glottal exercise, and it should be done at high speed to be effective. The items are to be drilled as shown below.

dɛɛŋ thăam sĭi   dɛɛŋ thăam sĭi, chây máy.   mây chây. sĭi thăam dɛɛŋ.

nɔ́ɔŋ bɔ̀ɔk phîi	nɔ̀y chɔ̂ɔp păa	taa thák nɔ̀y	nɔ̀y thák păa
taa thôot yaay	mɛ̂ɛ tɔ̀ɔp phɔ̂ɔ	náa tɔ̀ɔp tùm	náa sòŋ nɔ́ɔy
phîi kròot nɔ̀y	sĭi khɔ̌ɔ dɛɛŋ	lăan ráp ʔaa	taa tii yaay
lûuk thăam mɛ̂ɛ	tùm khɔɔy păa	ʔɛ́ɛt tii păa	lăan hɛ̌n yâa
nɔ́ɔy khɔ̌ɔ ʔɛ́ɛt	luŋ thăam mɛ̂ɛ	nɔ́ɔy hây pùu	tôy khɔ̌ɔ náa
phɔ̌ɔ chɔ̂ɔp tôy	ʔaa chûay păa	dɛɛŋ hǎa ʔaa	pâa lían luŋ
lăan kròot taa	tùm klìat nɔ̀y	păa tii lăan	dɛɛŋ hɛ̌n pùu
yaay phóp phɔ̌ɔ	păa chɔ̂ɔp sĭi	pùu ráp dɛɛŋ	nɔ̀y ráp phîi
phîi thăam ʔaa	phɔ̌ɔ rák lûuk	luŋ bɔ̀ɔk sĭi	ʔɛ́ɛt rák taa
nɔ́ɔy rîak lăan	ʔaa thôot nɔ̀y	nɔ̀y klua mɛ̂ɛ	tùm hây nɔ́ɔŋ
pâa chɔ̂ɔp dɛɛŋ	taa chuan tùm	nɔ́ɔy rák păa	pùu rîak yâa
yaay kròot nɔ̀y	nɔ̀y klìat sĭi	luŋ hǎa nɔ́ɔŋ	păa sɔ̌ɔn sĭi
lăan khɔɔy tùm	lûuk phóp tùm	tùm sòŋ dɛɛŋ	tùm sòŋ phɔ̌ɔ
náa chûay nɔ́ɔy	pùu thăam yâa	yaay ráp luŋ	lăan ráp pùu
phɔ̌ɔ thôot sĭi	ʔɛ́ɛt khɔ̌ɔ mɛ̂ɛ	náa klua nɔ̀y	nɔ̀y phóp náa
pâa chuan lăan	tôy chuan ʔaa	tùm tʉan pùu	mɛ̂ɛ sòŋ lăan
phîi rîak nɔ́ɔŋ	yâa chɔ̂ɔp nɔ̀y	păa hây ʔɛ́ɛt	dɛɛŋ tii náa
pùu thăam nɔ́ɔy	sĭi klìat pâa	sĭi sɔ̌ɔn pùu	nɔ́ɔŋ hǎa nɔ̀y
ʔɛ́ɛt khɔɔy luŋ	ʔɛ́ɛt thák náa	mɛ̂ɛ tɔ̀ɔp taa	sĭi tii phîi
lăan klìat păa	nɔ̀y sɔ̌ɔn dɛɛŋ	nɔ̀y khɔ̌ɔ pùu	náa lían tùm
nɔ́ɔy chûay luŋ	tùm thôot ʔaa	taa lían sĭi	yâa sɔ̌ɔn nɔ̀y
ʔaa kròot lûuk	lûuk thák păa	ʔaa tʉan mɛ̂ɛ	náa tɔ̀ɔp sĭi
pâa khɔɔy nɔ́ɔy	ʔaa chuan sĭi	sĭi tɔ̀ɔp náa	luŋ hɛ̌n lăan
luŋ chûay nɔ́ɔŋ	pùu tʉan nɔ́ɔŋ	náa hɛ̌n lăan	taa sòŋ dɛɛŋ
phɔ̌ɔ bɔ̀ɔk ʔɛ́ɛt	nɔ́ɔy lían pâa	păa hây lûuk	pùu tɔ̀ɔp náa
yaay phóp nɔ́ɔy	sĭi klìat tùm	pùu tʉan taa	sĭi hǎa ʔɛ́ɛt
ʔaa thôot lăan	luŋ bɔ̀ɔk nɔ́ɔy	păa rák lăan	tùm rîak pùu
nɔ́ɔŋ rîak phîi	tôy thăam păa	yâa klua pùu	yâa tʉan tôy
lăan klua yaay	nɔ́ɔy hɛ̌n dɛɛŋ	sĭi hây yaay	lăan rák náa
ʔɛ́ɛt kròot taa	păa chûay tùm	mɛ̂ɛ phóp náa	pùu sɔ̌ɔn păa
păa chuan nɔ́ɔy	nɔ́ɔŋ klua pâa	pùu lían nɔ̀y	sĭi thák tôy
náa khɔɔy nɔ́ɔŋ			

๕๘.๓ โครงสร้างของประโยค

เติมน้ำมัน ๓๐ บาท

เติมน้ำมันให้เต็ม

เติมน้ำอีกหน่อย

เติมลม ๓๐ ปอนด์

สูบลม ๓๐ ปอนด์

น้ำมันเครื่อง

น้ำมันเบนซิน

น้ำมันก๊าด

น้ำมันใส่ผม

น้ำมันหมู

ยางหน้าข้างซ้าย

ยางหน้าข้างขวา

ยางหลังข้างขวา

ยางหลังข้างซ้าย

ยางอะไหล่

เครื่องอะไหล่

๕๘.๔ แบบฝึกหัดการฟังเสียงสูงต่ำ

อ่างทอง

บุรีรัมย์

ฉะเชิงเทรา

ชัยนาท

ชัยภูมิ

จันทบุรี

เชียงใหม่

เชียงราย

ชลบุรี

ชุมพร

กาฬสินธุ์

กำแพงเพชร

กาญจนบุรี

ขอนแก่น

กระบี่

ลำปาง

ลำพูน

เลย

ลพบุรี

แม่ฮ่องสอน

มหาสารคาม

นครนายก

นครปฐม

นครพนม

นครราชสีมา

นครสวรรค์

นครศรีธรรมราช

น่าน

นราธิวาส

หนองคาย

นนทบุรี

ปทุมธานี

ปัตตานี

พังงา

พัทลุง

58.3 Patterns.

tɔɔm námman sǎam sìp bàat.	Put in 30 baht worth of gas.
tɔɔm námman hây tem.	Fill it up with gas.
tɔɔm náam ʔìik nɔ̀y.	Put in a little more water.
tɔɔm lom sǎam sìp pɔɔn.	Put in 30 pounds of air.
sùup lom sǎam sìp pɔɔn.	Pump in 30 pounds of air.
námman khrûaŋ.	Motor oil.
námman bensin.	Gasoline.
námman káat.	Kerosine.
námman sày phǒm.	Hair oil.
námman mǔu.	Lard.
yaaŋ nâa khâŋ sáay.	The front left tire.
yaaŋ nâa khâŋ khwǎa.	The front right tire.
yaaŋ lǎŋ khâŋ khwǎa.	The right rear tire.
yaaŋ lǎŋ khâŋ sáay.	The left rear tire.
yaaŋ ʔalày.	Spare tire.
khrûaŋ ʔalày.	Spare parts.

58.4 Tone identification.

Thai provinces.

ʔaaŋthɔɔŋ	Ang Thong.	lopburii	Lop Buri.
buriiram	Buri Ram.	mɛɛhɔŋsɔɔn	Mae Hong Son.
chachɔɔŋsaw	Chachoengsao.	mahaasaarakhaam	Maha Sarakham.
chaynaat	Chai Nat.	nakhɔɔnnayok	Nakhon Nayok.
chayyaphuum	Chaiyaphum.	nakhɔɔnpathom	Nakhon Pathom.
can (tha) burii	Chanthaburi.	nakhɔɔnphanom	Nakhon Phanom.
chiaŋmay	Chiang Mai.	nakhɔɔnraatchasimaa	Nakhon Ratchasima.
chiaŋraay	Chiang Rai.	nakhɔɔnsawan	Nakhon Sawan.
chonburii	Chon Buri.	nakhɔɔnsiithammaraat	Nakhon Si Thammarat.
chumphɔɔn	Chumphon.	naan	Nan.
kaanlasin	Kalasin.	naraathiwaat	Narathiwat.
kamphɛɛŋphet	Kamphaeng Phet.	nɔɔŋkhaay	Nong Khai.
kaan (cana) burii	Kanchanaburi.	non (tha) burii	Nonthaburi.
khɔɔnkɛn	Khon Kaen.	pathumthaanii	Pathum Thani.
krabii	Krabi.	pattanii	Pattani.
lampaaŋ	Lampang.	phaŋŋaa	Phangnga.
lamphuun	Lamphun.	phatthaluŋ	Phatthalung
ləəy	Loei.		

๕๘.๕   บทสนทนา

ก.   เติมน้ำมัน ๓๐ บาท

    ข.   ธรรมดาหรือพิเศษครับ

ก.   เอาอย่างธรรมดา ดูน้ำกับน้ำมันเครื่องด้วยนะ

    ข.   เติมน้ำกลั่นแล้วก็น้ำในหม้อน้ำแล้วครับ
        น้ำมันเครื่องขาดลิตรหนึ่ง เติมไหมฮะ

ก.   ไม่ต้อง พรุ่งนี้จะเอารถมาอัดฉีด
    และเปลี่ยนน้ำมันเครื่อง
    อ้อ เกือบลืม รู้สึกว่ายางหน้าข้างซ้ายอ่อนไป
    ช่วยสูบลมให้หน่อย เดี๋ยวยางแบนจะลำบาก
    เพราะแม่แรงก็ไม่มี กุญแจถอดล้อก็ไม่มี

    ข.   ครับ เชิญทางโน้นครับ ใช้ลมกี่ปอนด์ครับ

ก.   ยางหน้า ๒๒ ปอนด์ ยางหลัง ๒๔

    ข.   สูบลมยางอะไหล่ไหมฮะ

ก.   ฮึ่ม สูบด้วย

    ข.   เรียบร้อยแล้วครับ

ก.   ขอบใจ

๕๘.๖   ความแตกต่างระหว่างเสียงสูงต่ำ

เสื้ออยู่บนกลอง   เสืออยู่บนเสื่อ   กล้องอยู่บนกล่อง

184

58.5 Dialog.

A. təəm námman săam sìp bàat.

Put in 30 baht worth of gas.

B. thammadaa rɨ́ phísèet khráp.

Regular or extra?

A. ʔaw yàaŋ thammadaa.

Regular.

duu náam ka námman khrɨ̂aŋ dûay ná.

Check the water and oil, too.

B. təəm nám klàn lɛ́ɛw kɔ̂ náam

nay mɔ̂ɔ náam lɛ́ɛw khráp.

I've put in distilled water and filled
the radiator.

námman khrɨ̂aŋ khàat lít nɨŋ.

The oil is down one liter.

təəm máy háʔ.

Shall I add some?

A. mây tôŋ.   phrûŋ níi ca ʔaw rót maa

It won't be necessary. Tomorrow I'm going to

ʔàt chìit lɛ́ʔ plìan námman khrɨ̂aŋ.

get a grease job and an oil change.

ʔɔ̂ɔ, kɨ̀ap lɨɨm.

Oh, I almost forgot.

rúusɨk wâa yaaŋ nâa khâŋ sáay ʔɔ̀ɔn pay.

I think the front left tire is low.

chûay sùup lom hây nɔ̀y.

Please put some air in it.

dǐaw yaaŋ bɛɛn ca lambàak,

It'll soon be flat and I'll be in trouble,

phrɔ́ʔ mɛ̂ɛ rɛɛŋ kɔ̂ mây mii,

because I haven't got a jack

kuncɛɛ thɔ̀ɔt lɔ́ɔ kɔ̂ mây mii.

or a lug wrench.

B. khráp. chəən thaaŋ nóon khráp.

Yes, sir. Over there, please.

cháy lom kìi pɔɔn khráp.

How many pounds do you use?

A. yaaŋ nâa yîi sìp sɔ̌ɔŋ pɔɔn,

22 pounds in the front tires,

yaaŋ lăŋ yîi sìp sìi.

and 24 in the rear ones.

B. sùup lom yaaŋ ʔalày máy háʔ.

Shall I put air in the spare tire?

A. hɨ̂ɨm. sùup dûay.

Yes. Pump it, too.

B. rîaprɔ́ɔy lɛ́ɛw khráp.

All finished, sir.

A. khɔ̀ɔpcay.

Thanks.

58.6 Tone distinctions.

sɨ̂a yùu bon klɔɔŋ.

The shirt is on the drum.

sɨ̌a yùu bon sɨ̀a.

The tiger is on the mat.

klɔ̂ŋ yùu bon klɔ̀ŋ.

The pipe is on the box.

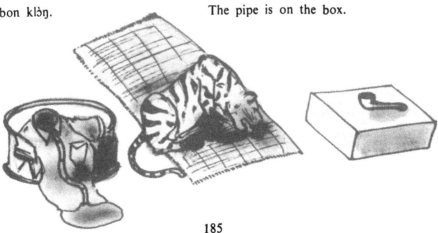

เสืออยู่บนเสื้อใช่ไหม
ไม่ใช่
เสื้ออยู่ที่ไหน
บนกลอง
แล้วอะไรอยู่บนเสื้อ
เสือ

เสืออยู่บนกลองใช่ไหม
ไม่ใช่
เสื้ออยู่ที่ไหน
บนเสื้อ
แล้วอะไรอยู่บนกลอง
เสือ

กล้องอยู่บนกลองใช่ไหม
ไม่ใช่
กล้องอยู่ที่ไหน
บนกล่อง
แล้วอะไรอยู่บนกลอง
เสือ

เสืออยู่บนกล่องใช่ไหม
ไม่ใช่
เสื้ออยู่ที่ไหน
บนกลอง
แล้วอะไรอยู่บนกล่อง
กล้อง

เสืออยู่บนกล่องใช่ไหม
ไม่ใช่
เสื้ออยู่ที่ไหน
บนเสื้อ
แล้วอะไรอยู่บนกล่อง
กล้อง

กล้องอยู่บนเสื้อใช่ไหม
ไม่ใช่
กล้องอยู่ที่ไหน
บนกล่อง
แล้วอะไรอยู่บนเสื้อ
เสือ

๕๘.๗ แบบฝึกหัดไวยากรณ์

ก.

เย็นนี้หน่อยจะไปเที่ยว เขาเคยทำ
กับข้าวให้ฉัน วันนี้ฉันต้องทำเอง

ไม่ต้องหรอก
บอกให้หน่อยทำไว้ให้ก่อนไป

เย็นนี้ศรีจะไปเที่ยว เขาเคยเปิดประตู
หน้าบ้านให้ฉัน วันนี้ฉันต้องเปิดเอง

ไม่ต้องหรอก
บอกให้ศรีเปิดไว้ให้ก่อนไป

เย็นนี้ต้อยจะไปเที่ยว เขาเคยกางมุ้ง
ให้ฉัน วันนี้ฉันต้องกางเอง

ไม่ต้องหรอก
บอกให้ต้อยกางไว้ให้ก่อนไป

เย็นนี้แดงจะไปเที่ยว เขาเคยหุงข้าวให้ฉัน
วันนี้ฉันต้องหุงเอง

ไม่ต้องหรอก
บอกให้แดงหุงไว้ให้ก่อนไป

เย็นนี้แอ๊ดจะไปเที่ยว เขาเคยรีดเสื้อให้
ฉัน วันนี้ฉันต้องรีดเอง

ไม่ต้องหรอก
บอกให้แอ๊ดรีดไว้ให้ก่อนไป

sᵾa yùu bon sᵾa,
chây máy.
mây chây.
sᵾa yùu thîi nǎy.
bon klɔɔŋ.
lɛ́ɛw ʔaray yùu bon sᵾa.
sᵾa.

sᵾa yùu bon klɔ̀ŋ,
chây máy.
mây chây.
sᵾa yùu thîi nǎy.
bon klɔɔŋ.
lɛ́ɛw ʔaray yùu bon klɔ̀ŋ.
klɔ̀ŋ.

sᵾa yùu bon klɔɔŋ,
chây máy.
mây chây.
sᵾa yùu thîi nǎy.
bon sᵾa.
lɛ́ɛw ʔaray yùu bon klɔɔŋ.
sᵾa.

sᵾa yùu bon klɔ̀ŋ,
chây máy.
mây chây.
sᵾa yùu thîi nǎy.
bon sᵾa.
lɛ́ɛw ʔaray yùu bon klɔ̀ŋ.
klɔ̀ŋ.

klɔ̂ŋ yùu bon klɔɔŋ,
chây máy.
mây chây.
klɔ̂ŋ yùu thîi nǎy.
bon klɔ̀ŋ.
lɛ́ɛw ʔaray yùu bon klɔɔŋ.
sᵾa.

klɔ̂ŋ yùu bon sᵾa,
chây máy.
mây chây.
klɔ̂ŋ yùu thîi nǎy.
bon klɔ̀ŋ.
lɛ́ɛw ʔaray yùu bon sᵾa.
sᵾa.

58.7 Grammar drills.

a. Response drill.

yen níi nɔ̀y ca pay thîaw.
kháw khəəy tham kàphâaw hây chán.
wan níi chán tɔ̂ŋ tham ʔeeŋ.
  mây tɔ̂ŋ lɔk.
  bɔ̀ɔk hây nɔ̀y tham wáy hây kɔ̀ɔn pay.

Noy is going out this evening.
She usually cooks my dinner for me.
I'll have to do it myself today.
  No you won't.
  Tell Noy to cook it before she goes
  and leave it for you.

yen níi sǐi ca pay thîaw.
kháw khəəy pə̀ət pratuu nâa bâan hây chán.
wan níi chán tɔ̂ŋ pə̀ət ʔeeŋ.
  mây tɔ̂ŋ lɔk.
  bɔ̀ɔk hây sǐi pə̀ət wáy hây kɔ̀ɔn pay.

Sri is going out this evening.
She usually opens the front gate for me.
I'll have to open it myself today.
  No you won't.
  Tell Sri to open it before she goes
  and leave it open for you.

yen níi tɔ̂y ca pay thîaw.
kháw khəəy kaaŋ múŋ hây chán.
wan níi chán tɔ̂ŋ kaaŋ ʔeeŋ.
  mây tɔ̂ŋ lɔk.
  bɔ̀ɔk hây tɔ̂y kaaŋ wáy hây kɔ̀ɔn pay.

Toy is going out this evening.
She usually puts up the mosquito net for me.
I'll have to put it up myself today.
  No you won't.
  Tell Toy to put it up for you before she
  goes and leave it up.

yen níi dɛɛŋ ca pay thîaw.
kháw khəəy hǔŋ khâaw hây chán.
wan níi chán tɔ̂ŋ hǔŋ ʔeeŋ.
  mây tɔ̂ŋ lɔk.
  bɔ̀ɔk hây dɛɛŋ hǔŋ wáy hây kɔ̀ɔn pay.

Daeng is going out this evening.
She usually cooks the rice for me.
I'll have to cook it myself today.
  No you won't.
  Tell Daeng to cook it before she goes
  and leave it for you.

yen níi ʔɛ́ɛt ca pay thîaw.
kháw khəəy rîit sᵾa hây chán.
wan níi chán tɔ̂ŋ rîit ʔeeŋ.
  mây tɔ̂ŋ lɔk.
  bɔ̀ɔk hây ʔɛ́ɛt rîit wáy hây kɔ̀ɔn pay.

At is going out this evening.
She usually irons my shirt for me.
I'll have to iron it myself today.
  No you won't.
  Tell At to iron it before she goes
  and leave it for you.

ข.

คุณขับรถเป็นไหม

    ไม่เป็น การขับรถไม่ใช่ของง่าย

คุณตัดผมเป็นไหม

    ไม่เป็น การตัดผมไม่ใช่ของง่าย

คุณทำกับข้าวเป็นไหม

    ไม่เป็น การทำกับข้าวไม่ใช่ของง่าย

คุณเขียนภาษาจีนเป็นไหม

    ไม่เป็น การเขียนภาษาจีนไม่ใช่ของง่าย

คุณตัดเสื้อเป็นไหม

    ไม่เป็น   การตัดเสื้อไม่ใช่ของง่าย

๕๘.๘ การสนทนาโต้ตอบ

เรือ

บิน

เรือบิน

รถเมล์

ชั้นหนึ่ง

ชั้นสอง

ชั้นสาม

ไนท์คลับ

บาร์

หนัง

ละคร

ดนตรี

ร้อง

เพลง

ร้องเพลง

ศาสนา

ศาสนาพุทธ

ศาสนาคริสต์

ปลูก

เลี้ยง

ข้าวสาลี

ข้าวโพด

ผ้าย

ภูเขา

แม่น้ำ

ทะเล

ทะเลสาบ

ชายทะเล

ชายหาด

ป่า

โบว์ลิ่ง

กอล์ฟ

เทนนิส

ว่ายน้ำ

b. Response drill.

khun khàp rót pen máy.	Can you drive a car?
mây pen.	No.
kaan khàp rót mây chây khɔ̌ɔŋ ŋâay.	Driving a car isn't an easy thing to do.
khun tàt phǒm pen máy.	Can you give someone a haircut?
mây pen.	No.
kaan tàt phǒm mây chây khɔ̌ɔŋ ŋâay.	Cutting hair isn't an easy thing to do.
khun tham kàpkhâaw pen máy.	Can you cook?
mây pen.	No.
kaan tham kàpkhâaw mây chây khɔ̌ɔŋ ŋâay.	Cooking isn't an easy thing to do.
khun khǐan phasǎa ciin pen máy.	Can you write Chinese?
mây pen.	No.
kaan khǐan phasǎa ciin mây chây khɔ̌ɔŋ ŋâay.	Writing Chinese isn't an easy thing to do.
khun tàt sûa pen máy.	Can you make shirts?
mây pen.	No.
kaan tàt sûa mây chây khɔ̌ɔŋ ŋâay.	Making shirts isn't an easy thing to do.

58.8 Conversation. 58.8

The teacher should ask each student about various things in his own country. The new words listed below will suggest topics to talk about.

rɯa	Boat, ship.	plùuk	To plant crops.
bin	To fly.	líaŋ	To raise animals.
rɯa bin	Airplane.	khâaw sǎalii	Wheat.
rót mee	Bus.	khâaw phôot	Corn, maize.
chán nɯ̀ŋ	First class.		
chán sɔ̌ɔŋ	Second class.	fâay	Cotton.
chán sǎam	Third class.		
		phuukhǎw	Mountains.
náy khláp	Night club.	mɛ̂ɛ náam	River.
baa	A bar.		
		thalee	Sea, ocean.
nǎŋ	Movie.	thalee sàap	Lake.
lakhɔɔn	A play.	chaay thalee	Seashore.
		chaay hàat	Beach.
dontrii	Music.		
		pàa	Forest, jungle.
rɔ́ɔŋ	To cry out, yell.		
phleeŋ	A song.	boolîŋ	Bowling.
rɔ́ɔŋ phleeŋ	To sing.		
		kɔ́ɔp	Golf.
sàatsanǎa	Religion.		
sàatsanǎa phút	Buddhism.	thennít	Tennis.
sàatsanǎa khrít	Christianity.		
		wâay náam	To swim.

189

๕๘.๕ วลีท้ายประโยค

หรือ   น่ะซิ   ล่ะ (๑)   ล่ะ (๒)   หรอก   นี่

ก. คุณจะไปอย่างไร

     ข. จะเดินไป

ก. จะเดินไปหรือ

     ข. เดินไปน่ะซิ บอกแล้วอย่างไรล่ะ

ก. ไม่ต้องเดินไปหรอก

     ข. ทำไมไม่ต้องเดินไปล่ะ

ก. ไปแท๊กซี่ก็ได้

     ข. ก็ผมจะเดินไปนี่

ก. ตกลงคุณจะเอาอย่างไร

     ข. ก็เดินไปน่ะซิ

๕๘.๑๐ การเขียน

lɔ̌ə, nâsi, lâ (1), lâ (2), lɔk, nî.

   In the following dialog, there is a slight argument over two alternatives. A thinks it would be more convenient to go by taxi and may even consider walking a little foolish; but B insists on walking since he feels the exercise would be good for him.

A. khun ca pay yaŋŋay.   How are you going to go?
 B. ca dəən pay.   I'm going to walk.
A. ca dəən pay lɔ̌ə.   You're going to walk?
 B. dəən pay nâsi.   Yes, walk.
  bɔɔk lɛɛw ŋay lâ.*   That's what I said, isn't it?
A. mây tôŋ dəən pay lɔk.   You don't have to walk.
             (Said with a dipping tone on **walk**.)
 B. thammay mây tôŋ dəən pay lâ. Why don't I?
A. pay thɛ́ksîi kô dây.   You can take a taxi.
 B. kô phǒm ca dəən pay nî.   But I'm going to walk (and what I've decided to do is the only relevant consideration; anyway, I have my reasons and your line of thinking is beside the point).

A. tòkloŋ khun ca ʔaw yaŋŋay.** Okay, so which are you going to do?
 B. kô dəən pay nâsi.   *Walk.* (Your argument has had no effect on me whatsoever; and after my 'nî' statement, it's a bit impertinent of you to ask again.)

58.10 Writing.   58.10

   Practice reading and writing lesson 18 of Book 1 in Thai. Review 36.10 for an explanation of the spelling of **yàak.**

---

* bɔɔk lɛɛw ŋay lâ. The English translation gives the overall feeling, but ŋay lâ does not correspond to isn't it. This is not like the lâ type questions of 48.9; in fact it isn't a question at all. Its force is to point out something obvious: 'You needn't ask. I've already told you **that's how it is.**'

** tòkloŋ here is calling for a new decision in light of A's information. 'Now that you've had a chance to reconsider, what's your decision?'.

บทที่ ๕๙

๕๙.๑ คำศัพท์

ตั้งใจ	เหลือ
สังเกต	เหลือน้อย
สังเกตเห็นว่า	เตรียม
ทั้ง..... และ.....	นึกขึ้นมาได้
เกรงใจ	สำคัญ
ตรวจ	เรื่องสำคัญ
หม้อแบตเตอรี่	ทำให้

๕๙.๒ แบบฝึกหัดการสลับเสียงสูงต่ำ

ใคร		อะไร	ที่ไหน	วันไหน	ตอนไหน
ลุง	กิน	ปลา	ครัว	จันทร์	เย็น
ปู่	สั่ง	ไก่	ตลาด	ศุกร์	บ่าย
พี่	ทอด	กุ้ง	บ้าน	แม่	เที่ยง
น้อง	ซอ	เนือ	ร้าน	พุธ	เช้า
หลาน	ขาย	หมู	ถนน	เสาร์	สาย

LESSON 59

59.1 Vocabulary and expansions.

tâŋcay	To intend (literally 'to set the heart').
săŋkèet	To notice.
săŋkèet hěn wâa ...	To notice that ... .
tháŋ ... lέʔ ...	Both ... and ... . (With negative, either ... or ... .)
kreeŋcay	To have a feeling of imposing on someone.
trùat	To inspect.
môɔ béttərii	A car battery.
lǔa	To be left over, remaining.
lǔa nɔ́ɔy	Only a little is left.
triam	To prepare.
núk khûn maa dây	It occurred to him, he remembered (not to be confused with **cam**).
sǎmkhan	To be important.
rûaŋ sǎmkhan	An important matter.
tham hây	To cause, make.

59.2 Tone manipulation.

Chain response drill.

The students should play the game described in 57.2 with the expanded matrix below (15,625 tunes).

khray		ʔaray	thîi nǎy	wan nǎy	tɔɔn nǎy
luŋ	kin	plaa	khrua	can	yen
pùu	sàŋ	kày	talàat	sùk	bàay
phîi	thɔ̀ɔt	kûŋ	bâan	mɛ̂ɛ	thîaŋ
nɔ́ɔŋ	sɯ́ɯ	nɯ́a	ráan	phút	cháaw
lǎan	khǎay	mǔu	thanǒn	sǎw	sǎay

๕๕.๓ โครงสร้างของประโยค

มีทั้งแม่แรงและกุญแจถอดล้อ   เตรียมขับรถกลับ
มีทั้งเด็กและผู้ใหญ่   เตรียมทำกับข้าว
มีทั้งกลางวันและกลางคืน

ไม่มีทั้งแม่แรงและกุญแจถอดล้อ   ฉันนึกขึ้นได้ว่า
ไม่มีทั้งเด็กและผู้ใหญ่   ฉันจำได้ว่า
ไม่มีทั้งกลางวันและกลางคืน

๕๕.๔ แบบฝึกหัดการฟังเสียงสูงต่ำ

เพชรบูรณ์	สระบุรี
เพชรบุรี	สตูล
พิจิตร	สิงห์บุรี
พิษณุโลก	ศรีสะเกษ
แพร่	สงขลา
พระนคร	สุโขทัย
พระนครศรีอยุธยา	สุพรรณบุรี
ภูเก็ต	สุราษฎร์ธานี
ปราจีนบุรี	สุรินทร์
ประจวบคีรีขันธ์	ตาก
ระนอง	ธนบุรี
ราชบุรี	ตรัง
ระยอง	ตราด
ร้อยเอ็ด	อุบลราชธานี
สกลนคร	อุดรธานี
สมุทรปราการ	อุทัยธานี
สมุทรสาคร	อุตรดิตถ์
สมุทรสงคราม	ยะลา

59.3 Patterns.

mii tháŋ mɛ̂ɛrɛɛŋ lɛ́ʔ kuncɛɛ thɔ̀ɔt lɔ́ɔ.	I have both a jack and a lug wrench.
mii tháŋ dèk lɛ́ʔ phûu yày.	There were both children and adults.
mii tháŋ klaaŋwan lɛ́ʔ klaaŋkhʉʉn.	There is (someone or something there) both day and night.
mây mii tháŋ mɛ̂ɛrɛɛŋ lɛ́ʔ kuncɛɛ thɔ̀ɔt lɔ́ɔ.	I don't have either a jack or a lug wrench.
mây mii tháŋ dèk lɛ́ʔ phûu yày.	There were neither children nor adults.
mây mii tháŋ klaaŋwan lɛ́ʔ klaaŋkhʉʉn.	There is (no one or nothing there) either day or night.
triam khàp rót klàp.	He prepared to drive back.
triam tham kàpkhâaw.	She prepared to cook dinner.
chán núk khʉ̂n dây wâa	I just remembered that ... .
chán cam dây wâa	I can remember that ... .

59.4 Tone identification.

Thai provinces (concluded).

phetchabuun	Phetchabun.	saraburii	Saraburi.
phetburii	Phetchaburi.	satuun	Satun.
phicit	Phichit.	siŋburii	Sing Buri.
phitsanulook	Phitsanulok.	siisakeet	Si Sa Ket.
phrɛɛ	Phrae.	soŋkhlaa	Songkhla.
phranakhɔɔn	Phra Nakhon.	sukhoothay	Sukhothai.
(phranakhɔɔnsii) ʔayutthayaa	Phra Nakhon Si Ayutthaya.	suphanburii	Suphan Buri.
phuuket	Phuket.	suraat (thaanii)	Surat Thani.
praciinburii	Prachin Buri.	surin	Surin.
pracuap (khiiriikhan)	Prachuap Khiri Khan.	taak	Tak.
ranɔɔŋ	Ranong.	thonburii	Thon Buri.
raat (cha) burii	Ratchaburi.	traŋ	Trang.
rayɔɔŋ	Rayong.	traat	Trat.
rɔɔyʔet	Roi Et.	ʔubon (raatchathaanii)	Ubon Ratchathani.
sakonnakhɔɔn	Sakon Nakhon.	ʔudɔɔn (thaanii)	Udon Thani.
samutpraakaan	Samut Prakan.	ʔuthaythaanii	Uthai Thani.
samutsaakhɔɔn	Samut Sakhon.	ʔuttaradit	Uttaradit.
samutsoŋkhraam	Samut Songkhram.	yalaa	Yala.

๕๘.๕ บทบรรยาย

คุณประเสริฐตั้งใจว่าพรุ่งนี้เขาจะส่งรถไปอัดฉีดและเปลี่ยนน้ำมันเครื่อง แต่
วันนี้เขาสังเกตเห็นว่ายางหน้าข้างซ้ายอ่อนไป   เขาจึงตกลงใจจะไปสูบลมที่ปั๊ม
น้ำมันก่อน ถ้ายางแบนเขาจะลำบากเพราะไม่มีทั้งแม่แรงและกุญแจถอดล้อ

เมื่อไปถึงปั๊มน้ำมันเขารู้สึกเกรงใจที่จะสูบลมอย่างเดียว   เขาจึงเติมน้ำมัน
ก่อนสามสิบบาทและให้เด็กที่ปั๊มน้ำมันตรวจหม้อน้ำและหม้อแบ็ตเตอรี่ให้ด้วย เมื่อ
เด็กเติมน้ำในหม้อน้ำและน้ำกลั่นในหม้อแบ็ตเตอรี่แล้ว   เด็กบอกเขาว่าควรจะเติม
น้ำมันเครื่องด้วย เพราะเหลือน้อยแล้ว แต่เขายังไม่ให้เติม เขาบอกกับเด็กว่าจะ
ส่งรถมาอัดฉีดและเปลี่ยนน้ำมันเครื่องพรุ่งนี้   หลังจากจ่ายเงินแล้ว เขาก็เตรียมขับ
รถกลับ แต่นึกขึ้นมาได้ว่าเขายังไม่ได้สูบลม ซึ่งเป็นเรื่องสำคัญที่ทำให้เขาต้องขับ
รถมาที่ปั๊มน้ำมันในวันนี้

๕๘.๖ ความแตกต่างระหว่างเสียงสูงต่ำ

พ่อเฆี่ยนม้า   ลูกชายเขียนม้า
แม่เฆี่ยนหมา   ลูกสาวเขียนหมา

khun prasòot tâŋcay wâa phrûŋ níi kháw ca sòŋ rót pay ʔàt chìit léʔ plìan námman khrûaŋ. tὲε wan níi kháw săŋkèet hěn wâa yaaŋ nâa khàŋ sáay ʔòon pay. kháw cuŋ tòkloŋ cay ca pay sùup lom thîi pám námman kòon. thâa yaaŋ bεεn kháw ca lambàak, phrɔ́ʔ mây mii thâŋ mὲεrεεŋ léʔ kuncεε thɔ̀ɔt lɔ́ɔ.

mûa pay thěŋ pám námman kháw rúusùk kreeŋcay thîi ca sùup lom yàaŋ diaw. kháw cuŋ tɔɔm námman kɔɔn săam sìp bàat léʔ hây dèk thîi pám námman trùat mɔ̂ɔ náam léʔ mɔ̂ɔ béttɔrîi hây dûay. mûa dèk tɔɔm náam nay mɔ̂ɔ náam léʔ nám klàn nay mɔ̂ɔ béttɔrîi lέεw, dèk bɔ̀ɔk kháw wâa khuan ca tɔɔm námman khrûaŋ dûay, phrɔ́ʔ lǔa nɔ́ɔy lέεw. tὲε kháw yaŋ mây hây tɔɔm. kháw bɔ̀ɔk kàp dèk wâa ca sòŋ rót maa ʔàt chìit léʔ plìan námman khrûaŋ phrûŋ níi. lăŋcàak càay ŋən lέεw, kháw kô triam khàp rót klàp. tὲε núk khûn maa dây wâa kháw yaŋ mây dây sùup lom, sûŋ pen rûaŋ sămkhan thîi tham hây kháw tɔ̂ŋ khàp rót maa thîi pám námman nay wan níi.

phɔ̂ɔ khîan máa.	The father is beating the horse.
mὲε khîan mǎa.	The mother is beating the dog.
lûuk chaay khîan máa.	The son is drawing a horse.
lûuk sǎaw khîan mǎa.	The daughter is drawing a dog.

197

พ่อเฆี่ยนหมาใช่ไหม	พ่อเขียนม้าใช่ไหม	พ่อเขียนหมาใช่ไหม
ไม่ใช่	ไม่ใช่	ไม่ใช่
พ่อทำอะไร	พ่อทำอะไร	พ่อทำอะไร
เฆี่ยนม้า	เฆี่ยนม้า	เฆี่ยนม้า
แล้วใครเฆี่ยนหมา	แล้วใครเขียนม้า	แล้วใครเขียนหมา
แม่	ลูกชาย	ลูกสาว
แม่เฆี่ยนม้าใช่ไหม	แม่เขียนหมาใช่ไหม	แม่เขียนม้าใช่ไหม
ไม่ใช่	ไม่ใช่	ไม่ใช่
แม่ทำอะไร	แม่ทำอะไร	แม่ทำอะไร
เฆี่ยนหมา	เฆี่ยนหมา	เฆี่ยนหมา
แล้วใครเฆี่ยนม้า	แล้วใครเขียนหมา	แล้วใครเขียนม้า
พ่อ	ลูกสาว	ลูกชาย
ลูกชายเขียนหมาใช่ไหม	ลูกชายเฆี่ยนม้าใช่ไหม	ลูกชายเฆี่ยนหมาใช่ไหม
ไม่ใช่	ไม่ใช่	ไม่ใช่
ลูกชายทำอะไร	ลูกชายทำอะไร	ลูกชายทำอะไร
เขียนม้า	เขียนม้า	เขียนม้า
แล้วใครเขียนหมา	แล้วใครเฆี่ยนม้า	แล้วใครเฆี่ยนหมา
ลูกสาว	พ่อ	แม่
ลูกสาวเขียนม้าใช่ไหม	ลูกสาวเฆี่ยนหมาใช่ไหม	ลูกสาวเฆี่ยนม้าใช่ไหม
ไม่ใช่	ไม่ใช่	ไม่ใช่
ลูกสาวทำอะไร	ลูกสาวทำอะไร	ลูกสาวทำอะไร
เขียนหมา	เขียนหมา	เขียนหมา
แล้วใครเขียนม้า	แล้วใครเฆี่ยนหมา	แล้วใครเฆี่ยนม้า
ลูกชาย	แม่	พ่อ

๕๕.๗ คำถามบทบรรยาย

คุณประเสริฐตั้งใจว่าจะส่งรถไป		ยางหน้าข้างซ้ายใช่ไหม	ใช่
อัดฉีดใช่ไหม	ใช่	คุณประเสริฐตกลงใจจะไปสูบลม	
เขาจะเปลี่ยนน้ำมันเครื่องด้วย		ใช่ไหม	ใช่
ใช่ไหม	ใช่	เขาไปสูบลมที่โรงแรมใช่ไหม	ไม่ใช่
คุณประเสริฐสังเกตเห็นว่ายางอ่อน		เขาไปสูบที่ปั๊มน้ำมันใช่ไหม	ใช่
ไปใช่ไหม	ใช่	เขาเติมน้ำมันด้วยใช่ไหม	ใช่
ยางหลังข้างขวาใช่ไหม	ไม่ใช่	เขาเติมน้ำมันสามสิบลิตรใช่ไหม	ไม่ใช่

198

phɔɔ khĭan mǎa,
chây máy.
    mây chây.
phɔɔ tham ʔaray.
    khĭan máa.
lɛ́ɛw khray khĭan mǎa.
    mɛ̂ɛ.

mɛ̂ɛ khĭan máa,
chây máy.
    mây chây.
mɛ̂ɛ tham ʔaray.
    khĭan mǎa.
lɛ́ɛw khray khĭan máa.
    phɔɔ.

lûuk chaay khĭan mǎa,
chây máy.
    mây chây.
lûuk chaay tham ʔaray.
    khĭan máa.
lɛ́ɛw khray khĭan mǎa.
    lûuk sǎaw.

lûuk sǎaw khĭan máa,
chây máy.
    mây chây.
lûuk sǎaw tham ʔaray.
    khĭan mǎa.
lɛ́ɛw khray khĭan máa.
    lûuk chaay.

phɔɔ khĭan máa,
chây máy.
    mây chây.
phɔɔ tham ʔaray.
    khĭan máa.
lɛ́ɛw khray khĭan máa.
    lûuk chaay.

mɛ̂ɛ khĭan mǎa,
chây máy.
    mây chây.
mɛ̂ɛ tham ʔaray.
    khĭan mǎa.
lɛ́ɛw khray khĭan mǎa.
    lûuk sǎaw.

lûuk chaay khĭan máa,
chây máy.
    mây chây.
lûuk chaay tham ʔaray.
    khĭan máa.
lɛ́ɛw khray khĭan máa.
    phɔɔ.

lûuk sǎaw khĭan mǎa,
chây máy.
    mây chây.
lûuk sǎaw tham ʔaray.
    khĭan mǎa.
lɛ́ɛw khray khĭan mǎa.
    mɛ̂ɛ.

phɔɔ khĭan mǎa,
chây máy.
    mây chây.
phɔɔ tham ʔaray.
    khĭan máa.
lɛ́ɛw khray khĭan mǎa.
    lûuk sǎaw.

mɛ̂ɛ khĭan máa,
chây máy.
    mây chây.
mɛ̂ɛ tham ʔaray.
    khĭan mǎa.
lɛ́ɛw khray khĭan máa.
    lûuk chaay.

lûuk chaay khĭan mǎa,
chây máy.
    mây chây.
lûuk chaay tham ʔaray.
    khĭan máa.
lɛ́ɛw khray khĭan mǎa.
    mɛ̂ɛ.

lûuk sǎaw khĭan máa,
chây máy.
    mây. chây.
lûuk sǎaw tham ʔaray.
    khĭan mǎa.
lɛ́ɛw khray khĭan máa.
    phɔɔ.

59.7   Questions on the narrative.   **59.7**

khun prasɤ̀ɤt tâŋcay wâa ca sòŋ rót pay ʔàt chìit, chây máy.   chây.

kháw ca plìan námman khrûaŋ dûay, chây máy.   chây.

khun prasɤ̀ɤt sǎŋkèet hěn wâa yaaŋ ʔɔ́ɔn pay, chây máy.   chây.

yaaŋ lǎŋ khǎŋ khwǎa, chây máy.   mây chây.

yaaŋ nâa khǎŋ sáay, chây máy.   chây.

khun prasɤ̀ɤt tòkloŋ cay ca pay sùup lom, chây máy.   chây.

kháw pay sùup lom thîi rooŋrɛɛm, chây máy.   mây chây.

kháw pay sùup thîi pám námman, chây máy.   chây.

kháw təəm námman dûay, chây máy.   chây.

kháw təəm námman sǎam sìp lít, chây máy.   mây chây.

(More.)   199

คุณประเสริฐตั้งใจว่าจะส่งรถไปอัดฉีด
    วันนี้ใช่ไหม   ไม่ใช่ เขาตั้งใจว่าจะส่งไปพรุ่งนี้
เวลาอัดฉีดเขาจะเติมน้ำมันเครื่อง
    ใช่ไหม   ไม่ใช่ เขาจะเปลี่ยนน้ำมันเครื่อง
วันนี้ยางหลังข้างขวาของรถเขาอ่อนไป
    ใช่ไหม   ไม่ใช่ ยางหน้าข้างซ้าย
เขาเลยเปลี่ยนยางใช่ไหม   ไม่ใช่ เขาไปสูบลม

เด็กที่ปั๊มน้ำมัน ไม่ได้ตรวจ
    น้ำมันเครื่องใช่ไหม   ไม่ใช่ ตรวจ
น้ำมันเครื่องยังเต็มอยู่ใช่ไหม   ไม่ใช่ เหลือน้อยแล้ว
เขาซื้อน้ำมันก๊าดใช่ไหม   ไม่ใช่ เขาซื้อน้ำมันเบนซิน
เขาซื้อน้ำมันห้าสิบบาทใช่ไหม   ไม่ใช่ เขาซื้อสามสิบบาท
เขาซื้อสามสิบลิตรใช่ไหม   ไม่ใช่ เขาซื้อสามสิบบาท

ใครจะส่งรถไปอัดฉีด   คุณประเสริฐ
เขาจะส่งไปเมื่อไหร่   พรุ่งนี้
วันนี้เขาสังเกตเห็นอะไร   ยางหน้าข้างซ้ายของรถเขาอ่อนไป
แล้วเขาทำอย่างไร   เอาไปสูบลม
เขาเอาไปสูบลมที่ไหน   ที่ปั๊มน้ำมัน
เขาสูบลมกี่ปอนด์   ยี่สิบสองปอนด์
แล้วเขาเติมอะไรอีกหรือเปล่า   เติม
เติมอะไรบ้าง   เติมน้ำในหม้อน้ำ น้ำกลั่นในหม้อ
                                       แบ๊ตเตอรี่และน้ำมันเบนซิน

เติมน้ำมันเบนซินเท่าไหร่   สามสิบบาท
คุณประเสริฐมีแม่แรงไหม   ไม่มี
ถ้ายางแบนเขาจะทำอย่างไร   ไม่ทราบ

khun prasɔ̀ɔt tâŋcay wâa ca sòŋ rót pay ʔàt chìit wan níi, chây máy.

weelaa ʔàt chìit, kháw ca təəm námman khrûaŋ, chây máy.

wan níi yaaŋ lǎŋ khâŋ khwǎa khɔ̌ŋ rót kháw ʔɔ̀ɔn pay, chây máy.

kháw ləəy plìan yaaŋ, chây máy.

dèk thîi pám námman mây dây trùat námman khrûaŋ, chây máy.

námman khrûaŋ yaŋ tem yùu, chây máy.

kháw sɯ́ɯ námman káat, chây máy.

kháw sɯ́ɯ námman hâa sìp bàat, chây máy.

kháw sɯ́ɯ sǎam sìp lít, chây máy.

khray ca sòŋ rót pay ʔàt chìit.

kháw ca sòŋ pay mɯarày.

wan níi kháw sǎŋkèet hěn ʔaray.

lɛ́ɛw kháw tham yaŋŋay.

kháw ʔaw pay sùup lom thîi nǎy.

kháw sùup lom kìi pɔɔn.

lɛ́ɛw kháw təəm ʔaray ʔìik rɯ́ plàaw.

təəm ʔaray bâaŋ.

təəm námman bensin thâwrày.

khun prasɔ̀ɔt mii mɛ̂ɛrɛɛŋ máy.

thâa yaaŋ bɛɛn, kháw ca tham yaŋŋay.

mây chây. kháw tâŋcay wâa ca sòŋ pay phrûŋ níi.

mây chây. kháw ca plìan námman khrûaŋ.

mây chây. yaaŋ nâa khâŋ sáay.

mây chây. kháw pay sùup lom.

mây chây. trùat.

mây chây. lɯ̌a nɔ́ɔy lɛ́ɛw.

mây chây. kháw sɯ́ɯ námman bensin.

mây chây. kháw sɯ́ɯ sǎam sìp bàat.

mây chây. kháw sɯ́ɯ sǎam sìp bàat.

khun prasɔ̀ɔt.

phrûŋ níi.

yaaŋ nâa khâŋ sáay khɔ̌ŋ rót kháw ʔɔ̀ɔn pay.

ʔaw pay sùup lom.

thîi pám námman.

yîi sìp sɔ̌ɔŋ pɔɔn.

təəm.

təəm náam nay mɔ̂ɔ náam. nám klàn nay mɔ̂ɔ bɛ́ttərîi, lɛ́ʔ námman bensin.

sǎam sìp bàat.

mây mii.

mây sâap.

๕๕.๘ การสนทนาโต้ตอบ

๕๕.๕ วลีท้ายประโยค

หรือ   น่ะซิ   ล่ะ (๑)   ล่ะ (๒)   หรอก   นี่

ก. คุณจะซักอย่างไร
   ข. จะซักแห้ง

ก. จะซักแห้งหรือ
   ข. ซักแห้งน่ะซิ บอกแล้วอย่างไรล่ะ

ก. ไม่ต้องซักแห้งหรอก
   ข. ทำไมไม่ต้องซักแห้งล่ะ

ก. ซักน้ำก็ได้
   ข. ก็ผมจะซักแห้งนี่

ก. ตกลงคุณจะเอาอย่างไร
   ข. ก็ซักแห้งน่ะซิ

ก. คุณจะพูดภาษาอะไร
   ข. จะพูดภาษาไทย

ก. จะพูดภาษาไทยหรือ
   ข. พูดภาษาไทยน่ะซิ บอกแล้วอย่างไรล่ะ

ก. ไม่ต้องพูดภาษาไทยหรอก
   ข. ทำไมไม่ต้องพูดภาษาไทยล่ะ

ก. พูดภาษาอังกฤษก็ได้
   ข. ก็ผมจะพูดภาษาไทยนี่

ก. ตกลงคุณจะเอาอย่างไร
   ข. ก็พูดภาษาไทยน่ะซิ

202

The students should ask questions about the pictures on pages 97, 123, and 177.

59.9 Particles. 59.9

lɔ̌ə, nâsi, lâ (1), lâ (2), lɔk, nî (continued).

In the following dialog, **A** thinks it would be cheaper and easier if **B** washed his suit in water, but **B** thinks it would look better if it were dry-cleaned.

A. khun ca sák yaŋŋay.	How are you going to clean it?
B. ca sák hɛ̂ɛŋ.	I'm going to dry-clean it.
A. ca sák hɛ̂ɛŋ lɔ̌ə.	You're going to dry-clean it?
B. sák hɛ̂ɛŋ nâsi.	Yes, dry-clean it.
bɔ̀ɔk lɛ́ɛw ŋay lâ.	That's what I said, isn't it?
A. mây tɔ̂ŋ sák hɛ̂ɛŋ lɔk.	You don't have to dry-clean it.
B. thammay mây tɔ̂ŋ sák hɛ̂ɛŋ lâ.	Oh yeah? Why not?
A. sák náam kɔ̂ dây.	You can *wash* it.
B. kɔ̂ phǒm ca sák hɛ̂ɛŋ nî.	Look. It's my suit and I've decided to have it dry-cleaned.
A. tòkloŋ khun ca ʔaw yaŋŋay.	Okay, so which are you going to do?
B. kɔ̂ sák hɛ̂ɛŋ nâsi.	*Dry-clean it.*

B, a Farang, is going to the bank. He knows they speak good English there, but he thinks one should make an effort to speak Thai while living in Thailand.

A. khun ca phûut phasǎa ʔaray.	What language are you going to speak?
B. ca phûut phasǎa thay.	Thai.
A. ca phûut phasǎa thay lɔ̌ə.	You're going to speak Thai?
B. phûut phasǎa thay nâsi.	Yes, Thai.
bɔ̀ɔk lɛ́ɛw yaŋŋay lâ.	That's what I said.
A. mây tɔ̂ŋ phûut phasǎa thay lɔk.	You don't have to speak Thai.
B. thammay mây tɔ̂ŋ phûut phasǎa thay lâ.	Yeah? Why not?
A. phûut phasǎa ʔaŋkrìt kɔ̂ dây.	You can speak *English*.
B. kɔ̂ phǒm ca phûut phasǎa thay nî.	Look. I'm going to speak Thai.
A. tòkloŋ khun ca ʔaw yaŋŋay.	Come on. What are you going to do?
B. kɔ̂ phûut phasǎa thay nâsi.	*Speak Thai.*

ก. คุณจะบอกแดงอย่างไร
    ข. จะไปหาเขาที่บ้าน

ก. จะไปหาเขาที่บ้านหรือ
    ข. ไปหาเขาที่บ้านน่ะซิ บอกแล้วอย่างไรล่ะ

ก. ไม่ต้องไปหาเขาที่บ้านหรอก
    ข. ทำไมไม่ต้องไปหาเขาที่บ้านล่ะ

ก. โทร.ไปบอกเขาก็ได้
    ข. ก็ผมจะไปหาเขาที่บ้านนี่

ก. ตกลง คุณจะเอาอย่างไร
    ข. ก็ไปหาเขาที่บ้านน่ะซิ

๕๕.๑๐ การเขียน

It would be more convenient to give Daeng the news by phone, but **B** feels that, in this particular case, personal contact is called for.

A. khun ca bɔ̀ɔk dɛɛŋ yaŋŋay.

  B. ca pay hǎa kháw thîi bâan.

A. ca pay hǎa kháw thîi bâan lɔ̌ə.

  B. pay hǎa kháw thîi bâan nâsi.
     bɔ̀ɔk lɛ́ɛw yaŋŋay lâ.

A. mây tôŋ pay hǎa kháw thîi bâan lɔk.

  B. thammay mây tôŋ pay hǎa kháw
     thîi bâan lâ.

A. thoo pay bɔ̀ɔk kháw kɔ̂ dây.

  B. kɔ̂ phǒm ca pay hǎa kháw thîi bâan nî.

A. tòkloŋ khun ca ʔaw yaŋŋay.

  B. kɔ̂ pay hǎa kháw thîi bâan nâsi.

How are you going to tell Daeng?

  I'm going to call on him at his house.

You're going to call on him at his house?

  Yes, call on him at his house.
  Like I said.

You don't have to go call on him at his house.

  And just why don't I have to go call on him
  at his house?

You can phone him just as well.

  Look. I've got my reasons, and I've decided
  to go call on him at his house.

So what are you going to do, now?

  Call on him at his house, like I've been
  saying all along.

59.10 Writing.

Practice reading and writing lessons 19 and 20 of Book 1 in Thai. For the spelling of **wan phárɯhàt** review 49.10.

บทที่ ๖๐

๖๐ ก.

๖๐ ข. เรียงความ

ร้านขายของต่าง ๆ ในประเทศไทย

ในประเทศไทยมีร้านขายของหลายชนิด เช่น ร้านขายอาหารสดซึ่งเรียกว่า ตลาดสด ร้านขายยา ร้านขายเครื่องสำอาง ร้านขายผ้า ร้านขายเครื่องเรือน และ ร้านขายเครื่องเหล็กเป็นต้น ร้านขายของที่มีของหลายชนิดอยู่ในร้านเดียวกัน คนไทยบางคนเรียกว่า ซุปเปอร์มาร์เก็ตและดีพาร์ตเมนต์สโตร์เช่นเดียวกับฝรั่ง

ตลาดสด เป็นที่ที่เราจะไปหาซื้อของสำหรับใช้ในการทำอาหารเช่น เนื้อ หมู ไก่ กุ้ง ปู ปลา และผักสดต่าง ๆ

ร้านขายยา มีอยู่ทั่วไป เราจะหาซื้อยาได้ทุกชนิดทั้ง ยาฉีด ยากิน และยาที่ ใช้ใส่บาดแผลต่าง ๆ

ร้านขายเครื่องสำอาง คือร้านที่ขายเครื่องแต่งตัวสำหรับผู้หญิง เช่น แป้ง น้ำหอม ลิปสติค เป็นต้น แต่บางร้านจะมีเสื้อและกระโปรงสำเร็จรูปขายด้วย

ร้านขายผ้าจะมีผ้าต่าง ๆ ทั้งของไทยและของต่างประเทศ มีทั้งผ้าราคาถูก และแพงซึ่งต้องแล้วแต่ชนิดของผ้าจะเป็นชนิดดีหรือไม่ดี การหาซื้อผ้าในเมืองไทย ไม่ยากนัก เพราะมีร้านขายผ้าอยู่ทั่วไป

สด	บาด	ลิปสติค
เครื่องสำอาง	แผล	สำเร็จ
	บาดแผล	
เครื่องเรือน		รูป
เครื่องเหล็ก	แต่ง	สำเร็จรูป
	แต่งตัว	
ซุปเปอร์มาร์เก็ต	เครื่องแต่งตัว	ต่างประเทศ
ดีพาร์ตเมนต์สโตร์	แป้ง	แล้วแต่
ยาฉีด	หอม	ยาก
	น้ำหอม	

206

LESSON 60

(Review)

60.a Review sections 2, 5, 6, 7, and 9 of lessons 56 – 59.

60.b Reading selection.

ráan khǎay khɔ̌ɔŋ tàaŋtàaŋ nay prathêet thay

nay prathêet thay mii ráan khǎay khɔ̌ɔŋ lǎay chanít, chên ráan khǎay ʔaahǎan sòt sɐ̌ŋ rîak wâa talàat sòt, ráan khǎay yaa, ráan khǎay khrɐ̂aŋ sǎmʔaaŋ, ráan khǎay phâa ráan khǎay khrɐ̂aŋ rɐan, lɛ́ʔ ráan khǎay khrɐ̂aŋ lèk pen tôn. ráan khǎay khɔ̌ɔŋ thîi mii khɔ̌ɔŋ lǎay chanít yùu nay ráan diaw kan khon thay baaŋ khon rîak wâa súppɔ̀ɔ maakêt lɛ́ʔ diipháatmén satoo chên diaw kàp faràŋ.

talàat sòt pen thîi thîi raw ca pay hǎa sɐ́ɐ khɔ̌ɔŋ sámràp cháy nay kaan tham ʔaahǎan, chên nɐ́a, mǔu, kày, kûŋ, puu, plaa, lɛ́ʔ phàk sòt tàaŋtàaŋ.

ráan khǎay yaa mii yùu thûa pay. raw ca hǎa sɐ́ɐ yaa dây thúk chanít tháŋ yaa chìit, yaa kin, lɛ́ʔ yaa thîi cháy sày bàat phlɛ̌ɛ tàaŋtàaŋ.

ráan khǎay khrɐ̂aŋ sǎmʔaaŋ khɐɐ ráan thîi khǎay khrɐ̂aŋ tèŋtua sámràp phûu yǐŋ, chên pɛ̂ɛŋ, nám hɔ̌ɔm, lípsatìk pen tôn. tɛ̀ɛ baaŋ ráan ca mii sɐ̂a lɛ́ʔ kraprooŋ sǎmrèt rûup khǎay dûay.

ráan khǎay phâa ca mii phâa tàaŋtàaŋ tháŋ khɔ̌ɔŋ thay lɛ́ʔ khɔ̌ɔŋ tàaŋ prathêet. mii tháŋ phâa rakhaa thùuk lɛ́ʔ phɛɛŋ sɐ̌ŋ tôn lɛ́ɛwtɛ̀ɛ chanít khɔ̌ŋ phâa ca pen chanít dii rɐ̌ɐ mây dii. kaan hǎa sɐ́ɐ phâa nay mɐaŋ thay mây yâak nák, phrɔ́ʔ mii ráan khǎay phâa yùu thûa pay.

sòt	To be fresh.
khrɐ̂aŋ sǎmʔaaŋ	Cosmetics, toilet articles.
khrɐ̂aŋ rɐan	Furniture.
khrɐ̂aŋ lèk	Hardware.
súppɔ̀ɔ maakêt	Supermarket.
diipháatmén satoo	Department store.
yaa chìit	Medicine for injection.
bàat	To cut or wound.
phlɛ̌ɛ	A cut, wound, or sore.
bàat phlɛ̌ɛ	A cut, wound, or sore.
tèŋ	To adorn, decorate.
tèŋtua	To adorn the body (get dressed, apply cosmetics, etc.).
khrɐ̂aŋ tèŋtua	Things used to adorn the body (clothes, cosmetics, etc.).
pɛ̂ɛŋ	Powder, flour, starch.
hɔ̌ɔm	To smell good.
nám hɔ̌ɔm	Perfume.
lípsatìk	Lipstick.
sǎmrèt	To complete, be successful.
rûup	Form, shape.
sǎmrèt rûup	Ready made.
tàaŋ prathêet	Foreign countries.
lɛ́ɛwtɛ̀ɛ	Depending on.
yâak	To be difficullt.

207

ร้านขายเครื่องเรือนก็มีโต๊ะเครื่องแป้ง โต๊ะอาหาร โต๊ะทำงาน ชุดรับแขก ตู้ เตียง และของอื่น ๆ ให้เราเลือกซื้อได้หลายอย่าง

ร้านขายเครื่องเหล็กมีของใช้ชนิดต่าง ๆ ที่ทำด้วยเหล็ก เช่น มีด กรรไกร ท่อน้ำ ค้อน ตะปู และอื่นๆ อีกมาก

ร้านขายของที่เรียกว่า ซุปเปอร์มาร์เก็ตคือร้านขายของที่มีทั้งอาหารสดซึ่งใช้ ในการทำอาหาร อาหารกระป๋อง และของใช้ที่ต้องใช้ประจำวัน เช่น สบู่ ยาสีฟัน ผงซักฟอกเป็นต้น

ร้านขายของอีกอย่างหนึ่งที่เรียกว่า ดีพาร์ตเมนต์สโตร์ ซึ่งเป็นห้างใหญ่ๆ มีของขายทุกอย่างนับตั้งแต่ เสื้อผ้า เครื่องสำอาง รองเท้า ถ้วยชาม ดินสอ ปากกา หนังสือ วิทยุ และเครื่องรับโทรทัศน์ด้วย

โต๊ะเครื่องแป้ง	
โต๊ะทำงาน	ค้อน
ชุด	ตะปู
ชุดรับแขก	
ตู้	ประจำ
	ประจำวัน
เตียง	ผง
	ฟอก
และอื่นๆ	ผงซักฟอก
กรรไกร (ตะไกร)	นับ
ท่อน้ำ	ห้าง

ráan khăay khrûaŋ rɯan kɔ̂ mii tóʔ
khrûaŋ pɛ̂ɛŋ, tóʔ ʔaahăan, tóʔ tham ŋaan,
chút ráp khɛ̀ɛk, tûu. tiaŋ, léʔ khɔ̌ɔŋ ʔɯ̀ɯn-
ʔɯ̀ɯn hây raw lɯ̂ak sɯ́ɯ dây lăay yàaŋ.

ráan khăay khrûaŋ lèk mii khɔ̌ɔŋ
cháy chanít tàaŋtàaŋ thîi tham dûay lèk, chên
mîit, kankray, thɔ̂ɔ náam, khɔ́ɔn, tapuu, léʔ
ʔɯ̀ɯnʔɯ̀ɯn ʔìik mâak.

ráan khăay khɔ̌ɔŋ thîi rîak wâa súp-
pɘ̂ɘ maakêt khɯɯ ráan khăay khɔ̌ɔŋ thîi mii
tháŋ ʔaahăan sòt sɛ̌ŋ cháy nay kaan tham
ʔaahăan, ʔaahăan krapɔ̌ŋ, léʔ khɔ̌ɔŋ cháy thîi
tɔ̂ŋ cháy pracam wan, chên sabùu, yaa sǐi fan,
phɔ̌ŋ sák fɔ̂ɔk pen tôn.

ráan khăay khɔ̌ɔŋ ʔìik yàaŋ nɯŋ thîi
rîak wâa diipháatmén satoo sɛ̌ŋ pen hâaŋ
yàyyày mii khɔ̌ɔŋ khăay thúk yàaŋ náp
tâŋtɛ̀ɛ sɯ̂a phâa, khrûaŋ sǎmʔaaŋ, rɔŋtháaw,
thûay chaam, dinsɔ̌ɔ, pàakkaa, naŋsɯ̌ɯ,
wítthayúʔ léʔ khrûaŋ ráp thoorathát dûay.

tóʔ khrûaŋ pɛ̂ɛŋ	Dressing table.
tóʔ tham ŋaan	Desk.
chút	A set of something.
chút ráp khɛ̀ɛk	A living room set.
tûu	Cabinet.
tiaŋ	Bed.
léʔ ʔɯ̀ɯnʔɯ̀ɯn	And so forth.
kankray (takray)	Scissors.
thɔ̂ɔ náam	A water pipe.
khɔ́ɔn	A hammer.
tapuu	Nails.
pracam	To be regularly attached to.
pracam wan	Daily.
phɔ̌ŋ	A powdery substance, dust.
fɔ̂ɔk	To wash.
phɔ̌ŋ sák fɔ̂ɔk	Soap powder, detergent powder.
náp	To count.
hâaŋ	A large store.

209

THE THAI SYSTEM OF WRITING

a. Consonants.

The **44** consonants of the Thai alphabet appear below in a pseudo-phonetic chart (the phonetic labels are not accurate in every case). This is the most convenient way to present them since it clearly shows the system in back of the alphabetic ordering. The order is given by reading the chart from left to right until a double line is reached, and then proceeding to the next line below. The letter following ŋɔɔ, for example, is cɔɔ, and the one following mɔɔ is yɔɔ.

	Voiced stops (mid)	Voiceless stops (mid)	High aspirate stops	High fricatives	Low aspirate stops	Low fricatives	Irregular low aspirate stops	Nasals (low)	Sonorants (low)	Sibilants (high)	Miscellaneous
Velars	ก k	ข kh	ฃ kh	ค kh	ฅ kh	ฆ kh		ง ŋ			
Palatals		จ c	ฉ ch		ช ch	ซ s	ฌ ch	ญ y, n	ย y	ศ s	ห h
Irregular dentals	ฎ d	ฏ t	ฐ th		ฑ th		ฒ th	ณ n	ร r	ษ s	ฬ l
Dentals	ด d	ต t	ถ th		ท th		ธ th	น n	ล l	ส s	อ ʔ
Labials	บ b	ป p	ผ ph	ฝ f	พ ph	ฟ f	ภ ph	ม m	ว w		ฮ h

b. Vowels.

The correspondence of Thai vowel symbols to sounds is shown in the following chart. There are between 9 and 24 vowel sounds and between 15 and 36 vowel symbols, depending on what one chooses to count. ꜷꜵꜵ is used for the initial consonant and ꜷꜵꜵ for the non-specific final.

	LONG			SHORT					
	With Final		Without Final	With Final					Without Final
	y	Other		y	w	m		Other	
a	อา			ไอ	ใอ	เอา	อำ	อัน	อะ | อ
ə	เอย	เอิน	เออ						เออะ
e		เอ			เอ็น				เอะ
o		โอ			อน				โอะ
ua	อวน		อัว						อัวะ
ia		เอีย							เอียะ
ɯa		เออ							เออะ
ɛ		แอ							แอะ
ɔ		ออ							เอาะ
ɯ	อืน		อือ				อึ		
i		อี					อิ		
u		อู					อุ		

212

c. Tones.

The following chart shows the way the five tones are written with the three types of initials in the three types of syllables.

	MID			HIGH			LOW		
	Live	Long Dead	Short Dead	Live	Long Dead	Short Dead	Live	Long Dead	Short Dead
–	กา						คา นา		
`	ก่า	กาด	กั๊ด	ข่า หน่า	ขาด หนาด	ขัด หนัด			
^	ก้า	ก้าด	กั้ด	ข้า หน้า			ค่า น่า	คาด นาด	คั่ด นั่ด
´	ก๊า	ก๊าด	กั๊ด				ค้า น้า	ค้าด ค๊าด น๊าด	คั้ด นั้ด
⌄	ก๋า			ขา หนา					

213

GLOSSARY

The following alphabetical order is followed in the glossary: ʔ a b c d e ə ɛ f h i k l m n ŋ o ɔ p r s t u ʉ w y. The number immediately following each entry refers to the section where it is first used.

ʔaa 26.4 Father's younger sibling (aunt, uncle).

ʔâa 44.9 To open the mouth.

ʔaaceentinâa 57.4 Argentina.

ʔaacian 51.9 To vomit, throw up.

ʔaahǎan 3.3 Food.

ʔaakàat 45 Weather, air (the space above the ground).

ʔàan 13.5 To read.

ʔàaŋ láaŋ nâa 44.4 Wash basin.

ʔàaŋthɔɔŋ 58.4 Ang Thong (a province of Thailand).

ʔàap náam 52.9 To bathe, take a bath.

ʔaaràp 57.4 United Arab Republic.

ʔàat 41.3 May, might, maybe.

ʔâaw 47.7 An exclamation of surprise.

ʔaayúʔ 51.8 Age.

ʔalày 58.5 Spare.

ʔameerikaa 17.2 America.

ʔameerikan 9.3 American.

ʔamphəə 57.5 District, county (subdivision of a province).

ʔanúsǎwwarii 42.4 Monument.

ʔanúsǎwwarii chaysamɔɔraphuum 42.4 The Monument of Victory.

ʔanúsǎwwarii prachaathíppatay 42.4 The Monument of Democracy.

ʔaŋkrìt 9.2 England, English.

ʔaŋkhaan (See following entries.)

daaw ʔaŋkhaan Mars.

wan ʔaŋkhaan 19.4, 27.8 Tuesday.

ʔapháatmén 47.5 Apartment.

ʔaray 6.5 What? Something, anything.

ʔarɔy 23.3 To taste good.

ʔàt 55, 58.5 To compress.

ʔàt chìit 58.5 To lubricate a car.

ʔathít 26.7 Week.

phráʔ ʔathít Sun.

wan ʔathít 19.4, 27.8 Sunday.

ʔaw 17.3 To take, accept.

ʔâw 32.9 An exclamation used to announce that a demonstration is ready to start. All right?

ʔèek 53.3 First rank.

ʔeeŋ 26.3, 44.2 Self, by oneself, just (after demonstratives).

ʔeerawan 6.3 Erawan (a hotel in Bangkok).

ʔee yuu ʔee 11.7 AUA. American University Alumni Association.

ʔèt 4.8 One (in 21, 31, etc.).

ʔìik 8.3 Another, one more, more.

ʔìik thii 8.3 Again, another time.

ʔìm 23.3 To have eaten enough, to be full.

ʔindia 57.4 India.

ʔindooniisia 57.4 Indonesia.

ʔiràan 57.4 Iran.

ʔitaalii 57.4 Italy.

ʔìtsaraaʔeen 57.4 Israel.

ʔoolíaŋ 23.2 Black, iced coffee.

ʔooyúaʔ 23.2 Black, hot coffee.

ʔòp 8.4 To roast or bake.

ʔɔɔ 19.3 Oh, I see.

ʔɔɔk 29.7 To exit, to go or come out, to pay out.

ʔɔɔk sǐaŋ 48.10 To pronounce.

ʔɔɔn 40.6, 58.5 To be soft, tender, young, weak.

ʔɔɔtsatreelia 57.4 Australia.

ʔɔɔtsatria 57.4 Austria.

ʔɔpfít 37.7 Office.

ʔûan 1.5 To be fat.

ʔubon (râatchathaanii) 59.4 Ubon Ratchathani (a province of Thailand).

ʔudɔɔn (thaanii) 59.4 Udon Thani (a province of Thailand).

ʔuthaythaanii 59.4 Uthai Thani (a province of Thailand).

ʔùtnǔn 31.4 To patronize, support.

ʔùtsǎahàkam 56.4 Industry.

ʔùttaradìt 59.4 Uttaradit (a province of Thailand).

ʔùun 42.5 Other.

baa 58.8 A bar (place that sells drinks).

bàa 2.6 Shoulder (the horizontal part, not the tip).

bâa 38.2 Crazy.

bâan 10 House, home.

baaŋ 33.2 To be thin.

baaŋ 49.5 Some. (See 49.3)

bâaŋ 17.3 Some. (See 49.3)

baaŋkapìʔ 54.4 Bang Kapi (an amphoe in Phra Nakhon province; unofficially, the area along Sukhumvit Road).

baaŋ khěen 54.4 Bang Khen (an amphoe in Phra Nakhon province).

baaŋ lamphuu 42.4 An area in Bangkok.

baaŋ rák 54.4 Bang Rak (an amphoe in Phra Nakhon province).

baaŋ sɛ̌ɛn 29.4 Bang Saen (a resort beach in Chon Buri province).

bàat 7.8 Baht, ticals (the monetary unit of Thailand).

bàat 60 To cut or wound.

bàay 14.4 Afternoon.

bamìi 48.8 Egg noodles.

banday 51.4 Stairway.

banthát 39.4 A line of print, a ruled line.

banthúk 56.5 To note, to record.

baŋkháp 34.4 To force.

baw 53.2 To be light in weight.

bay 1.6, 22.5 A leaf. Classifier for containers (dishes, glasses, etc.).

beekhɔ̌n 25.b, 27.9 Bacon.

beenyîam 57.4 Belgium.

bensin 58.5 Benzine, gasoline.

bəə 13.3 Number. (See 13.1)

bɔ̀ɔk· 39.6 To withdraw (money).

bɛɛ 57.9 To spread out, unfold.

bɛɛ muu 57.9 To open the hand.

bɛɛn 58.5 Flat.

bɛ̀ɛp 51.5 Type, style.

bɛ̀ɛp fùk hàt 48.10 A drill or exercise in a textbook.

béŋ 28.3 Bank.

bia 23.3 Beer.

bìip 9.6 To squeeze.

bin 50, 58.8 To fly.

bòk 50 Land (as opposed to sea).

bon 8.3 On, the upper part of.

khâŋbon 8.3 Upstairs.

boolîŋ 58.8 Bowling.

bòt 43.9 A lesson in a textbook, the text or lines of a play.

bɔ̀ɔk 18.3 To tell.

bɔɔriween 51.5 Area, vicinity.

bɔ̀y 25 Often.

braasin 57.4 Brazil.

burìi 14.7 Cigarette.

buriiram 58.4 Buri Ram (a province of Thailand).

câ 1.2 Polite particle, confirmative. (See 1.1 and 3.1)

cá 4.2 Polite particle. (See 1.1)

càʔ, ca 11.3 Will.

càak 32.9 From, to separate from.

caam 29.6 To sneeze.

caan 12.6, 22.3 A plate.

câaŋ 42.5 To hire.

càay 47.5 To pay out, spend.

cam 56.7 To remember, recognize.

campen 52.5 To be necessary.

can (See following entries.)

phráʔ can The moon.

wan can 17.4 Monday.

can (tha) burii 58.4 Chanthaburi (a province of Thailand).

caŋwàt 50 Province.

càp 12.6 To catch, grab.

caraǝnkruŋ 41.1 New Road (a road in Bangkok).

càt 45 Strong, intense, extreme.

câw 44.5 Prince, ruler.

câwkhɔ̆ɔŋ 44.5 Owner.

cèp 51.9 To hurt, be hurt.

cèt 3.8 Seven.

cɛ̂ɛŋ 56.5 To make known, inform, report.

chaa 23.3 Tea (the product or drink).

cháa 14.3 To be slow.

chaam 21.5 A bowl.

cháaŋ 37.4 Elephant.

   cháaŋ phùak 37.4 White elephant.

châat 25 Nationality.

cháaw 14.4 Morning.

chaay 7.3 Male (people only).

chaay 45 Edge, border.

   chaay hàat 58.8 Beach.

   chaay thalee 45 Seashore.

chăay 18.10, 43.5 To shine a light.

chàchəəŋsaw 58.4 Chachoengsao (a province of Thailand).

chán 48.5 A layer, storey, class, grade.

chaná? 56.7b To win.

chanít 55 Kind, type, variety.

chaphɔ́? 45 Especially or exclusively for.

chát 34.3 To be plain, clear, distinct.

châw 46.5 To rent.

chây 9.3 To be the one meant, to be so, to be a fact. That's right.

cháy 13.5 To use.

   khon cháay 46.5 Servant.

chaynâat 58.4 Chai Nat (a province of Thailand).

chayyaphuum 58.4 Chaiyaphum (a province of Thailand).

chên 45 As, like, for example.

   chên diaw kàp 55 The same as, in like manner.

chét 12.6 To wipe.

chəən 11.3 To invite. Go ahead. Please do. Help yourself.

chə́ət 41.5 (From the English 'shirt'.)

   sûa chə́ət 41.5 A dress shirt.

chiaŋmày 58.4 Chiang Mai (a province of Thailand).

chiaŋraay 58.4 Chiang Rai (a province of Thailand).

chíi 57.5 To point.

chìit 58.5 To inject, inoculate, spray.

chín 24.3 A piece of something.

chomphûu 38.4 Rose-apple.

chonburii 58.4 Chon Buri (a province of Thailand).

chɔ́ɔn 12.6, 49.8 Spoon.

chɔ̂ɔp 7.4 To like.

chûamooŋ 27.3 Hour.

chuan 35 To invite.

chûay 17.3 To help. (See 17.1 and 41.9)

chumphɔɔn 58.4 Chumphon (a province of Thailand).

chút 60 A set of something.

   chút ráp khɛ̂ɛk 60 A living room set.

chûak 28.7 Rope, string.

chʉ̂ʉ 18.3 Name, to be named.

ciin 14.2 Chinese.

cìip 29.6 To pleat, to flirt.

ciŋ 43.5 To be true.

cîŋcòk 36.5 House lizard.

cîŋrìit 39.4 Cricket.

cìp 29.6 To sip.

con 45 Until.

còtmăay 54.7 A letter, mail.

cɔ̀ɔt 26.3 To park, bring to a stop.

cuan 29.3 Almost, approaching, getting close to.

cùt 41.9 To light a fire.

cʉŋ 42.5 So, therefore, consequently.

cʉ̀ʉt 24.7 To be tasteless.

dàa 27.6 To curse, scold.

daaw 27.9 Star.

   khày daaw 27.9 Fried eggs.

dâaw 56.5 Foreign.

   tàaŋ dâaw 56.5 Foreigner.

dâay 11.6 Thread.

dam 16.6 Black.

dan 31.4 To push.

daŋ 54.5 Like, as, according to.

dây 8.3 Can, be able.

dây 18.1 To get.

dây 48.5 Preceding a verb, this shows the accomplishment or completion of the verb. (See 48.1)

dâyyin 56.7 To hear.

dèk 7.1 Child (boy or girl, not son or daughter; see lûuk).

denmàak 57.4 Denmark.

dəən 6.3 To walk.

  dəən thaaŋ 50 To travel.

dɛɛŋ 14.4 Red.

dèɛt 17.4 Sunlight, sunshine.

diaw 19.3 Single, only one, one and the same.

dǐaw 22.3 In a moment.

dǐawnii 35.6 Now.

dichán 8.2 I (woman speaking). (See 8.1)

dii 1.5 To be good.

diipháatmén satoo 60 Department store.

dinsɔ̌ɔ 16.3 Pencil.

dontrii 58.8 Music.

dooy 47.5 By means of, with, by.

dooysǎan 50 To take passage.

  khon dooysǎan 50 Passenger.

  khâa dooysǎan 50 Fare.

dɔ́ktəə 53.3 Doctor (Ph.D., not medical).

dɔɔk bua 39.4 The lotus flower.

dùan 50 To be urgent, express.

dûay 17.3 Also, too. (See 17.1)

dûay 42.9 A particle used in requests. (See 42.9)

dûaykan 21.3 Together.

dusìt 54.4 Dusit (an amphoe in Phra Nakhon province).

duu 32.2 To look at.

dɨan 26.7 Month.

dɨŋ 11.6 To pull.

dɨ̀ɨm 55 To drink.

fáa 14.4, 44.5 Sky.

  sǐi fáa 14.4 Light blue.

fǎa phanǎŋ 51.4 Wall (of a room or house).

fâay 58.8 Cotton.

fák thɔɔŋ 49.4 Pumpkin.

fan 33.3 Teeth.

faŋ 18.5 To listen to.

faràŋ, fáràŋ 24.1 European, American, Australian, etc. Occidental.

faràŋsèet 57.4 France, French.

fâw 46.5 To guard, watch, keep an eye on.

fay 16.3 Fire, light.

  fay fáa 44.5 Electricity.

fílíppin 57.4 The Philippines.

finlɛɛn 57.4 Finland.

fiw 43.3 A fuse.

flɛ̀t 46.5 A flat, an apartment.

fǒn 18.10, 45 Rain.

fɔ́ɔk 60 To wash, to suds.

  phǒŋ sák fɔ́ɔk 60 Soap powder, detergent powder.

fút 41.3 A foot in length.

fɨ̀k hàt 48.10 To practice.

hâ (há) 32.9 Short form of khâ (khá).

háʔ 31.3 Short form of khráp.

hâa 1.8 Five.

hǎa 13,3 To look for.

hâaŋ 34.3, 60 A business firm, commercial establishment, large store.

haawaay 42.5 Hawaii.

hǎay cay 44.9 To breathe.

halǒo 53.5 Hello (used only for answering the phone).

hǎn 44.9 To turn in place (not in line of motion).

hây 17.3 To give. (See 17.1)

hěn 7.4 To see.

hèt 48.4 Mushrooms.

hɛm 25.b, 27.9 Ham.

hɛ̂ɛŋ 8.4 To be dry.

hɛ̀ŋ 56.7 Place, classifier of places.

hìmáʔ 45 Snow.

hǐn 22.5 Rock, stone.

hǐw 21.3 To hunger or thirst for.

  hǐw khâaw 21.1 To be hungry.

hǐw náam 21.1 To be thirsty.

hm̂m 3.5 A confirmative. Yes. (See 3.1)

hòk 2.7 Six.

hòt 41.5 To shrink.

hôŋ 3.2 A room.

hôŋ kin khâaw 46.8, 51.5 Dining room.

hôŋ náam 7.3 Bathroom.

hôŋ nɔɔn 46.8, 48.2 Bedroom.

hôŋ ráp khɛ̀ɛk 46.8 51.5 Living room.

hɔ̀ɔ 43.5 To wrap, classifier for things wrapped.

hɔ̀ɔ phák 38.4 Dormitory.

hɔ̌ɔm 23.2 To smell good.

hǔa 16.4, 37.10 Head.

hǔa hǐn 26.4 Hua Hin (a resort beach in Prachuab Khiri Khan province).

hǔa hɔ̌ɔm 39.4 Onion.

hǔalamphooŋ 41.4 Bangkok's central railway station and surrounding district.

hǔa phàkkàat lǔaŋ 49.4 Carrot.

hǔarɔ́ʔ 32.4, 51.9 To laugh.

hǔŋ 38.5 To cook (especially rice).

hùp 44.9 To close the mouth.

hǔu 16.4 Ears.

kaafɛɛ 23.3 Coffee.

kaan . . . 47.5 The action of . . . .

kaan khlaŋ 56.4 Finance.

kaan tàaŋ prathêet 56.4 Foreign affairs.

kaan (caná) burii 58.4 Kanchanaburi (a province of Thailand).

kaanlasǐn 58.4 Kalasin (a province of Thailand).

kaaŋ 38.5 To spread out, hang out.

káat 58.3 (From the English 'gas'.)

námman káat 58.3 Kerosene.

kâaw 3.8 Nine.

kâaw 14.6 A step, to step.

kalaahǒom 56.4 Defense.

kalàm dɔ̀ɔk 49.4 Cauliflower.

kalàm plii 48.4 Cabbage.

kam 57.9 To clench the fist.

kam mʉʉ 57.9 To clench the fist.

kamlaŋ 30 In the process of.

kamlaŋ ca 32.3 To be about to, on the point of.

kamphɛɛŋ 51.4 Wall (enclosing a yard or city).

kamphɛɛŋphét 58.4 Kamphaeng Phet (a province of Thailand).

kan 6.5, 53.9 The other, each other, mutually, together, as a group.

kankray 60 Scissors.

kanyaayon 36.8 September.

kaŋkeeŋ 27.5 Trousers.

kaŋkeeŋ chán nay 37.9 Underpants.

kàp 6.9 With, and.

kàp khâaw 47.5 The side dishes eaten with rice.

karákkadaakhom 36.8 July.

karunaa 53.5 To be kind, merciful. 'Please.' (See 53.1)

kasèet 56.4 Agriculture.

kàt 9.6 To bite.

kaw 28.6 To scratch lightly.

kàw 38.9 To be old (not new).

kâwʔîi 19.4, 38.9 Chair.

kawlǐi 57.4 Korea.

kày 7.4 Chicken.

kèŋ 15 To be skillful or good at something.

kèp 44.5 To collect, keep, store.

kèp tóʔ 52.9 To clear the table.

kəən 42.5 To exceed.

kəən pay 42.5 Too, excessively.

kə̀ət 9.6 To be born.

kɛɛ 40 He, she (respectful).

kɛ̀ɛ 40 To be old (opposite of young, not the opposite of new).

kɛ̂ɛ 26.3 To repair, make right, to correct.

kɛ̂ɛm 16.4 The cheeks.

kɛɛŋ 13.6 Curry.

kɛ̂ɛw 13.6, 21.5 Glass, a glass.

khâ 1.3 Polite particle, confirmative. (See 1.1 and 3.1).

khá 2.3 Polite particle. (See 1.1)

khâa 42.5 Expenses, fee, cost, value.

khâa câaŋ 42.5 Wages (for hiring someone).

khâa dooysǎan 50 Fare.

khâa thamniam 57.5 Fee.

khǎa 34.7 Leg.

khâam   56.5   To cross.

khâaŋ   4.1   A side.

khàat   43.5   To be torn, broken, lacking.

khâaw   21.3   Rice, grain.

  khâaw phôot   58.8   Corn, maize.

  khâaw sǎalii   58.8   Wheat.

khǎaw   14.4   White.

khǎay   11.4   To sell.

kham   19.3   Word.

  kham sàp   54.10   Vocabulary.

khǎm   51.9   To be funny.

khamanaakhom   56.4   Communications.

khamooy   46.5   A thief, to steal.

khan   28.1   Classifier for cars.

khanàat   44.5   Size.

khanǒm   23.1   Pastry, sweets, dessert.

  khanǒmpaŋ   23.7   Bread.

khanǔn   47.4   Jackfruit.

khàp   26.3   To drive.

kháp   32.3   Tight.

khàw   28.4   The knees.

khâw   29.7   To enter, to go or come in.

kháw   1.9   He, she, they (people only).

khâwcay   8.3   To understand.

kháwtəə   48.7   The counter or bar.

khày   24.3   Eggs.

  khày ciaw   48.8   Omelette.

  khày daaw   27.9   Fried eggs.

  khày lûak   27.9   Very soft boiled eggs.

  khày tôm   48.8   Boiled eggs.

khây   38.2   A fever.

  pen khây   38.2   To have a fever.

khǎy   29.6   To unlock, to wind a clock.

khǎy   43.5   Animal fat, tallow.

khěmkhàt   33.4   A belt.

khəəy   37.2, 46.7 Having experienced.
(See 46.1)

khὲεk   46.8, 51.5   Guests.

khὲεn   13.6   Arm, sleeve.

khεεnadaa   57.4   Canada.

khěŋ   23.3   To be hard (not soft).

khìa   17.3   To remove or dislodge something
with light stroking movements of the
finger or some instrument.

khian   44.6   To whip, beat.

khǐan   13.5   To write.

khǐaŋ   33.5   A chopping board.

khǐaw   14.4   Green.

khîi kìat   31.4   To be lazy.

khîi nǐaw   36.4   To be stingy.

khiim   33.5   Pliers.

khít   25.9   To figure, think.

  khít thěŋ   39.10 To think about someone
(used in the same situations where **to
miss someone** is used in English).

khon   2.9   Person, people.

khón khwáa   26.4   To research.

khoŋ   41.5   Most likely, sure to, bound to.

khoorâat   27.4   Korat (a city in Nakhon
Ratchasima province).

khɔ̌ɔ   2.3   To ask for.

  khɔ̌ɔ thôot   2.3   Excuse me, I'm sorry.

khɔ̂n   55   More than half.

  khɔ̂nkhâaŋ ca   55   Rather, quite.

khɔ̌ɔn   60   A hammer.

khɔ̌ɔn kὲn   21.4   Khon Kaen (a province
of Thailand).

khɔ̌ɔŋ   22.2   Thing.

khɔ̌ɔŋ, khɔ̌ɔŋ, khɔ́ŋ   36.2, 40   Of (possessive).

khɔ̌ɔpcay   25   Thanks (used with intimates or
social inferiors).

khɔ̌ɔpkhun   3.3   Thanks.

khɔɔ sɔ̌ɔ   14.8   The Christian era (an abbreviation of **khrítthasàkkaràat**).

khɔɔy   26.3   To wait for. ⸌

khɔ̂y   46.5   Gradually, little by little.

  mây khɔ̂y   46.5   Hardly, not very.

khráŋ   56.5   A time, occaision.

khráp   1.3   Polite particle, confirmative.
(See 1.1 and 3.1)

khray   7.9   Who?

khrók   33.5   A mortar.

khrooŋ   54.10   Frame, skeleton.

  khrooŋ sâaŋ   54.10   Structure.

khrɔ̂ɔpkhrua   48.5   Family.

khrua   13.4   Kitchen.

220

khruu 34.4 Teacher.

khrûu 53.5 A short period of time, a while.

khrûaŋ 57.3 Implements.

khrûaŋ ʔalày 58.3 Spare parts.

khrûaŋ bin 50 Airplane.

khrûaŋ chǎay nǎŋ 57.3 A movie projector.

khrûaŋ dùum 55 Drinks.

khrûaŋ kɛɛŋ 57.3 The spices for making a curry.

khrûaŋ khrua 57.3 Kitchen utensils.

khrûaŋ lèk 60 Hardware.

khrûaŋ mǎay 38.4 A symbol.

khrûaŋ ruan 57.3, 60 Furniture.

khrûaŋ sǎmʔaaŋ 60 Cosmetics, toilet articles.

khrûaŋ thoorasàp 57.3 A telephone.

khrûaŋ thoorathát 57.3 Television set.

khrûaŋ yen 57.3 Air conditioner.

khrûŋ 21.8 Half.

khuan 41.5 Should, ought to.

khùan 13.6 To scratch (painfully).

khùap 51.8 A year of age (used for children only).

khùat 21.5 Bottle.

khúk khàw 28.4 To kneel.

khun 4.3 A respectful title, you. (See 4.1 and 6.1)

khùt 29.6 To dig.

khûu 31.3 A pair (classifier).

khùut 29.6 To scrape off.

khûn 29.1 To ascend, go or come up, increase.

khuu 50 To be as follows or defined, namely.

khuun 31.8 Night.

khuun 57.5 To return, give back.

khwǎa 4.2 Right (side).

khwaam 55, 57.3 Essence, stuff, -ness,-ity. (See 57.1, 57.3)

khwaam ciŋ 57.3 Truth, actually, in fact.

khwaam hěn 57.3 Opinion.

khwaay 6.5 Water buffalo.

kìi 14.6 How many?

kíi, kîi 44.2 A moment ago.

kiloo (kram) 28.7 A kilogram (2.205 pounds).

kiloo (méet) 28.7 A kilometer (.621 miles).

kin 11.4 To eat.

klaaŋ 24.3 Center, middle, in the middle of.

klaaŋ khuun 46.5 Night time.

klaaŋ wan 24.3 Midday, day time.

klàn 58.5 To distill.

klàp 12.3 To return.

klàp rót 27.3 To turn the car around.

klay 28.7 To be far.

klây 11.3 To be near.

klìat 58.2 To hate.

klɔ̌ŋ 47.6 A small box.

klɔ̂ŋ 47.6 A tobacco pipe, camera, binoculars, telescope, microscope.

klɔ̂ŋ sùup yaa 52.8 A tobacco pipe.

klɔ̂ŋ thàay rûup A camera.

klɔɔŋ 47.6 Drum.

klua 58.2 To fear.

klûay 46.4 Bananas.

klûay hɔ̌ɔm 46.4 Fragrant bananas.

klua 23.7 Salt.

koon nùat 32.4 To shave.

kɔ̂ 14.6 Also, too. (See 46.5)

kɔ̀ɔn 11.3 Before, first.

kɔ̂ɔn 33.3 A lump. Classifier for things in lumps.

kɔ́ɔp 58.8 Golf.

krabìi 58.4 Krabi (a province of Thailand).

krabɔ̀ɔk chìit yuŋ 43.4 A flit gun.

kracòk 51.4 Window pane, mirror.

kradaan 41.9 A board, plank.

kradaan dam 41.9 A blackboard.

kradaan prakàat 52.4 A bulletin board.

kradàat 16.3 Paper.

kradàat chamráʔ 43.4 Toilet paper.

krapɔ̌ŋ 48.3 A can, a tin.

kraprooŋ 42.8 A skirt.

krasuaŋ 56.4 Government ministry.

krathiam 49.4 Garlic.

kreeŋcay 59.5 To have a feeling of imposing on someone.

kroŋ 46.6 A cage.

kròot 51.9 To be mad at someone.

kruŋ thêep 28.7 Bangkok.

kúaytǐaw 23.3 Noodles.

kumphaaphan 33.8 February.

kuncɛɛ 58.5 A key, wrench.

kûŋ 7.4 Shrimps.

kùak 23.6 Shoes (vulgar).

kùap 29.1 Almost, approximately, being close to.

kwàa 6.5 More (than), –er (than).

kwâaŋ 41.5 To be wide, broad.

lâ 4.3 A particle used to direct a previous question to a new topic. 'And what about ...?' (See 4.1 and 47.7)

lâ 39.5, 48.9, 54.9 – 59.9 A particle used with a question to press for an answer. 'Why on earth...?' (See 39.2 and 54.9)

lâ 58.9, 59.9 A particle used to emphasize the finality of the information.

lá 34.3 Per.

lǎa 41.5 A yard in length.

láan 19.8 A million.

lǎan 11.4 Nephew, niece, grandchild. (Younger relation two steps removed.)

lâaŋ 8.3 Lower.
  khâŋ lâaŋ 8.3 Downstairs.

láaŋ 46.2 To wash (not used with 'hair' or 'clothes').

lâat krabaŋ 54.4 Lat Krabang (an amphoe of Phra Nakhon province).

laaw 57.4 Laos.

lǎay 26.3 Several.

lakhɔɔn 58.8 A play.

lambàak 47.5 Inconvenient, difficult.

lampaaŋ 58.4 Lampang (a province of Thailand).

lamphuun 58.4 Lamphun (a province of Thailand).

lamyay 46.4 Lamyai (a kind of fruit).

lǎŋ 4.2 The back.
  khâŋ lǎŋ 4.2 In back of.
  lǎŋ càak 36.2 After.

lǎŋ 27.5 Classifier for houses.

lǎŋkhaa 34.4 Roof.

lǎŋ sǔan 42.4 A Soi between Wireless and Rajdamri Roads.

làp 56.7 To close the eyes.

làw 55 A group.
  làw níi 55 These.

lâw 49.5 To tell, relate.

lêek 12.3 Number.
  lêek thîi 12.3 A number used as a designation.

leekhǎanúkaan 54.5 A secretary.

lèk 33.5 Iron.

lék 2.5 To be little.

lêm 27.5 Classifier for books.

lên 44.8 To play.

lǒə 2.3, 58.9, 59.9 A particle used to ask for a confirmation. 'Am I right in assuming that ...?'

ləəy 27.3 To be beyond.
  ləəy pay 27.3 To go beyond, to go past.
  mây...ləəy 4.5 Not ... at all.

ləəy 35.6 Therefore, so.

ləəy 58.4 Loei (a province of Thailand).

lɛ́ʔ 15 And.

lɛ́ɛw 4.3 And then, subsequently.
  lɛ́ɛw kɔ̂ 22.3 And, and then.

lɛ́ɛw 8.3 Already. (See 8.1)

lɛ́ɛwtɛ̀ɛ 60 Depending on.

lìam 57.9 An angle, corner, edge.

líaŋ 58.2 To treat, raise (as a child).

líaw 6.3 To turn (in line of motion).

lìik lìaŋ 34.4 To avoid.

líncìi 27.4 Litchi, lichee nuts.

lípsatìk 60 Lipstick.

lít 28.7 Liter (1.057 quarts).

lom 16.3 Wind, air (in motion or under pressure).

lòm 2.4 A muddy place.

lóm 2.4 To fall over, topple.

loŋ 27.3, 29.2 To descend, go or come down, diminish.
  loŋ chɯ̂ɯ 57.5 To enter one's name.
  loŋ thabian 56.1 To register.

lóp 57.9 To erase, subtract.

lópburii 58.4 Lop Buri (a province of Thailand).

lót 41.5 To reduce in price or weight.

lòk 41.2, 42.2, 58.9, 59.9 A particle used to straighten out a wrong impression. Usually used with the negative. 'But that's not the way it is.'

lɔ́ɔ 28.1 Wheel.

lɔɔŋ 44.9 To try out.

lɔ̀ɔt 33.3 A tube. Classifier for things in tubes.

    lɔ̀ɔt fay 43.5 An electric light bulb.

lûak 27.9 To scald.

    khày lûak 27.9 Very soft boiled eggs.

lŭam 32.2 Loose.

lûat 51.5 Wire.

    múŋ lûat 51.5 Wire screens.

lúk 43.8 To rise.

luŋ 11.4 Older brother of father or mother, uncle.

lûuk 7.5 Child (son or daughter, not boy or girl; see **dèk**).

lûuk 22.5 A 'ball' of something. A classifier for 'ball' like things.

    lûuk hǐn 22.5 A marble.

    lûuk ŋɔ́ʔ 47.4 Rambutan (a kind of fruit).

lǔa 59.5 To be left over, remaining.

lûak 55 To choose.

lûan 54.5 To shift, slide, or move in position, time, or grade.

lǔaŋ 14.4 Yellow.

luɯm 17.3 To forget.

luɯm 44.9 To open the eyes.

maa 8.1 To come.

máa 41.6 Horse.

mǎa 27.3 Dog.

mâak 3.3 Very, a lot.

maaleesia 57.4 Malaysia.

máay 17.3 Wood, a stick.

    máy banthát 52.4 A ruler.

    máy cîm fan 44.4 Toothpick.

    máy khìit 17.3 Matches.

    máy kwàat 43.4 Broom.

mahǎasǎarakhaam 58.4 Maha Sarakham (a province of Thailand).

mahàatthai 56.4 Interior (as in the Ministry of Interior).

mák (ca) 50 Regularly, habitually, usually.

makhǔa 48.4 The tomato-eggplant family of vegetables.

    makhǔa thêet 48.4 Tomato.

malakɔɔ 46.4 Papaya.

mamûaŋ 47.4 Mango.

man 24.1 The potato-yam family of vegetables.

    man faràŋ 24.1 Potato.

    man thêet 49.4 Yam.

    man thɔ̂ɔt 24.3 Fried potatoes, potato chips.

man 28.7 The fat of an animal.

man 54.8 Pronoun for things, animals, and disrespectfully for humans. It.

manaaw 22.3 Limes.

maŋkhút 46.4 Mangosteen (a kind of fruit).

maphráaw 42.2 Coconut.

màj 11.3 To be new, anew.

mây 1.5 Not.

    mây dây 13.5, 48.1 Didn't, it is not the case. (See 13.1)

    mây khɔ̂y 46.5 Not very, hardly.

    mây ... nák 50 Not very ... .

    mây ... sák thii 56.7c Never.

mây 3.4 To burn.

máy 1.5 A question particle. (See 1.1)

máykhìit See **máay**.

mǎy 41.5 Silk.

    mǎy thay 41.5 Thai silk.

mêek 17.4 Clouds.

meesǎayon 34.8 April.

méet 28.7 Meter (39.37 inches).

mét 22.5 A seed. Classifier for 'kernel' like things.

mɛ̂ɛ 17.4 Mother.

    mɛ̂ɛ khrua 37.10, 58.7 A female cook.

    mɛ̂ɛ náam 50, 58.8 River.

    mɛ̂ɛ rɛɛŋ 58.5 A car jack.

mɛ̂ɛhɔ̂ŋsɔ̌ɔn 58.4 Mae Hong Son (a province of Thailand).

mɛɛw 44.8 Cat.

mɛ̂m 36.1 Ma'am. The usual term used by servants when speaking to or about a Farang lady.

mia lǔaŋ 37.4 Major wife.

mii 7.4 To have, there is.

miinaakhom 34.8 March.

mîit 33.5 Knife.

minburii 54.4 Min Buri (an amphoe in Phra Nakhon province).

míthunaayon 37.8 June.

mítsataə 53.7 Mr.

mókkaraakhom 33.8 January.

mooŋ 21.8 O'clock (daytime hours).

mòt 32.3 To be all gone, to the last one.

mɔ̀ʔsǒm 28.4 To be appropriate.

mɔ̂ɔ 58.5 A pot.

  mɔ̂ɔ béttərîi 59.5 A car battery.

  mɔ̂ɔ náam 58.5 A car radiator.

mɔ̌ɔ 32.2 Medical doctor.

  mɔ̌ɔ nûat 36.4 Masseur, masseuse.

mɔ̌ɔn 19.4, 46.2 Pillow.

mɔɔŋ 56.7 To look at. (See 56.1)

mɔɔtəəsay 46.7 Motorcycle.

muan 33.7 Classifier for cigarettes.

mûaŋ 14.4 Purple.

múŋ 38.5 Mosquito net.

  múŋ lûat 51.5 Wire screens.

mǔu 7.4 Pig, pork.

mɯ̂a 24.2 When.

  mɯ̂a kíi níi 44.2 This preceding moment.

  mɯ̂arày 24.2 When?

mɯ̌ankan, mɯ́ankan 22.3 Likewise.

mɯaŋ 34.3 Town, city, country.

  mɯaŋ nɔ̂ɔk 39.1 Foreign countries. Abroad.

mɯɯ 16.4 Hands.

mɯ̀ɯn 16.8 Ten thousand.

mɯ̂ɯt 18.3 To be dark.

ná 14.3 A particle used with questions to get a second answer. 'What was that again?' (See 14.1)

ná 7.9, 19.3, 46.9, 48.9 A particle requesting the listener to give some indication that he has heard. 'Do you follow me?', 'Get it?' (See 7.1 and 19.1)

naa 1.4, 45 Rice field.

nâa 1.4, 41.5 Face, surface, page.

  khâŋ nâa 4.2 In front of.

nâa 51.5 Good for . . . , interesting to... .

nâa rák 37.4 Cute, loveable.

nâa yùu 51.5 Nice to live in.

nâa 45 Season.

  nâa fǒn 45 The rainy season.

  nâa nǎaw 45 The cold season.

  nâa rɔ́ɔn 45 The hot season.

nǎa 33.3 To be thick.

naalikaa 11.8 Watch, clock, o'clock (in the 24 hour system).

náam 7.3 Water, liquid, juice, fluid.

  náam ʔàt lom 55 Carbonated drinks.

  nám hɔ̌ɔm 60 Perfume.

  nám khɛ̌ŋ 23.3 Ice.

  nám klàn 58.5 Distilled water.

  námman 28.7 Oil, gasoline.

  námman bensin 58.5 Gasoline, benzine.

  námman káat 58.3 Kerosene.

  námman khrɯ̂aŋ 58.5 Motor oil.

  námman mǔu 58.3 Lard.

  námŋən 16.6 Blue.

  nám phrík 25 A hot sauce.

  námtaan 23.7 Sugar.

naan 26.2 To be long in time.

nâan 58.4 Nan (a province of Thailand).

nâatàaŋ 16.3 Window (the opening and shutters, not the glass).

naathii 11.8 Minute.

nǎaw 17.4 Cold (weather).

naay 34.3 Mr., master, boss.

  naay hâaŋ 34.3 The boss of a firm. (See 34.1)

  naay nâa 49.5 An agent.

  naay phan ʔèek 53.3 Colonel.

  naay phan thoo 53.3 Lieutenant colonel.

  naay phan trii 53.3 Major.

  naay rɔ́ɔy ʔèek 53.3 Captain.

  naay rɔ́ɔy thoo 53.3 First lieutenant.

  naay rɔ́ɔy trii 53.3 Second lieutenant.

  naay sìp 57.5 Corporal, sergeant.

  naay sìp ʔèek 57.3 Sergeant.

  naay sìp thoo 57.3 Corporal.

  naay sìp trii 57.3 Private first class.

nàk 28.7 To be heavy.

nák 50 So, very.

   mây . . . nák 5o Not very . . .

nakhɔɔn 54.10 City.

   nakhɔɔnnayók 58.4 Nakhon Nayok (a province of Thailand).

   nakhɔɔnpathǒm 58.4 Nakhon Pathom (a province of Thailand).

   nakhɔɔnphanom 58.4 Nakhon Phanom (a province of Thailand).

   nakhɔɔnrâatchasimaa 58.4 Nakhon Ratchasima (a province of Thailand).

   nakhɔɔnsawǎn 58.4 Nakhon Sawan (a province of Thailand).

   nakhɔɔnsǐithammarâat 58.4 Nakhon Si Thammarat (a province of Thailand).

nám (See náam.)

nân 6.7 There.

nán 2.9 That, the one mentioned.

nâŋ 20 To sit.

nǎŋ 32.2 Moving pictures.

naŋsɯ̆ɯ 14.3 Book.

   naŋsɯ̆ɯ phim 44.8 Newspaper.

náp 60 To count.

naraathíwâat 58.4 Narathiwat (a province of Thailand).

nâsi 49.9, 51.9, 58.9, 59.9 A particle used to emphasize the obviousness of the information. 'Of course.'

nát 53.5 To make an appointment.

nay 29.7 In.

nǎy 3.3 Where? Which?

   nǎy duu sí 43.5 Let me see it.

náy khláp 58.8 Night club.

neethɔ̂ɔlɛɛn 57.4 The Netherlands.

nəəy 24.1 Butter.

   nəəy khɛ̌ŋ 24.3 Cheese.

nɛ́ʔnam 49.5 To suggest, advise, introduce.

nɛ̂ɛ 24.3 To be certain.

nî 39.6, 54.9 – 59.9 A particle indicating that the utterance is a defense against an accusation. '. . ., that's why.'

nĭam 29.6 To be shy.

nîi 3.2 Here.

níi 6.3 This.

nítnɔ̀y 14.3 A little bit.

níw 16.4, 41.5 Fingers, toes, inches.

niwsiilɛɛn 57.4 New Zealand.

nom 23.7 Milk, cream.

non (tha) burii 58.4 Nonthaburi (a province of Thailand).

nôon 3.3 Over there.

nóon 6.2 That (farther away than nán).

nɔ̂ɔk 24.3 Outside of, abroad.

   nɔ̂ɔkcàak 40 Outside of, besides.

nɔ̀ɔmáay 33.4 Bamboo shoots.

nɔɔn 7.1 To lie down.

   nɔɔn làp 56.7 To sleep.

nɔ́ɔŋ 11.4 Younger brother or sister.

nɔ̌ɔŋ cɔ̀ɔk 54.4 Nong Chok (an amphoe in Phra Nakhon province).

nɔ̌ɔŋkhaay 58.4 Nong Khai (a province of Thailand).

nɔɔrawee 57.4 Norway.

nɔ́ɔy 47.5 To be small in number or amount.

nɔ́ɔynàa 22.4 Custard apple.

nɔ̀y 14.3 A little.

nɔ̀y 14.3, 41.9, 42.9 A particle used to add politeness to an imposition. 'Do it just a little.'

nûŋ 42.8 To wear or put on a lower garment.

nǔu 4.2 Mouse. (See 4.1)

núa 7.4 Meat, beef.

nùay 34.6 To be tired, fatigued.

núk 39.4 To think.

nɯ̀ŋ, nɯŋ 2.8 One, a.

ŋaan 9.3 Work, party, ceremony.

ŋâay 46.7 To be easy.

ŋán 30 Short for thâa yaŋŋán.

ŋən 33.5 Silver, money.

ŋîap 34.6 To be quiet.

ŋûaŋ nɔɔn 8.6 To be sleepy.

ŋuu 44.9 Snake.

ŋɯ̀a 51.9 Sweat.

   ŋɯ̀a ʔɔ̀ɔk 51.9 To sweat.

pàa 2.6, 58.8 Forest, jungle.

pâa 21.6 Father or mother's older sister, aunt.

păa 9.6 Father, papá (used mainly with foreigners).

pàak 16.4 Mouth.

    pàak náam 24.4 Paknam (a town at the mouth of the Chao Phya River).

paakiisathăan 57.4 Pakistan.

pàakkaa 52.8 Pen.

    pàakkaa mùk sum 52.4 A fountain pen.

pám 29.3 A pump.

    pám námman 29.3 A gas pump, a gas station.

panamaa 57.4 Panama.

pàt 17.6 To brush or dust off.

pathumthaanii 58.4 Pathum Thani (a province of Thailand).

pathumwan 54.4 Pathum Wan (an amphoe in Phra Nakhon province).

pàttanii 58.4 Pattani (a province of Thailand).

pàw 9.6 To blow (with the mouth).

pay 6.3 To go.

pay 28.3 Too, excessive.

    kəən pay 42.5 Too, excessive.

pen 2.3, 10 To be someone or something.

pen 26.3 To be mentally able, to know how.

pen 38.3 To have or be in some unnatural condition.

pépsii 21.4 Pepsi Cola.

pèt 27.9 Duck.

pòət 17.6 To open, turn on.

pêɛŋ 60 Powder, flour, starch.

pèɛt 3.8 Eight.

phaa 32.3 To take someone somewhere.

phàa 2.6 To split, cut open.

phâa 9.6 Cloth.

    phâa chét fùn 43.4 A dust cloth.

    phâa chét tua 44.4 Towel.

    phâa hòm 43.4 Blanket.

    phâa mâan 43.4 Curtains.

    phâa puu thîi nɔɔn 43.4 Bed sheets.

    phâa puu tó? 44.4 Tablecloth.

    phâa sîn 42.8 Thai style skirt.

phàan 33.3 To pass a fixed object.

phaaynay 49.5 Within.

paahŏnyoothin 17.8 Phaholyothin (a road in Bangkok).

phàk 48.8 Leaf vegetables.

    phàk chii 49.4 Parsley.

    phàk kàat 9.6 Lettuce.

    phàkkàat hɔɔm 48.4 Common lettuce.

    phàk khŏom 49.4 Spinach.

phamâa 14.2 Burmese.

phan 13.7 A thousand.

phanrayaa 38.7 Wife.

phaŋŋaa 58.4 Phangnga (a province of Thailand).

phárwhàt (See following entries.)

    daaw phárwhàt Jupiter.

    wan phárwhàt 19.4 Thursday.

phasăa 14.3 Language.

phàt 22.3 To stir fry, a fried mixture.

phát 16.3 To blow (as the wind).

    phátlom 16.3 An electric fan.

pháttakhaan 55 A large restaurant.

phátthaluŋ 58.4 Phatthalung (a province of Thailand).

phátthanaakaan hèŋ châat 56.4 National Development.

phátthayaa 45, 56.7 Pataya (a seaside resort in Chon Buri province).

phăw 29.4, 31.4 To burn something.

    phăw sòp 29.4 To cremate a corpse.

phayabaan 52.3 To tend, to nurse.

phayanchaná? 57.10 Consonants.

phayathai 41.4 Phyathai (a road in Bangkok).

phayayaam 54.8 To try, make an attempt.

pheedaan 51.4 Ceiling.

phèt 24.7 To be hot (peppery).

phétburii 59.5, 41.4 Phetchaburi (a province of Thailand, also a road in Bangkok).

phétchabuun 59.4 Phetchabun (a province of Thailand).

phòəm 47.5 To increase.

phôŋ, phûŋ 18.6 Just now, just a minute ago.

phé? 8.4 A goat.

phɛ̌ɛ 26.6 To lose to someone (as in a game).

phɛ̌ɛn thîi 52.4 A map.

phɛɛŋ 28.3 Expensive.

phɛ̂ɛt 53.5 Medical doctor (formal).

phɛ̀n 22.5 A 'sheet' of something. Classifier for 'sheet' like things.

phícìt 59.4 Phichit (a province of Thailand).

phîi 9.6 Older brother or sister.

phim 44.8 To print.

   naŋsɯ̌ɯ phim 44.8 Newspaper.

phísèet 58.5 Special.

phítsanúlôok 59.4 Phitsanulok (a province of Thailand).

phǐw nǎŋ 27.4 Skin.

phleeŋ 58.8 A song.

phlɔɔncìt 9.2 Ploenchit (a road in Bangkok).

phlɛ̌ɛ 60 A cut, wound, or sore.

phǒm, phóm 8.2 I (man speaking). (See 8.1)

phǒm 3.2 Hair (of the head only).

phǒnlamáay 24.3 Fruit.

phǒŋ 60 A powdery substance, dust.

   phǒŋ sák fɔ̀ɔk 60 Soap powder, detergent powder.

phóp 11.3 To see, meet, find.

phɔɔ 23.3 Enough.

   phɔɔ cay 55 To be satisfied.

   phɔɔ cháy dây 31.3 Good enough to use, passable.

   phɔɔ dii 52.5 Just right.

phɔɔ 32.9 As soon as.

phɔ̂ɔ 7.5 Father.

phɔ̌ɔm 1.5 To be thin.

phɔɔn 54.10 Blessings.

phɔɔ sɔ̌ɔ 14.8 The Buddhist era (an abbreviation of phútthasàkkaràat).

phrákhanǒoŋ 54.4 Phra Khanong (an amphoe in Phra Nakhon province).

phránakhɔɔn 54.4 Phra Nakhon (a province of Thailand).

(phránakhɔɔnsǐi) ʔayútthayaa 59.4 Phra Nakhon Si Ayutthaya (a province of Thailand).

phrɛ̂ɛ 59.4 Phrae (a province of Thailand).

phrík 23.1 Peppers, chilies.

   phrík thay 23.7 Pepper.

phrom 43.4 A rug.

   phrom puu phɯ́ɯn 43.4 A rug.

phrɔ́ʔ 23.2 To sound good.

phrɔ́ʔ 27.3 Because.

phrûŋ níi 28.8 Tomorrow.

phrɯ́tsacikaayon 33.8 November.

phrɯ́tsaphaakhom 34.8 May.

phút (See following entries.)

   daaw phút Mercury.

   wan phút 17.4 Wednesday.

phûu 7.3 Person (rarely used alone).

   phûu chaay 7.3 Boy, man.

   phûu yǐŋ 7.3 Girl, woman.

phuukèt 59.4 Phuket (a province of Thailand).

phuukhǎw 58.8 Mountains.

phuum, phuumíʔ 53.3 Earth, place (in compounds).

   phuumísàat 53.3 Geography.

phûut 8.3 To speak.

phɯ̀a 44.5 In case.

phɯ̂a (ca) 54.5 In order to.

phɯ̀ak 37.4 Albino.

phɯ̂an 30 Friend.

phɯ́ɯn 38.5 Floor.

pii 30 Year.

pìi 9.6 A wind instrument.

pîŋ 27.9 To toast.

pìt 19.3 To close, turn off.

plaa 7.4 Fish.

   plamɯ̀k 48.9 Squid.

   plathuu 8.4 A fish resembling a herring or a mackerel.

plàaw 11.3 Empty. Used to reject a wrong assumption. No.

plɛɛ 24.3 To mean, to translate.

plìan 58.5 To change.

plɔ̀ɔk mɯ̌ɔn 44.4 Pillow case.

plɔ̀ɔtphay 46.5 To be safe.

plùuk 58.8 To plant crops.

pòkkatì? 27.9 Normally, ordinarily.

pootukèet 57.4 Portugal.

pɔ̀ɔm pràap satruu phâay 54.4 Pom Prap Sattru Phai (an amphoe in Phra Nakhon province).

pɔɔn 58.5 A pound.

pɔ̂ɔn 29.6 To feed someone.

pracam 60 To be regularly attached to.
  pracam wan 60 Daily.

praciinburii 59.4 Prachin Buri (a province of Thailand).

pracùap (khiiriikhǎn) 59.4 Prachuap Khiri Khan (a province of Thailand).

prakàat 52.4 To announce.
  kradaan prakàat 52.4 Bulletin board.

pramaan 42.5 Approximately.

prathêet 45 Country.

pratuu 16.3 Door.
  pratuu nâa bâan 51.4 Front gate.

pratuunáam 41.4 The intersection of Phetburi and Rajdamri roads.

prawàt 53.3 Account, story, history.
  prawàttisàat 53.3 The field or subject of History.

prayòok 54.10 Sentence.

prayòot 45 Use, usefulness.

praysanii 28.3 Post office.

prɛɛŋ 33.4 A brush, to brush.
  prɛɛŋ lóp kradaan dam 52.4 Blackboard eraser.

prìap thîap 22.4 To compare.

prinyaa 53.3 An academic degree.

pùat 37.10 To ache.

puu 27.9 Crab.

pùu 9.6 Father's father, grandfather.

puun 19.6 Gun.

ráan 3.3 Shop, store.

râat (cha) burii 59.4 Ratchaburi (a province of Thailand).

râat (cha) damnəən 41.4 Ratchadamnern (a road in Bangkok).

râat (cha) damrì? 11.2 Ratchadamri (a road in Bangkok).

râat (cha) prasǒŋ 11.3 Rajprasong (the intersection of Ratchdamri and Ploenchit).

râat (cha) theewii 41.4 Ratchatevi (the intersection of Phetburi and Phyathai roads).

raaw 28.3 Approximately.

raaykaan 26.9 A list of items.

rabiaŋ 51.4 Veranda, porch.

rák 58.2 To love.

rakhaa 31.3 Price, cost.

ráksǎa 34.4 To take care of, treat.

ranɔɔŋ 59.4 Ranong (a province of Thailand).

ráp 26.3 To receive, pick up someone.
  ráp sòŋ 50 To pick up and deliver, to take passengers.

rápprathaan 21.1 To eat (formal).

ráprɔɔŋ 38.4 To guarantee.

rátsia (rútsia) 57.4 Russia, U.S.S.R.

raw 24.3 We, I, you. (See 24.1)

rawaŋ 46.5 To be careful.

ray 2.3 Short for of ?aray.

rayá? 45 A stretch of distance or time.

rayɔɔŋ 59.4 Rayong (a province of Thailand).

rew 21.3 To be fast.

rə̂əm 45 To begin.

rɛ̂ɛk 49.5 To be first.

rɛɛŋ 43.5 Strength, power.
  mɛ̂ɛ rɛɛŋ 58.5 A car jack.
  rɛɛŋ thian 43.5 Candle power, watt.

rîak 14.3 To call.

rian 11.3 To study.

rîaprɔ́ɔy 58.5 To be in good condition, all set.

rîit 38.5 To press, iron.

rôok 38.2 Disease.

rooŋ 11.3 A large shed or hall.
  rooŋ nǎŋ 52.3 Movie theater.
  rooŋ phayabaan 52.3 Hospital.
  rooŋ rian 11.3 School.
  rooŋ rɛɛm 4.3 Hotel.
  rooŋ rót 46.8 Garage.

rópkuan 33.4 To bother.

rót 26.3 Any wheeled vehicle.
  rót fay 27.2 Train.
  rót mee 27.2 Bus.
  rót théksîi 27.3 Taxi.
  rót yon 26.1 Automobile.

rɔŋtháaw 31.3 Shoes.

rɔɔ 22.3 To wait for.

rɔ́ɔn 2.5 To be hot.

rɔ́ɔŋ 58.8 To cry out, yell.

rɔ́ɔŋhâay 51.9 To cry, weep.

rɔ́ɔy 12.8 A hundred.

rɔ́ɔyʔèt 59.4 Roi Et (a province of Thailand).

ruam 55 To combine, include.

rûam rɐdii 42.4 A Soi behind Wireless Road.

rûŋ 57.5 Dawn.

   rûŋ khûn 57.5 The next day.

rúu 13.3 To know (a subject). (See 13.1)

   rúucàk 6.3 To know a person, place, or thing, to be acquainted with. (See 13.1)

   rúusɐ̀k 58.5 To feel.

rûup 57.9 A picture, form, shape.

rɐa 50, 58.8 Boat, ship.

   rɐa bin 58.8 Airplane.

rɐan 51.5 House (used in certain combinations only).

rɐ̂aŋ 39.7 A story, a matter, classifier for stories or happenings.

rɐ̌ɐ, rɐ́ 7.9 Or.

rɐɐn (See following entry.)

   marɐɐn nii 29.8 The day after tomorrow.

saaʔudii ʔaareebia 57.4 Saudi Arabia.

sǎaladɛɛŋ 11.2 Saladaeng (the intersection near Lumpini Park).

sǎam 1.8 Three.

   sǎamlɔ́ɔ 28.3 Samlor, tricycle taxi.

sǎamii 38.7 Husband.

sâaŋ 54.10 To build.

sâɐp 13.3 To know (information). (See 13.1)

sàat 53.3 A suffix meaning 'field of knowledge'. -ology.

sǎathaaranasùk 56.4 Public Health.

sǎathɔɔn 22.4 Sathon (a road in Bangkok).

sàatsanǎa 58.8 Religion.

   sàatsanǎa khrít 58.8 Christianity.

   sàatsanǎa phút 58.8 Buddhism.

sǎaw 19.9 Young woman, unmarried woman.

saay 22.5 Sand.

sàay 29.6 To move back and forth.

sáay 4.3 Left (side).

sǎay 14.4 Late morning.

sabaay 2.3 To be comfortable, feel nice.

sabùu 33.3 Soap.

sadùak 49.5 Convenient.

sák 41.5 To wash clothing, launder.

   sák hɛ̂ɛŋ 41.5 To dry-clean.

   sák náam 41.5 To wash in water, to rinse.

sák 31.3 At least, or so, anyway, and maybe more later.

   sák thii 56.7c Even once.

   mây .... sák thii 56.7c Never.

sakonnakhɔɔn 59.4 Sakon Nakhon (a province of Thailand).

salàp 54.10 To alternate.

salàt 27.9 Salad.

sǎmʔaaŋ (See following entry.)

   khrûaŋ sǎmʔaaŋ 60 Cosmetics, toilet articles.

samǎy 51.5 An era.

   samǎy mày 51.5 Modern times.

   samǎy kɔɔn 51.3 Old-fashioned times.

samɔ̌ɔ 30 Always.

samǐan 57.5 Clerk.

sǎmkhan 59.5 To be important.

sǎmnaw 57.5 A copy.

sǎmphanthawoŋ 54.4 Samphanthawong (an amphoe in Phra Nakhon province).

sǎmràp, sǎmràp 47.5 For doing something, for someone, as for.

sǎmrèt 60 To complete, be successful.

   sǎmrèt rûup 60 Ready-made.

samùt 52.4 A notebook.

samùtpraakaan 59.4 Samut Prakan (a province of Thailand).

samùtsǎakhɔɔn 59.4 Samut Sakhon (a province of Thailand).

samùtsǒŋkhraam 59.4 Samut Songkhram (a province of Thailand).

sàn 51.9 To tremble, vibrate.

sân 3.5 To be short in length.

sanǎam 51.5 A yard, court, field.

   sanǎamlǔaŋ 41.4 'The Royal Arena.' A large oval field near the Grand Palace.

   sanǎam yâa 51.5 Lawn.

sàŋ 11.4 To order, to leave a message.

229

sǎŋkèet 59.5 To notice.

sàp 54.10 Word, term.

sapeen 57.4 Spain.

saphaan khwaay 42.4 Saphan Khwai (an area in Bangkok).

sapháy 40 A female in-law.

sapɔ̀ɔt khláp 32.9 Sports Club.

sàpparót 46.4 Pineapple.

sarà? 57.10 Vowels.

saràburii 59.4 Saraburi (a province of Thailand).

sataaŋ 26.1 One hundredth part of a baht, money.

sathǎanii 27.3 Station.

  sathǎanii rót fay 27.3 Railway station.

  sathǎanii tamrùat 56.5 Police station.

sathǎanthûut 9.3 Embassy.

satáat 43.3 To start a car.

satuun 59.4 Satun (a province of Thailand).

sǎw (See following entries.)

  daaw sǎw Saturn.

  wan sǎw 17.4 Saturday.

sawàaŋ 49.9 To be light, bright.

sawéttɔ̂ə (See following entry.)

  sûa sawéttɔ̂ə 44.3 A sweater.

sawàtdii 1.3 A greeting used for either meeting or parting. Greetings, hello, goodbye.

sawiideen 57.4 Sweden.

sawítsəəlɛɛn 57.4 Switzerland.

sày 7.4 To put in or on.

sèetthakaan 56.4 Economics.

sen 41.3 Centimeter.

sen 56.5 To sign.

sên 22.5 A line. Classifier for 'string' like things.

  sên mìi 48.8 Very fine rice noodles.

sèt 22.3 To finish, be finished.

sɛ̌ɛn 18.8 A hundred thousand.

sɛɛnwít 24.3 Sandwich.

sɛ̀ɛt 14.4 Orange (the color).

sì 43.5 A particle used to suggest an action.

sì 34.4, 43.9, 47.9 A particle used to request or urge an action when the action itself

is the point of the request. (See 47.9)

sì 18.3, 44.9, 47.9, 54.9 56.9, 57.9 A particle used to request an action when the result of the action, not the action itself, is the point of the request. (See 47.9)

sǐa 26.3, 42.1, To be spoiled, out of order, to spend.

sǐaŋ 48.10 Sound.

  sǐaŋ sǔuŋ tàm 48.10 Tones.

sìi 2.8 Four.

  sìi yɛ̂ɛk 6.3 Intersection (four forks).

sǐi 14.4 Color.

  sǐi tòk 41.5 The color runs or fades.

sǐi 33.3 To rub, scrub.

  sǐi fan 31.4 To brush the teeth.

sǐi ?ayútthayaa 42.4 Si Ayuthaya (a road in Bangkok).

siilɔɔn 57.4 Ceylon.

sǐisakèet 59.4 Si Sa Ket (a province of Thailand).

sǐŋburii 59.4 Sing Buri (a province of Thailand).

sǐŋhǎakhom 36.8 August.

sǐŋkapoo 57.4 Singapore.

sìp 3.8 Ten.

sôm 26.4 Oranges, tangerines, grapefruits, etc.

  sôm ?oo 26.4 Pomelo.

  sôm khǐaw wǎan 46.4 The common green orange of Thailand.

sǒnthanaa 46.10 Conversation.

sòŋ 17.3 To send. (See 17.1)

sǒŋkhlǎa 59.4 Songkhla (a province of Thailand).

soodaa 23.4 Soda water.

sòot 48.5 Unmarried.

  chaay sòot 48.1 Bachelor.

sòp 29.4 A corpse.

sòt 60 To be fresh.

sɔ̂m 49.8 A fork.

sɔ̌ɔn 41.9 To teach.

sɔ̌ɔn 54.10 Arrow.

sɔɔŋ 34.7 An envelope, a pack of cigarettes.

sɔ̌ɔŋ 1.8 Two.

sɔɔy 12.3 Soi, lane.

sûam 7.1 Toilet.

sùan 45 A part.

  sùan mâak 45 For the most part, the majority.

  sùan ... nán 55 As for ... .

sǔan 37.10 A garden or orchard.

sǔan lum 32.9 Lumpini Park (a park in Bangkok).

sǔay 46.9 To be pretty.

sùk (See following entries.)

  daaw sùk Venus.

  wan sùk 17.4 Friday.

sùkhǎa 7.1 Toilet (formal).

sùkhǒothay 59.4 Sukhothai (a province of Thailand).

sùkhǔmwít 12.3 Sukhumvit (a road in Bangkok).

súp 24.3 Soup.

sùphanburii 59.4 Suphan Buri (a province of Thailand).

súppɔ̀ɔ maakêt 60 Supermarket.

sùrâat (thaanii) 59.4 Surat Thani (a province of Thailand).

surin 59.4 Surin (a province of Thailand).

suriwoŋ 37.3 Suriwong (a road in Bangkok).

sùt 34.3 The end, extreme, utmost.

sǔun 12.3 Zero.

sǔuŋ 2.5 To be tall.

sùup 33.4 To draw on, pump, smoke.

sùa 19.4, 46.6 Mat.

sûa 31.2 Upper garment, shirt, blouse coat, sweater.

  sûa chɔ́ɔt 41.5 A dress shirt.

  sûa haawaay 42.5 A sport shirt.

  sûa nǎaw 44.3 A coat.

  sûa nay 37.9 An undershirt.

  sûa phâa 32.3 Clothing.

  sûa sawéttɔ̀ɔ 44.3 A sweater.

sǔa 46.6 A tiger.

sèksǎa 32.4 To educate.

  sèksǎathíkaan 56.4 Education.

sûŋ 45, 54.5 Relative pronoun (that, which).

súu 7.4 To buy.

suun (See following entry.)

  mûa wan suun níi 29.8 The day before yesterday.

taa 11.6 Eyes.

taa 58.2 Mother's father, grandfather.

tàak 46.2 To expose to the sun, air, or wind.

  tàak ʔaakàat 45 To expose oneself to the weather. To take an airing or vacation.

tàak 59.4 Tak (a province of Thailand).

taam 22.3 To follow.

taam 45 Along, at the various ... .

tàaŋ To differ.

  tàaŋ dâaw 56.5 Foreigner.

  tàaŋ prathêet 56.4, 60 Foreign countries.

  tàaŋtàaŋ 48.8 Various.

takrâa phǒŋ 44.4 Waste basket.

talàat 4.3 Market.

talɔ̀ɔt 55 Throughout.

tàm 48.10 Low (in pitch, elevation, or status).

tamnèŋ 36.4 Rank, position.

tamrùat 27.3 Police.

taŋ 26.9 The usual pronunciation of sataaŋ.

tâŋ 29.6, 55 To set up, erect, situate.

  tâŋcay 59.5 To intend.

taŋhàak 36.5, 51.5 On the contrary, contrary to what you think, to be separate.

tâŋtɛ̀ɛ 46.5 Since.

tapuu 60 Nails.

tàt 3.2 To cut.

taw 49.6 Stove.

tàw 49.6 Turtle.

tem 58.5 To be full.

tênram 42.8 To dance.

tɔ̀ɔm 58.5 To add to, fill.

tɔɔrakii 57.4 Turkey (the country).

tɛ̀ɛ 15 But.

tɛ̀ɛk tàaŋ 38.4 To differ.

tɛɛŋ kwaa 48.4 Cucumber.

tɛɛŋ moo 46.4 Watermelon.

tɛɛŋ thay 47.4 Musk melon.

231

tɛ̀ŋ 60 To adorn, decorate.

  tɛ̀ŋ tua 60 To dress, apply cosmetics, etc.

  tɛ̀ŋŋaan 39.1 To marry, get married.

thâa 18.3 If.

  thâa yaŋŋán 22.3 In that case, if that's how it is.

  thâa ca 43.5 It appears, there is some evidence or reason to think ... .

thǎam 18.3 To ask.

thaan 21.3 Short for **rápprathaan.**

thaan 51.6 Alms.

  khɔ̌ɔ thaan 51.6 To beg.

thàan 43.5 Charcoal.

  thàan fay chǎay 43.5 A flashlight battery.

thaaŋ 4.3 Way, path.

tháaw 31.3 Feet.

thàay 53.4 The end, the last of a series.

thàay rûup 29.4 To photograph.

thabian 56.5 A registration.

thák 21.4 To greet, say hello to.

thalee 45 Sea.

  chaay thalee 58.8 Seashore.

  thalee sàap 58.8 Lake.

tham 9.3 To do, make.

  tham dûay 33.5 To be made of.

  tham ŋaan 9.3 To work.

thamniam 57.5 Custom, tradition.

  khâa thamniam 57.5 Fee.

thammadaa 38.9 Usual, common.

thammay 21.3 Why?

than 51.5 To be on time.

  than samǎy 51.5 Up to date.

thanaakhaan 28.2 Bank.

thanǒn 9.3 Road.

thanwaakhom 33.8 December.

tháŋ 25 All of.

  tháŋ ... lɛ́ʔ 55, 59.5 Both ... and.

tháŋ mòt 25 Altogether.

  tháŋ sɔ̌ɔŋ 25 Both.

thǎŋ 21.5 Bucket.

tháp 12.3 To superimpose, lay on top, run over.

thâw To be equal to, level with.

  thâw nán 15 Only.

  thâwrày 12.3 How much? How many?

thay 14.2 Thai.

thennít 58.7 Tennis.

thəʔ 52.9, 53.9 An imperative intended for the hearer's good.

thəə 37.10 You (to intimates or inferiors).

thəəm 2.6 Term.

thɛɛŋ 27.6 To stab.

théksîi 27.3 Taxi.

thɛ̌w 38.3 A row.

thian 43.5 Candle.

  thian khǎy 43.5 A candle made of tallow.

thîaŋ 14.4 Noon.

thîaw 22.2 To go from place to place.

thii 8.3 A time.

  thii lǎŋ 37.2 Afterwards, later.

  thii rɛ̂ɛk 49.5 The first time, at first.

  ʔìik thii 8.3 Again, another time.

thii 41.9, 42.9 A particle used to add politeness to an imposition. 'Do it just this once.'

thîi 3.3 At.

thîi 17.3 A place.

  thîi khìa burìi 17.3 Ash tray.

thîi 12.3 Used in front of a cardinal number to form the ordinal, -th.

  thîi sìi The fourth.

  thîisùt 34.3 The most, extremely.

thîi 36.7 Relative pronoun (who, that, which).

thíŋ 11.6 To throw away.

thonburii 59.4 Thon Buri (a province of Thailand).

thoo 53.3 Second rank.

thoo 24.3 Short form of **thoorasàp.**

thooralêek 54.5 Telegram, to telegraph.

thoorasàp 13.3 Telephone, to telephone.

thoorathát 52.8 Television.

thôot 2.3 58.2 To blame, punishment.

thɔ̂ŋthîaw 50 To tour, travel for pleasure.

thɔ̌ɔ náam 60 A water pipe.

thɔɔn 29.3 To give change to.

thɔɔŋ 18.4 Gold.

thɔ̀ɔt 56.6 To take off.

  thɔ̀ɔt lɔ́ɔ 58.5 To take off a wheel.

thɔ̂ɔt 11.4 To fry (in large pieces).

thɔ̌y 26.3 To back up.

thùa 37.4 Beans, peas, nuts.

thùa lantaw 48.4 Green peas.

thùa lisŏŋ 48.4 Peanuts.

thùa ŋɔ̂ɔk 37.4 Bean sprouts.

thûa 47.5 To be all over, throughout.

thûay 23.7 A cup.

thúk 36.9 Every.

thûm 23.8 O'clock (used only with hours from evening to midnight).

thǔŋ 1.6, 34.3 A sack, bag.

thǔŋtháaw 34.3 Stockings.

thǔŋ mʉʉ 34.2 Gloves.

thúráʔ 32.3 An item of business, an errand.

thúrákìt 50 Business.

thúrian 47.4 Durian.

thuu 8.4 A fish resembling a herring or mackerel.

thǔu 38.5 To scrub.

thùuk 16.3 To be correct. (See 16.2)

thùuk 28.1 To be cheap.

thǔŋ 6.3 To arrive at, reach.

thǔŋ ca 47.5 Even though.

thʉ̌ʉ tua 37.4 To be haughty.

tîa 2.5 To be short in height.

tiaŋ 19.4 Bed.

tii 1.6 To beat, hit.

tìt 43.5 To be attached to.

tìttɔ̀ɔ 48.5 To contact, get in touch with.

tóʔ 20 Table, desk.

tóʔ khrûaŋ pɛ̂ɛŋ 44.4 Dressing table.

tóʔ tham ŋaan 60 Desk.

tòk 41.5 To fall.

tòkloŋ 22.3 To come to an agreement, decide.

tôm 24.3 To boil something.

tôm yam 27.9 A hot, sour soup.

tôn 45 A beginning.

tôn hèet 34.4 The cause of something.

tôn máay 46.8 Trees.

tɔ̂ɔ 56.10 To counter, back and forth.

tɔ̂ɔ tɔ̀ɔp 56.10 To interchange, talk or write back and forth.

tɔ̂ŋ 18.3 To have to, must.

tɔ̂ŋkaan 19.3 To want, need.

tɔ̀ɔ 48.5 To join on to, continue on, connect.

tɔ̀ɔ ʔaayúʔ 56.5 To renew, to continue on the age of something.

tɔ̀ɔ rakhaa 35 To bargain.

tɔɔn 14.4 A section or period.

tɔɔn yen 14.4 Evening.

tɔ̀ɔp 58.2 To answer.

tɔ̀ɔp thɛɛn 36.4 To pay back.

tràat 59.4 Trat (a province of Thailand).

traŋ 59.4 Trang (a province of Thailand).

trii 53.3 Third rank.

triam 59.5 To prepare.

troŋ 4.3 To be straight.

troŋ kan khâam 56.1 Just opposite (in position), just the opposite (in meaning).

troŋ khâam kàp 56.5 Right across from, just opposite to.

trùat 59.5 To inspect.

tua 27.5 Body. Classifier for animals, chairs, tables, and articles of clothing.

tua kháw ʔʉ̀eŋ 40 He himself.

tua sàn 51.9 To shiver.

tulaakhom 37.8 October.

tûu 27.3 Cupboard, closet.

tûu yaam tamrùat 27.3 A police box.

tʉan 21.4 To remind, warn.

tʉ̀k 48.5 A building made of masonry.

tʉ̀ʉn 37.10, 46.7 To wake up.

wâa 14.3 A quotation signal. (See 14.1)

waan (See following entry.)

mûa waan níi 28.8 Yesterday.

wǎan 8.4 To be sweet.

wâaŋ 21.3 To be unoccupied, free.

wâat 57.9 To draw.

wâay náam 58.8 To swim.

wan 17.4 Day (either the daylight period or the 24 hour period).

wàt 38.2 A cold.

wáy 44.5 For future use or reference.

wăy 26.1 To be physically able, to be up to.

wayyakɔɔn 54.10 Grammar.

weelaa 21.3 Time.

ween 57.5 In turn, by shifts.

wɛ̌ɛn 42.6 A ring (for the finger).

wên 42.6 Lens, magnifying glass.

  wên taa 42.6 Eyeglasses.

wiatnaam 14.2 Vietnam.

wǐi 33.4 A comb, to comb.

witthayaa 53.5 Knowledge (used mainly in compounds).

witthayasàat 53.5 Science.

witthayúʔ 9.3 Radio, wireless.

woŋwian 11.2 A traffic circle.

wua 6.5 Cattle, cow, bull.

yaa 27.5 52.8 Medicine, tobacco.

yàa 30 Don't (the negative imperative).

yâa 40 Father's mother, grandmother.

yâa 46.2 Grass.

yàak 18.3 To want.

yâak 60 To be difficult.

yaannawaa 54.4 Yan Nawa (an amphoe in Phra Nakhon province).

yaam 27.3 A guard, watchman.

yaaŋ 58.5 Rubber, a tire.

  yaaŋ lóp 52.4 A rubber eraser.

yàaŋ 18.3 Kind, sort, variety.

  yàaŋ mâak 47.5 At most.

  yàaŋ nɔ́ɔy 47.5 At least.

  yàaŋ ray, yaŋray, yaŋŋay, ŋay 18.3 In what way? How?

yaaw 3.5 To be long.

yaay 58.2 Mother's mother, grandmother.

yáay 56.5 To relocate. (See 56.1)

yák khíw 46.9 To raise the eyebrows.

yalaa 59.4 Yala (a province of Thailand).

yaŋ 47.5 Still more, even.

yaŋ 21.3 Still, yet.

yày 2.5 To be big.

yen 2.5 To be cold (of things), cool (of weather).

yɔ́ʔyɛ́ 31.4 Plenty.

yəəraman 57.4 Germany.

yɛ̂ɛk 6.3 To fork, separate.

yiam 28.4 To visit.

yîi 6.8 Two (used only for the twenties).

yîihɔ̂ɔ 43.5 Brand, make, trademark.

yîipùn 57.4 Japan.

yím 34.3 To smile.

yǐŋ 7.3 Female (people only).

yók 41.9 To lift, to raise.

  yók khâaw 52.9 To bring on the food.

yókwén 36.4 To except.

yókyɔ̂ŋ 39.4 To honor, praise.

yɔɔm 42.5 To be willing.

yuŋ 36.5 Mosquito.

yúttitham 56.4 Justice.

yùu 3.3 To be some place.

yuusít 39.7 USIS, (United States Information Service.).

yuusɔ̂m 30 USOM (United States Operation Mission).

yɯɯm 19.6 To borrow, lend.

yɯɯn 26.3 To stand.

Printed at Kurusapha Ladprao Press by Nai Vivek Pangputhipong 1988

Milton Keynes UK
Ingram Content Group UK Ltd.
UKHW052239060824
446627UK00008B/262